Mystical Puzzle

by
Tanya Ebert

Mel,

If we always listened to
what everyone told us,
we would never learn
the truth.

Love & Light,
Tanya :)

Author contact: tanya@mysticalpuzzle.com

Order this book online at www.mysticalpuzzle.com

Published by Lulu.com

ISBN: 978-0-557-53713-6

Cover image © Photosani - Fotolia.com

Acknowledgments

This book is dedicated to everyone that has crossed my path; including the people who have abused me in one way or another. Without each and every single one of you, I would have not experienced all that I have and grown from it.

To my guardians, guides and angels, without you, I would have never made it to see how truly magical life is.

To my mom whom never gave up on me when I was an uncontrollable nightmare of a teenager.

To my friends and family that assisted me with daily tasks that I was unable to do on my own; I would have not made it through the days without your help and support.

To the doctors that did not get it; I would have never had the opportunity to learn that I could heal my leg without your help and with the help of spirit.

To my doctor who never once looked at her watch during my lengthy visits with her while her waiting room was piling up; I appreciate the time and effort you gave me.

To my chiropractor who lowered his rate so that I could afford treatment. You are the first doctor that took a little less so that I could gain a little more. I will never forget that.

To all the intuitives and healers that have assisted me on my journey. Without you, I would most likely be in a mental institute.

To the few that I had come out of the closet to before this book was published, thank you for accepting me just as I am.

A special thanks to Marnie, my horse Ce Ce, Boris, Audrey, Lance and my cat Molly, as I consider all of you my soul mates. You may not be a part of my life today, but you have had a significant part in my journey.

To all of you who seek to find your truth. I can only hope that by sharing my journey with you that you will be inspired to come out of your closet.

Preface

Even though I was in the most excruciating pain I had ever felt, and the doctors had no clue what was wrong with me, one week after my dirt bike accident, I looked at my friend with the biggest smile on my face and I told her that I did not know what, how or why, but something big was going to come from this accident. Something really big; I could feel it.

That smile was quickly wiped off my face. Over a year passed and the doctors still did not know how to fix me. I depended on so many to help me through my painful inhumane of an existence. Just as I was about to give up on life, something guided me to Sedona, Arizona. It was at this point that I was guided to start recording my daily experiences.

As my journey started to unfold, I then knew why I was recording everything. Not because of the traumas that I had lived but because I was experiencing something so phenomenal, that I am not sure that I have the words to describe it. Something that had me so frightened that I could not tell my friends or family. They were going to think that I had done one too many drugs and fell on my head far too many times. If my old self would think that my new self had totally lost it, how could I expect anyone else to understand?

I started to look for local authors with nonfiction stories that were out of this world so to speak. I knew that they were out there somewhere. I really needed to know that there was someone close to home that society would deem different. I came across two books, *"Blue Star – Fulfilling Prophecy"* by Miriam Delicado and *"Awakening the Divine Soul – Finding Your Life Purpose"* by Rosanna Ienco. Without knowing, these women have given me the strength and courage to come out of the closet so to speak and share my story.

By December of 2009, I decided to start at my birth and record everything that I remembered up until the present day. Everything made complete sense. I could see all the connections. I discovered that I am way stronger and resilient than I have ever given myself credit. Sometimes I can not believe that I am alive to tell the story. I worked on my book for four months straight, day in and day out and ended up with over nine hundred typed pages. That was skimming through my life.

I started to think, who was going to want to read all that. According to society, I was a no body. It is not as if I was a celebrity or famous. I put my book aside for six weeks. As I was stumped, I probably would have let it sit longer but my guides made it so that it was the only thing I was able to do for another six weeks. I tried to break it down and still came up with five hundred typed pages. That was still far too much for one book.

How much of my life are people interested in knowing about? Do they want to know about the journey I took from the time I was born until present day? Do they want to know all of the abuse and traumas that brought me to where I am today? I have experienced more in less than half a lifetime than the average human would in several.

One of my main concerns about sharing my journey was that no one would believe me and that they would think that I went crazy and belonged in a mental institution. Another concern was to protect myself, friends, and family of unwanted attention. For this reason, I have chosen to change the names involved with the exception of my own. Other than certain locations and people's names, every word in this book represents the true events of my life.

It makes no difference to me whether my entire journey is known and published. It was healing for me to start at the beginning and to see how everything unfolded from the time of my birth.

This book is a way for me to come out of the closet; to begin living my truth. To be what I came here to be. I have struggled with how humanity, my friends, and family will treat me after knowing my experiences, but I am now ready to embrace who I am and share it with those that are interested. I know there are more of you out there like me. I can only hope that this book gives you the courage to begin your journey of truth.

Writing this book seemed impossible. How on earth would little ole me write a book worth reading and manage to get it published? I had no idea how to do such a task. I just started to type. I know that I was meant to do this and I know that my guides will guide me along the way because honestly, I had no clue what I was doing. I put my full faith and trust in my guides and angels to help me with this project.

I was at a point that I had put so much work into my book that I had copies of it in my safe, on my external hard drive, a copy on disc at a friends and a copy on a memory stick. Even if I was going down the street for a minute and was coming right back home, I still brought a copy with me.

One of my worst nightmares was coming true when my nine hundred plus page document became corrupted and I could not access the file. I tried my back up copies and they were corrupted as well. I spent a day trying to recover the file and finally figured out a way to trick it. It was nerve wrecking to say the least to think about losing all of that work.

My book might make an English teacher cringe. I do not claim to be perfect. I decided not to hire an editor. Not because I was an incredible writer that had a high education under my belt, because that is far from the truth. It is because this is my personal story and I want to keep it in my personal words. The following is a portion of my journey in this thing we call life.

Tanya Ebert

CONTENTS

Acknowledgment   iii

Preface   v

Introduction   ix

Prologue   xi

Chapter

1   The Day That Will Forever Change My Life   1

2   The Struggle Continues   17

3   A Chance to Get My Life Back   33
        Reading with Kylee – Sep 12   41
        Reading with Sal – Sep 13   48

4   The Transformation – Tanya Who?   79
        Session with Becca – Oct 5   91
        Flashback   98

5   Finally! I Now Know Why I am So Different   105

6   Getting Use to My New Skin   119
        Session with Becca – Nov 6   125
        Session with Becca – Dec 22   139
        Session with Becca – Feb 5   145
        Reading with Brianna – Mar 26   153

7   Mental Health Comes For a Visit
     – My Friends Think I am Crazy   155
        Session with Becca – Mar 30   155
        Reading with Darla – Apr 5   160

8	Still Trying to Put the Puzzle Together	167
	Reading with Darla – Apr 12	167
	Reading with Victoria – Apr 21	171
	Reading with June – Apr 24	173
	Reading with Darla – Apr 26	173
	Reading with Jessica – Apr 30	174
	Session with Becca – May 7	176
	Reading with Jessica – May 21	179
	Reading with Victoria – May 26	180
	Reading with Brianna – June 8	181
	Reading with Victoria – June 23	184
	Reading with Candace and Sharon – July 4	186
9	Spiritual Retreat? Yeah Right! More like a Cult!	189
10	The Puzzle Continues	203
	Reading with June – Sep 9	208
	Reading with Victoria – Oct 8	220
11	Milestones	225
	Reading with June – Nov 2	226
	Reading with Lilli and Roger – Nov 9	228
	Reading with Marco – Nov 29	232
	Reading with Pricilla – Dec 27	238
Puzzle Pieces and Other Tidbits		247
Closing Comments		253
About the Author		255
Resources		256
References		259

Introduction

Imagine going through an experience so traumatizing that you felt completely shattered. Empty. Hollow. Nothing left but the shell of a body. You thought you had seen it all but this one took the cake. You felt the only choice was suicide. You found yourself crying and rocking back and forth pleading for help. Only you did not know who you were asking because no one was there but you.

Like magic there was a link staring back at you on your computer. You had this deep urge to click on it. Maybe this was the place that could help you. Maybe this was the answer you have been looking for. You picked up the phone and before you knew it, you were on a plane heading to the unknown.

On your way back home, you noticed something was different. You go to sleep one person only to wake up a completely different one. One that was no longer shattered. One that was so blissfully happy it was almost too much to handle. Everything could be falling apart all around you and the birds were still singing on your shoulders.

Something was guiding you. Something had taken over. Voices guide you to go to places. Voices guide you to your bedroom window; showing you things that you could never ever forget. You remember that voice. That was the same voice that guided you to save your sister from the fire when you were eleven years old.

You know damn well that you are not the same person that was here a month ago. "This is not my skin! What the hell am I? Who am I?" You looked up and started to yell, "What have you guys done to herrrrr! She is not strong and she is scared and terrified of the dark! She cannot be by herself; she needs help! She is dying. I need to know what the hell you guys did to her! Where is she!?"

You start to cry and frantically look for yourself in your own home. You looked under your bed and in your closets. "What is going on and where is she!?" You made it back to your bedroom and cried your eyes out.

She is gone! I really hoped she was doing alright. I wish I could just talk to her to ensure that she is no longer in emotional pain and that she is safe. I understand why she had to leave. She was so dead inside. She could not handle the fact that she may end up permanently crippled and that her adventurous life was gone, not to mention the pain.

Then try to explain it to those around you when you had no idea what was happening yourself. Mental Health was sure to come knocking on your door.

Mystical Puzzle

Join me on a challenging magical journey of my sudden awakening where my entire world changed over night. I never knew of such an existence. I was not looking for it. It found me!

Prologue

Whoever dealt the cards when I was born, should have shuffled the deck a little longer and maybe the hand I was dealt would have not been so bad. I arrived weighing a mere five pounds and five ounces at 8:21pm on June 9, 1972. I was a burden to my mom and unloved by my dad. My mom was only eighteen years old at the time.

You know how the pain feels when you lose a loved one to death. That is how I felt almost from the day I was born. A deep darkness followed me; even on the days that I was happy. The task of summing up the first thirty-six years of my life would be impossible. It is excessively complicated.

By the time I was fourteen years old, I was stealing my mom's car in the middle of the night to go for joy rides. I started to sell marijuana as well as smoked it daily. It did not take long before I was taking acid and smoking crack cocaine. One time I did a needle of cocaine as well. I remember a time that I use to complain that my mom drank too much alcohol and by fourteen years old, I became an alcoholic. From the time I was fourteen, every day was a party day. Between getting drunk and stoned, I still managed to graduate and hold a decent paying job.

At twenty-two years old, I decided that I could not live anymore. I could not take the pain that I carried with me. I felt as though nobody loved me and no one ever would. My dad did not love me and wanted nothing to do with me. If my own dad did not love me, why would another man? If I was going to be messed up, depressed and alone all my life, then what was the point in living?

How does one just let go of the facts? My own father never loved me or wanted anything to do with me. My mother was too busy getting drunk to take care of me, so I had to take care of her, my little sister, and myself. I was repeatedly sexually abused as a child, and raped as a teenager. Instead of being a teenager, I played house for six years with an abusive older boyfriend. My entire family is beyond dysfunctional. Most people during their entire life time do not witness what I saw in the first twenty-two years of my life! I did not belong in this screwed up place!

Although I do not recall a near death experience, I did die. I was on life support for a few days until my body could function on its own. I toned the drinking down for awhile after this incident but it did not take long before I was partying every day again.

In 1995, while I was in Vancouver, I came across a psychic and I was drawn to get a reading. I had never done that before so I did not know what to expect. As soon as the psychic touched my hand, she looked at me and said,

Mystical Puzzle

"You're psychic." I replied with, "I know. I do not know how to control it and I do not do anything with it."

During the reading, she was blowing me away with what she was telling me. She was telling me information that she definitely should not know about. There was only one thing that she said that I thought that she was way off. She told me that I was going to write my first book by the time I was forty years old. The only thing that came to mind when she said that was, yeah right lady! I *do not* read books. I was sure not going to write one! I smoke pot, drink, and party! Everything else she was dead on, except for that. So I thought.

Living in the city proved to be too much after returning from a year long backpacking trip in South East Asia. I moved to a small town called Hope in 2004. I was still partying all the time but had a growing interest in the outdoors. I started hiking, tandem sky diving, river rafting, canoeing, camping, and four wheeling every chance I had.

Although my life had been more than challenging, it had also been a barrel of fun! I am very much young at heart and quite often see from the eyes of a child. Let us just say that I know how to have fun. I know how to turn boring, into unconventional fun! There is a reason the kids like to hang out with me.

In January of 2007, I went to Connecticut for work, and stayed in New York for the weekend. I noticed a shop advertising psychic readings. I decided to go inside and get a reading. I honestly do not remember what the young woman told me other than she was extremely worried about me. She said that she did not know why but she was very anxious around me and said that we could have other sessions to explore deeper. I explained that I lived in Canada and was in New York on holiday. She said that we could do it over the phone but I declined.

She seemed very worried about me for some reason but for all I knew, it could just be a scam for me to pay more money for more sessions. Before leaving, she urged me to buy a couple of crystal quartz points and asked me to keep them in my purse or with me at all times. She also told me not to tell anyone that I had them. I do not know why but I did buy the quartz points and left the shop rather confused. I guess only time would tell if something crazy was going to happen to me. Little did I know at the time, five months down the road, life as I knew it, would be no more.

A few years ago had someone told me
what I am about to share with you,
I would have thought that they had a few screws loose.
Even though I had a strong sixth sense,
and had many experiences with spirits,
and other things that go bump in the night,
I still would have thought
that there were definitely a few pages stuck together.
It is only because I have experienced first hand
the following events;
that I believe.

Some of you may be reading this book
to help you understand your own journey
as some of my experiences may resonate with yours.
You may come across some experiences
that seem far too unreal to be true.
I for one do not believe everything I hear or read.
If it does not feel right to me, I pass it by.
I only ask that you keep an open mind.
Envelop what feels right and leave the rest.
For what may be true to me is not true to you
and that is perfectly ok.
What is important for you
is to be completely true to yourself.
Even if that means
not connecting with anything that I have shared.
I respect that fully.

This is my story...

CHAPTER 1

The Day That Will Forever Change My Life

You never know what adventure lies ahead of you each day you get up in the morning. When I awoke on June 23, 2007, I had no idea that my life would forever change. Here I thought that I had already been to hell and back several times. Apparently, it was time to go for another round.

Amber and I went to her Brother Toby's house to do an oil change on my dirt bike and a tune up on my truck. We wanted to get my truck ready for the four by four obstacle race that I was entering in September. I have watched the four wheel races for the past four years and had no doubt that I could beat the best time.

Amber volunteered to be my co-pilot. Our plans were to paint "T & A" on the roof of my truck. It stands for Tanya and Amber not tits and ass, so get your head out of the gutter! On my door, we are painting "Dirty Dora" as I love to explore the back mountain roads. On my tailgate, we are painting "The little truck that could."

I had never done an oil change on my dirt bike, but how hard could it be? It explained what to do in my manual. If we run into any problems, Toby would be there to guide us along. Amber videotaped me while I did the oil change.

Once I finished the oil change, I started up the bike and took it for a spin in Toby's huge yard. Amber was nattering about something but I was not really paying attention to what she had said. Toby went for a ride on my bike as well.

Instead of doing the tune up on my truck, I had the bright idea to go four wheeling in the mountains instead. Amber refused to go with me because she said that I was scary and that she was not mentally prepared. I told her I was not scary and she replied that I was because she has seen all my videos. How was she supposed to be my co-pilot if she was scared to get in the truck with me?

We convinced Toby to let Amber borrow his three wheeled ATC (All Terrain Cycle) and we went to Silver Lake as he lived near there. I had to stop my dirt bike for what seemed like forever waiting for Amber to catch up to me. Amber was making fun of all the safety gear that I was wearing but she would not drive past five kilometers an hour. She also mentioned that when they were kids, all they had was a helmet, and that was it.

We went to the boat launch area of Silver Lake and Amber filmed while I rode around. At the time, I had no idea what provoked me to think and say the following. "Should I try and do a wheelie? I'm going to wipe out!" I tried to do a wheelie and it did not work. "I'm scared! I do not know how to do wheelies. I know how to do them, but I do not really know how. You just give lots of gas and pop the clutch!"

I tried to do a wheelie again and the front tire went an inch off the ground. I decided to give it one more mother of a go. From a stand still, I revved up the gas to almost full throttle and let go of the clutch.

Oh, I did a wheelie all right! I shot the bike straight up in the air! As I was starting to bring it back down, I had realized that I was going to wipe out! I put my left leg out thinking that it would brace the fall. The thought that ran through my mind at that very second was, *oh shit! Legs do not do that!*

I crashed and screamed, "My knee Amber!" I lay on the ground screaming and crying. The only thing that I could think of was pain! The only thing that my brain was sending me was pain! I was going to pass out! I could not take this pain! *Focus Tanya! Focus! Breathe!* I started to breathe as if I was a woman that was giving birth. I did not know what else to do other than focus and breathe through the pain.

Eventually I calmed down and stopped screaming and crying. I did not dare move though. I just lay on the ground and relaxed. Amber had this all on videotape. She asked me to explain on camera what had happened. In my whiniest voice I said, "I did a wheelie and I did not know how to bring it back down! It was a good wheelie though!"

After lying on the ground for about twenty minutes, Amber pulled my riding pants down so that she could have a look at my knee. I am not a doctor but I knew my leg was severely injured! I did not know what was wrong but I knew that legs do not do what my leg had just done. Amber told me that if I were a golden retriever, my leg would cost three thousand dollars to fix. Amber was always good for a laugh.

We could not see anything wrong with my leg but it definitely felt like something was wrong. I did not know how I was going to get out of there. Amber seemed to think that I could ride out. I told her if she could get my bike started, I would try to ride out. She started my bike and I proceeded to ride to her brothers. Before we parted, she had told me not to wait for her and that she would be right behind me.

As soon as I tried to switch gears, I had realized that my knee was so screwed, that I could not switch them. I had to ride to Toby's in first gear. Amber got there soon after I did. Amber and Toby loaded my bike onto my truck. I asked Amber to take me to the hospital. There was something definitely wrong with my leg.

As I was trying to get in the passenger seat of my truck, Amber asked me what I was doing. "Getting ready to go to the hospital dumb ass!" She then informed me that she did not know how to drive a standard and that I had to drive. There was no way in hell this leg of mine could push in a clutch. As it was, I could hardly get myself inside the truck without excruciating pain! I screamed the whole time trying to get in!

"Well Amber, it looks like you are getting a crash course on driving standard. You have until the end of Toby's driveway to figure it out." She hopped the truck all the way out of the driveway and off we went to my house. I wanted to drop off my truck and bike and pick up my car, as it was an automatic. There was no way I was going to get Amber to back my truck into my garage. It was hard enough for her to get it in forwards. Every time she hopped the truck, my leg started to throb and I started to scream!

By the time we got to the hospital, what little wobbling I could do, I could do no more. I had x-rays done but nothing was broken and the doctor could not find anything wrong to cause all the pain. Amber took me back home and into bed by midnight. I had to teach her how to roll joints because I could not move.

We decided to watch the video footage from the day's event. I had never realized this at the time but I soon figured out where I received the idea to do a wheelie. Before we had gone to the lake, and I had just started up my bike after the oil change, Amber had asked me if I could pop a wheelie. She had said that when I was not really paying attention to her. I guess there was a part of me that did hear because an hour later, I tried to do a wheelie.

I did not know how I was going to sleep because I was in so much pain and I normally could not sleep on my back. Anytime I moved a millimeter, I would scream! This was insane! I did not know what I had done but there was something seriously wrong!

June 24

I phoned my boss to let her know that I had an accident and did not know when I would be back at work. I was supposed to leave for Connecticut in a couple of days for work and there was no way that I was going to be able to go. I was hoping that I would be all fixed and ready to go by the time I was supposed to go to California for work.

As Alex was out of school, he came over to take care of me. The only time I got out of bed was to go to the washroom. If there were a way that I could go to the washroom without getting out of bed, I would have. The effort and pain it took to get out of bed, crutch twenty feet to the toilet and get back to bed, was worse than climbing the summit of Mount Everest.

I could not lift my injured leg to crutch forward. The only way I could get it to move was by placing my crutches so far ahead of myself that my body would fall forward. I screamed the whole time but it was the only way I could get to the bathroom. My brain would not allow me to voluntarily move forward because of the pain, so I had to force it forward by almost falling.

I ended up peeing in a bucket in my bedroom because I could not bare the pain to get to the washroom. Amber came over to check on me and noticed the bucket. She picked it up giggling and smelled it.

"What are you doing?!"

"Nice trick with the apple juice Tanya!"

"That is my pee you dumb ass! In case you have not noticed, I cannot move. To get the apple juice would mean that I walked to the fridge!"

"Oh my god! I just smelled your piss?! Where is the bleach?!"

June 25

I spent another long painful day in bed. I could not turn my head to watch TV. There was only one position that I could lay in without feeling pain. The second I moved any part of my body, it felt as though I was electrocuted repeatedly!

Something was seriously wrong with my leg! It was somehow stuck. I could not straighten it and I could not fully bend it either, not to mention the excruciating pain! I did not know how I was going to get through another minute!

June 26

Alex was a god send. He was only nine years old and I did not know what I would have done without him. He had been making us food or buying it for us in town. He passed me everything that I needed and picked up groceries, as we needed them. The grocery store was only half a block away and I only gave him a small list. He played at the park or went swimming in the pool and checked in with me throughout the day.

I phoned my doctor because I am no doctor but I know my body and something was seriously wrong with my leg! I was able to get an appointment but I had no idea how I was going to get down twenty stairs when I could barely move twenty feet to the bathroom.

I cannot put into words the kind of pain and struggle that I was feeling. The only way I could get myself down the stairs was on my butt, step by step. I used one arm to lower myself down to the next step and used the other arm to brace my injured leg. It did not end there because I had to get inside my car and then somehow get out of it and then into the doctors office.

I explained to my doctor that I had x-rays done and the doctor at the hospital could not find anything wrong but something was most seriously wrong. She made an appointment for me to see a surgeon named Dr. Sukai on June 30th.

Amber stopped by and said I stunk. I had not had a bath or shower since the accident. I did not think she really understood the pain that I was going through. Obviously, I would have had a bath long ago if it were that easy. I had no clue how I was going to get in or out of the tub, when I could not lift my leg on its own or move it without the electrocuting pain!

I had figured out a way to get in the tub. As my toilet was beside the tub, I sat on the toilet, slid over to the edge of the tub, and lowered myself in the tub with one arm. I had to use my other arm to brace my injured leg from moving. Do not ask how I did this or where I found the strength to do it. I got back out the same way only I had to pull myself up with one arm instead of lower myself.

Well I will tell you one thing. I would not be bathing everyday. The pain and the energy and strength involved were insane. I would try to bath three times a week but the thought of having to go through that every single time, filled my head with helplessness.

Between Amber and Lorne, they had been rolling my joints for me. Ok, so I smoke pot everyday but the last few days I had been smoking pot excessively. Lorne rolled me ten joints and I just about cried because I told him that I would run out by the time he got home from work in twelve hours.

Lorne thought it was funny that I could not move while I was being rained on while lying in bed. He refused to shut the window for me. He actually got up and left my place for a half hour while I got wet.

It was bad enough having to beg him to please warm up my soup in the microwave and pass it to me. He thought that it would be just fine for me to eat my soup cold. Eventually I had convinced him to heat it up for me.

I really did not like having to depend on everyone for my basic needs. I never knew when someone would be by to help me when Alex was out playing. I pretty much lay in bed and hoped that someone would be coming by when I was hungry or thirsty.

June 29

Since I was stuck in bed, I had been finding myself getting thirsty and hungry while waiting for people to stop by. I stocked my bed and area with everything I needed within reach. I kept at least four bottles of water and food that did not need refrigerating. I also stocked up with smokes, joints, and candy.

I kept a water spray bottle in the bed with me as well. It was the only thing that I had to protect myself from my cat Molly. She would run and jump on my bed; bite and attack my injured knee and then take off. I could not chase after her anymore. All I could do was spray her away from me and my bed.

I kept a pee bucket in my bedroom because it was easier to go in the bucket than to crutch twenty feet to the bathroom. I often wondered how I maneuvered in and out of bed each time I needed to go. I was surprised that the police had not come to investigate all the crying and screaming each day.

I left the key to my apartment under the mat so that my friends could let themselves in. I really only got out of bed for bowel movements and a bath every couple of days. That little bit was excruciating in itself.

Melissa phoned Alex to see if he wanted to come home and take a break. Alex said that he could not go home because Auntie Tanya needed him. Aww, he is such a sweet kid. Seriously, he had helped me so much since the accident. My friends and family worked all day so without him, I would have been screwed!

June 30

Melissa drove me to meet Dr. Sukai the surgeon. He had x-rays done again and then told me that he did not know what was wrong. I told him that I could not lift or move my leg a millimeter and that I was in excruciating pain! I also told him that my leg was stuck.

His response was if there were anything wrong with my leg, there would be more bruising. He then told me that he did not know what was wrong; he was going on vacation and I needed to find someone else to figure it out. He told me that a nurse would come and put a brace on and I would not need my crutches because I could walk out of the hospital and then he walked away.

The nurse came to put the brace on and told me to straighten my leg. I told her that I could not straighten my leg because it was stuck! She put it on as best she could even though my leg was in a bent position. The metal rods inside of the brace were stabbing me in the leg. I could not walk so Melissa used a wheelchair from the hospital and pushed me to the car. I removed the brace because it did not fit properly as it was made for someone one foot taller. Melissa drove me back home.

Amber came to visit later in the day. With the biggest smile on my face, I told her that I did not know what, how or why but something big was going to come from this accident. Something really big, I could feel it.

Lorne came over too and the two of them thought it would be funny to spray me with the water bottle repeatedly knowing that I could not move or it would hurt. I had to sit there and just take it. They were quite amused by that! I was not!

Alex ended up taking care of me for nine days in a row. My nephew Michael came up and took care of me for the next week. I really did not know what I would have done without the kids helping me. Thank god, they were on summer break. Just having someone pass me things was huge in itself. In addition, Community Services was nice enough to loan me a wheelchair to help me get around if I wanted to leave my apartment.

It had been almost a month since my accident and I realized all of my gear was still sitting in the back of my truck. Someone could easily steal it. As Alex was over and I had heard someone in the garage, I asked him to go down and get one of the guys to help him bring up the gear. I figured it was either Lorne or Rod in the garage.

Alex came back up stairs and said that he was scared because someone was in the garage. I told him it was Rod or Lorne and they could help him with all of my stuff. He looked frightened and would not leave my apartment. "Buddy, get going; Rod or Lorne will help you." At that point, Alex had left my apartment.

I was wondering what was taking him so long so I got out of bed and realized that he never went downstairs. He was standing outside of my apartment door. I was right pissed off by this point and started to go down the stairs on my ass. It took what seemed like forever to do that, not to mention the energy and pain.

Once I was downstairs and in the garage, I realized that Rod's garage door was open a bit. I tried shutting it but it would not budge. It would not open any further or close. Rod or Lorne, whoever it was that was just down there must have left because they were no longer there. Something did not feel right. I looked over at my truck and something did not look right but I could not put my finger on it.

Alex emptied the gear out of my truck and brought it upstairs to my apartment while I sat on the stairs and waited for him. While he was doing that, Lorne came inside the apartment from outside. I had asked him if he was just in the garage and he informed me that he was not.

I told Lorne that Rod's garage door was stuck and that I thought that maybe someone had just tried to break in. I told him to have a look around to see if any of his stuff was missing. It turned out that one of his golf clubs and a set of tools were missing. Lorne fixed Rod's garage door while I tried to wake up Rod to get him to check his stuff. Rod never answered his door as usual.

The next day Rod checked out his stuff and everything seemed to be there. He asked me if I owned a gray, black, and orange backpack. "Yes, I do, why?" He found it underneath my truck. That backpack was supposed to be in a locked toolbox in the back of my truck. That meant that my toolbox with all my outdoor gear was broken into.

I made my way downstairs to the garage and discovered that the thief used Lorne's golf club to pry open my toolbox at the hinge. I guess he had heard Alex coming down the stairs and dropped my backpack and got the hell out of there.

Amber was over and witnessed first hand why I went pee in a bucket in my bedroom. The pain I went through to get to the washroom was unbelievable. I screamed and cried every little movement I made. Amber thought that I was being ridiculous and over exaggerating. She said to me, "If I hear you cry or scream one more time, I am out of here!"

I could not believe what I was hearing and broke down into tears. Amber got up and left. Why did no one believe me or understand what was happening? Something was wrong with my leg! I was suffering and no one was helping it to go away! Everyone including the doctors seemed to think that there was nothing wrong with me and that I should be able to walk!

Amber came back a couple of hours later with a gift because she said that I behaved so badly. That was her way of apologizing. She bought me some Kleenex to wipe my tears, a kit to fix my nails when they break, and some candy.

It had been just over a month and I had been stuck in bed in excruciating and unbearable pain. Betty took me to see my doctor. I found out that the next available appointment to see a surgeon from Hope to Vancouver was at the end of September.

This was ridiculous! I could not imagine having to suffer one more hour let alone months! I tried to explain to my doctor that my leg was stuck and there was something seriously wrong but she just did not hear me. She had not offered me anything other than Ibuprofen and Tylenol for the pain, which was of no help!

She sent me over to the pharmacy to get a proper sized brace put on. She said that I would be able to walk if I had a brace on. I did not understand how that was going to work, as I still could not lift my leg a millimeter off the ground. Betty and the pharmacist helped me down onto the floor.

The pharmacist asked me to straighten my leg so that he could put the brace on. Only that was one of my problems. I could not straighten my leg! Why did these people not get it?! Why were they not hearing me or listening to me! He could not get the brace on. I ended up stuck on the floor having no idea how they were going to get me on my feet while I held my leg in place.

I had a total emotional fit and started crying. I felt so useless and helpless on the floor. "I cannot do this any more! I cannot be crippled and I cannot do the pain. I am done! I am just plain done!" Betty and the pharmacist finally helped me off the floor and Betty took me home. I did not understand why my leg was so screwed up and no one got it!

~~~

Something rather strange happened. I knew that there were ghosts in the apartment that I lived in but I am starting to think that there was a cat ghost as well. I was lying in my bed during the day time and felt the bed depress beside me as though Molly had just jumped from the window sill. She did this all the time so I knew what it felt like.

Immediately after it happened I thought to myself, how did Molly get onto my window sill without me seeing her? I looked down on the floor expecting to see Molly and she was not there. I knew that she could not just disappear and if she were running, I would hear that. I called her and she came running into my bedroom from the living room. Whatever had jumped on my bed was not Molly. I was not afraid in any way. Usually I did not feel too good about those kinds of experiences, but for some reason the cat ghost did not scare me.

Maybe that was why Molly was so naughty. Maybe the cat ghost or other spirits were harassing her. She was always tripping out and following things that I could not see. When ever I sensed a presence, I always looked to see how Molly was behaving and she was usually more erratic during those times.

That was not the first time I had experienced spirits in this apartment. A few months back something creepy happened. I was listening to music on my computer in my bedroom. It was loud and I had my back turned to the entrance of my bedroom. Over the loud music, I heard my neighbor who lived down the hall yell, "Hello!" Close to my ear. It startled me because I could not figure out how she got into my apartment when I always kept the door locked.

I turned around expecting to see Charla and no one was there! Oh my god, you have to be kidding me! Oh Tanya! Just *forget* what happened and *do not* tell anyone! I had turned the music down and heard, "Hello!" A woman's voice shouted in my ear again but no one was in my apartment!

Ok, so I started to think that maybe it was not a ghost. Maybe it was on the song that I was listening to and my speakers were just projecting the sound beside my ear?! I started the song from the beginning and there were no "hello's," shouting through the music.

Oh, I did not feel good about this at all! I could feel her presence right at my back and she was not leaving! I had to leave my room and would not sit at my computer for the rest of the night. My cat was acting strangely too. I mean she always was strange, but she was definitely looking around at something that I could not see! I felt her presence for a couple of days and could not go on my computer until she left. It was so creepy!

Mystical Puzzle

By mid August, I was just starting to be able to lift my injured leg an inch off the floor and I was able to crutch around my apartment a little. I still spent most of my time in bed but I was able to move a few feet if I had to. The pain was still beyond excruciating. I did not know how I had survived that long as it had been six weeks of suffering for every second. I was in so much pain that I could not sleep at night. The existence that I was living was inhumane.

My neighbors Lorne and Rod helped me a lot. If I needed my garbage taken out, I would put it outside my apartment door and one of them would take it to the garbage bins in the garage for me. Between them, Amber and Alex, I pretty much got the basics done.

Over the course of the next month, I was starting to get around my apartment a little bit better. I was also starting to move around a little in bed without screaming. Do not get me wrong, I still suffered immensely every day but I was just starting to be able to do something other than lay in bed all day and all night.

I still required a lot of assistance. For example, I could not put my own sock and shoe on my left foot. I was hoping that by winter time I would be able to wear something on my feet other than sandals. I could not get a runner on at this point because I could not move my muscles in that way.

Putting underwear on was hard because my leg only bent so much. I had to try to loop my underwear over my foot and hope that they would not go on backwards. It was frustrating to try to dress myself. I had no problem with tops and clothes on my upper body but struggled and needed assistance with my lower body clothing.

It was a shame that summer had been flashing by and I was stuck in bed. I started going to the lake because I could park at the boat launch and the beach was only a few feet away. In order to go in the lake, I crutched into the water while who ever had come with me brought me my air mattress. Once I was deep enough, I handed them my crutches and fell onto the air mattress.

I could not gracefully lean onto the air mattress because it was too painful to do that and my body just would not do it. That was why I had to fall onto the mattress. I had to force my body into that position and just take the pain.

Once I was ready to get out of the water, my friend would hand me my crutches and take my air mattress for me. I could not get down on to the ground by myself or up on my own when I was on the ground, so I could not go to the lake by myself. However, with assistance, I could go.

I went to Kelowna for the weekend in September as my aunt and uncle were having a weekend family get together. I decided to go to the mall because I needed a small backpack. I thought that it would be much easier to carry things. That way I could keep my arms free for my crutches or wheelchair.

This was the first time that I had attempted to go somewhere like the mall by myself. I drove around the parking lot a few times looking for a stall that was close to an entrance. They were all taken. I got frustrated, started to cry, and left the mall.

I drove around Kelowna crying and upset because I could not go to the mall by myself. I smoked a joint because I figured I would have plenty of time to air out before I got back to my aunts. As I was driving around I thought, Screw that! I went back to the mall. I drove around again looking for a spot and managed to find one that was not too far from an entrance.

It was not easy pulling my wheelchair out of the car but I pulled it out eventually and sat myself in it. It was amazing how the littlest hill could give you so much speed if you were going down it and how hard it was to get up the slightest hill. The wheelchair tried to do wheelies when I was going up steep hills. I did not like that, as that was what got me in this mess in the first place.

I found a decent priced backpack. Now I would be able to carry things like a few groceries. With a backpack, I could pick up a few things by myself instead of always having to depend on everyone to take me. I could not carry stuff and crutch at the same time. It was hard enough to crutch never mind carry anything while I was doing it. If I were not in so much pain, it would be no big deal to get around. I felt good about going to the mall by myself. I tired easily but I did manage to do it by myself. It felt as though I had reached a milestone.

Once I arrived back at my family's home, they were playing yard games. I could not participate but going there was better than lying in bed all day at home. They had a hot tub so that was nice and relaxing. That I could do.

The following weekend was Briggie Days in Hope. My cousin Melissa brought me to the four wheeling obstacle race on Saturday and my friend Kaya brought me to the demolition derby on Sunday. This was the weekend that I was supposed to enter my truck in the obstacle race. Perhaps I should have done the tune up on my truck as planned instead of going for a dirt bike ride.

It was hard for me to maneuver the wheelchair by myself at the sports bowl because the ground was uneven and I still could not jerk my leg around. In fact, I could not touch my knee with a feather without screaming.

I saw my cousin Christopher at the race. He told me that he had an electric scooter wheelchair if I wanted to borrow it. I thanked him but told him that I was not going to need it. As soon as I could see a surgeon, they would fix me and I would be good to go. Christopher told me that God blessed him with the wheelchair and he was looking for someone in need to give it to. I was sure that there was someone out there that needed it more than me.

I met my surgeon, Dr. Cholt at the end of September. He suspected that I had a torn meniscus and said it would not be necessary for an MRI, as he would see everything when he went inside my knee. He had scheduled arthroscopic knee surgery for October 26th. That just happened to be Michael's birthday. I could finally put an end to this misery and get back to life! Because honestly, I had had enough of this being crippled business!

As I would not be able to go back to work any time soon, my position was awarded to another employee. After all the abuse and drama that I had put up with, I did not get to go to California after all. In a way, I was somewhat glad because originally, we were supposed to go for three months and they cut it down to three weeks. The project was nothing what I was told that it would be.

Not to mention my boss was purposely trying to sabotage me. I could never figure out why she would do that because in the end it would make her look bad. It was not until she gave her notice that it all made sense. She would not be there so it would not matter to her what happened. I always knew she was up to something; it just took me awhile to figure it out. I could not believe how dirty some people could actually be!

Had I not had the accident, my new boss would have been my friend Kara. She and I worked in the same department. Her position became open and Amber was awarded the position. That would have meant that Amber and I would have worked and traveled to California together. That would have been so much fun!

When Amber went to California, I stayed at her place to take care of her dogs and cat. Ok, so I always knew she had dogs but how could I be friends with someone and not know that they had a cat. I had never seen it ever. Apparently, he was a real scaredy cat. He would never come out when people were around.

By the time Amber came back, her cat loved me! I was definitely ready to go back home. One of her dogs was so anxious that it made my time around him very uncomfortable. He could not sit still and just paced back and forth.

Amber gave me a set of her house keys so that I could continue to let her dogs out to pee while she was at work. She had been full of stress and anxiety herself lately and I thought that it would help her out if I let her dogs out half way between her work shifts instead of her having to come home to do it on her breaks.

I also gave her a set of keys to my place. We must have really trusted each other because neither one of us was the type to give a set of keys to our home to a friend. When I was not at home, Amber could use my computer and she could just let herself in when she came for visits.

The Day That Will Forever Change My Life

My sister had told me that Michael's Great Uncle just lost one of his legs due to amputation. He was quite upset for obvious reasons but even more so because he was confined to his townhome. It was challenging enough being handicapped, but even worse when you could not leave your own home, and try to lead as normal a life as possible.

The light bulb went on! My cousin Christopher had an electric scooter wheelchair that he had been waiting to give someone. What a perfect match! This man had no money and was on welfare. I told my sister not to say anything because I did not want to get anyone's hopes up but I was going to phone Christopher to see if he still had the wheelchair. I phoned Christopher and yes, he still had the wheelchair. This was perfect! Christopher was more than excited that we found someone that was truly in need.

Christopher and I delivered the wheelchair to Todd. It was a tearful event when Todd graciously accepted the wheelchair. It was as though he was in a state of shock that someone would give him an electric wheelchair that was worth thousands of dollars and wanted nothing in return. Christopher said a prayer and we left.

Christopher mentioned that we had not visited in such a long time. I told him that I could not visit because I smoked a lot of pot and could not go without. He said that I could go for a walk and spray myself down before I came back in. He also said if that was what needed to take place for me to visit; he did not care because he just wanted to see me. Wow! That totally blew me away! Christopher or Father God Christopher as I liked to call him said I could smoke pot.

It was not that long ago that Christopher and I use to party together all the time. He was starting to mellow on the whole God thing. I was starting to see that he was still Christopher but he was Christopher that did not party anymore and he had a strong relation to God. He was not a junkie and he was helping so many people that were users and on the streets. I would rather have him just as he was than dead or a junkie. Even though the whole God thing was not my thing, I knew it was Christopher's thing and I was proud of the person that he had become.

On my facebook status I typed, "God works in mysterious ways." This was meant to happen. If Christopher never told me that he had the chair in the first place, and if my sister never mentioned that Uncle Todd lost his leg, this would have never happened. Something else I found out, Uncle Todd and I shared the same birthday.

Rex a man that I worked with replied to my facebook status, "Who are you and what have you done with Tanya?" Rex was very much a Christian. I really liked him though because he was non judgementive and let me be me, potty mouth and all.

~ ~ ~

I had finally received a handicap parking permit. That made it so much easier to get around. You have no idea how far the end of the parking lot was to a handicapped person. The thought of walking down one aisle in the grocery store seemed impossible to me. You really have no idea what it was like to go from active to almost null and void. I could not wait for my surgery so that I could walk again!

October 26

It had been four months since my accident and I was just starting to be able to crutch around using one crutch. It hurt a lot, but it allowed me to be just a little bit more independent. I was tired of relying on everyone to take care of me. I wanted to try to do as much as possible on my own.

I went for surgery as planned and was told that I would be walking in two to three weeks. Although he did tell me that while I was under anesthetics, he could not straighten my leg or bend it. I told them I was not faking it and it was stuck! If only people would have just listened to me in the first place!

I was in so much pain and my knee and leg were swollen so badly, that I could not imagine that I would actually be walking soon. The useless stuff they gave me for pain did nothing to alleviate it. My mom came over and took care of me for a few days. I swear to god the surgeon did not find what was wrong. My leg did not feel any better and I could not move it any more than before the surgery.

November 15

I had my follow up appointment with the surgeon. I was still in excruciating pain and every move I did was calculated, or I risked more pain. Dr. Cholt did not know why I was still in so much pain and suggested that I see a physio therapist. He told me to stop using the crutches and to start using a cane. Was he insane?! Something was seriously wrong with my leg and nobody got it! There was no way that I could get around with a cane as I could hardly get around with crutches! What part of that did he not understand?!

November 19

I started physio therapy. I went twice a week and I did exercises every two hours for ten to twenty minutes. The therapy and exercises were so painful that I had felt as though I was in another world. I could not think straight when I was in that kind of pain! This could not be right! It was not pain; it was pure suffering!

It had been five months since my accident and my work sent a get well card. No flowers, no fruit basket, no chocolate, but they did send me a card. It was nice to know how much they cared. To think I risked having a stroke in my thirties to bend over backwards for them.

December 17

I had a follow up appointment with my surgeon Dr. Cholt. He was surprised that I was still in the same condition. He thought that my hamstrings might need stretching. He preferred not to do that as there was a chance of nerve damage and the surgery was invasive. He also said that I would be required to spend a few days in the hospital after the surgery. Surgery had been set for January 25, 2008, if my leg was still not better.

I had to continue to go to physio and do my exercises. I swear to god that guy did not know what he was doing and had no clue what was wrong with me. My leg was stuck! Why did no one get that?!

~ ~ ~

I started to use my cane when I walked short distances. For any kind of distance like grocery shopping or up and down aisles, I used a wheelchair. The pain was still excruciating.

I suffered every day and did not know how much more I could take of it. Every couple of hours when I did my physio exercises, I was in excruciating pain. I still could not touch my knee with a feather without screaming. Even when I was just laying there doing nothing, I would still get sharp shooting pains in my knee.

I was really starting to freak out! I made an appointment to see Dr. Night. He was like the god of orthopedic surgeons. It would cost me five hundred and fifty dollars just to talk to him. The soonest appointment available was January 28, 2008. That was just great! My surgery was scheduled for January 25th, and I wanted to talk to Dr. Night before my surgery. I did not trust that Dr. Cholt knew what he was doing in my case. I had asked repeatedly to get an MRI and he refused to order one.

CHAPTER 2

The Struggle Continues

2008

I could no longer tolerate Molly's behavior. There was not a day that did not go by that she did not attack my injured leg and me. Every day she was still trying to rip my pictures off the wall and knock my stuff off my shelves. Every minute of life was hard enough! I did not need the added stress of my cat!

Molly viciously attacked me and I completely lost it. I tore after her like never before. I grabbed my bat and was hunting her down in my apartment like a mad woman. I pounded the bat into the floor all around her. She ran behind the couch where she knew I could not get her. I grabbed the end of the couch and swung it into the middle of the living room as if it was a pillow. That couch was no regular couch. It was heavy as it reclined on both ends.

I grabbed a hold of Molly and screamed as I had never screamed at her before. This was the first time in two years that she had actually been submissive towards me. She hunkered down on the ground and did not move an inch. She meowed as if to say, Ok stop it now! I give! I was in a crazy rage and did not know what to do. I had her pinned down with one hand and the bat in the other.

I threw the bat away from me and grabbed her with both hands. I was in such a rage that I felt like I could hurt her. Only I did not want to hurt her and I love animals. I loved her too but I could not take her crazy abusive behavior anymore. I threw her down and told her, if she knew what was good for her, she would stay the hell away from me!

I went to my bedroom and I bawled my eyes out! What was wrong with me?! I just about killed my cat! I could not handle this anymore! I could not go through the added daily stress that she brought. I had been hoping that each day that I woke up, that maybe that was the day that Molly would not be crazy anymore. I had waited two years and that day never came. There was not a day that had gone by since I took her home from the pet shop that she had not attacked me or drove me to insanity in some way.

I had dreaded having to make this decision. I needed to put her down. There was no way that I would be able to re-home her because I did not know one person that would put up with her behavior. I love her to bits but I was at the end of my rope. I could not imagine what someone would do to her if she pulled her usual crap and they did not have an attachment to her as I did.

I did not want to do it right away. I did not want her to think that she was being punished for what just happened. I wished I did not have to do it at all, but I was barely holding on to life and she was making it that much harder. As difficult of a cat that she was, I loved her so much and wanted her last days to remember me loving her, not in a crazy rage after her.

January 15

I saw Dr. Cholt, my surgeon. I confirmed with him that I would not be going through with the surgery scheduled on January 25th because I did not see Dr. Night until the January 28th. He was shocked that I had an appointment with Dr. Night. The only reason that I did not have to wait on the usual two year waiting list was that I was paying him five hundred and fifty dollars.

Dr. Cholt was clearly pissed off that Dr. Night was making that much money on one visit with me and that he had to have seven visits with me to make that same amount of money. The reason that I knew that was because that was what he had told me. Wow! You would think that he would appreciate someone of Dr. Night's expertise have a look at my leg since he had no clue what was wrong with it. Instead, he was jealous and envious of the money he was making. To be honest with you, I was not comfortable with Dr. Cholt performing the surgery. He really had no clue why my leg was the way it was, and he had been inside my knee once already.

It had been seven months since my accident and I was confused as to why I was still not walking properly. My leg was stuck and no one seemed to get that. My knee popped all the time as I was moving about. The more I used my leg, the more it hurt when I was not moving at all. My movements were still very calculated or else I was in excruciating pain. I dreaded physio and my exercises because it was like continuous torture all day, every day!

January 18

I was not looking forward to this day as this was the day that I was putting Molly down. I spent the day cuddling her and telling her how much I loved her. She seemed different that day as if somehow she knew. God I wish I did not have to do this.

I took Molly to the vet in the late afternoon. He shaved her where he was going to inject the needle. I scooped her hair as if it was the breath of life itself. He injected her and I watched her take her last breath. I just about collapsed to the floor. She was my every thing for the last two years and now she was no more.

I left the vet in an emotional mess. I got in my car and cried my way home, which was only a couple of blocks away. I could hardly drive and get myself to my apartment. I opened the door waiting for her to greet me but she never came. She was never coming to the door again. What had I done?! I did not know how I was ever going to leave my apartment again! I was so messed up!

I could not stop crying. I cried until my eyes were swollen shut. Lorne knocked on my door and insisted on coming in. I did not want to let him in because I did not want anyone to see the state that I was in. I felt completely lost and I did not feel like being made fun of because my cat was dead.

She was not just any cat. She was like my kid. She was a part of my life. She was the only thing in life that I could count on. When I opened my door, she would be there. I ended up letting Lorne in and he did not make fun of me. I eventually stopped crying. I could not imagine ever recovering from this. Lorne stayed until I fell asleep.

The next day I woke up and realized all over again that Molly was gone and never coming back. I started crying again until my eyes were swollen shut. I did not know how I was ever going to get through this. I felt as though I was never going to be able to leave my apartment in the state that I was in. I could not go a few minutes without breaking down into tears. I was an absolute mess!

Lorne came over and I managed to pull myself together and stopped crying. I ran out of smokes and there was no way that I could go out in this state, so Lorne went to the store for me. Lorne waited for me to fall asleep before leaving again.

When I woke up the following day, it was the same thing. Molly was gone! I could not function! I was an emotional mess! This routine of me being completely messed up, and Lorne coming over and staying with me until I fell asleep at night, continued on for a couple more days.

I was eventually able to get up in the morning and start my day without crying. I soon started to realize that Molly was in a better place, that I was not a cat killer, and that I really did try with her. Everyone that knew Molly and me told me that I made the right decision. Even Amber said that I did the right thing. That meant a lot to me, as I knew how much Amber loved animals and she use to be a vet technician.

I had Molly cremated and picked up her remains. Inside her urn of ashes, I placed her collar and a tinfoil ball as that was her favorite toy. Her food dish was still out along with all of her toys. I decided it was time to start packing up her stuff and putting it into storage. It was not easy. I also removed the locks off the cupboards that she used to get into.

Life was so different without her around. I really missed her and almost forgot how naughty she was, and how much she hurt me on a daily basis. I loved her so much! If only she did not attack me all the time. It was not as if I provoked her to attack. Something clicked inside of her and she switched into a vicious animal.

It was so hard for me because although she was vicious every day, she was also loving and entertaining. She certainly was no ordinary cat. Anyone that had ever come over to my place had mentioned that they had never seen a cat do the things that she did.

As if things could not get any worse. My Aunt Chandal, my mom's twin was in the hospital and we all needed to meet to discuss whether to take her off life support. She had a stroke. The doctors had been monitoring her brain activity and told us that if she ever did come out of coma, she would be a complete vegetable. We made a group decision that life was not life if you were a vegetable. After we spent some time with her, we were allowing the doctors to remove life support.

As all this was going on, I had found out that Amber's dad just lost his battle with cancer. When it rains, it pours. What was this? The week of death? Nana and I spent some time with Aunt Chandal before they unplugged the machines. Even though she was in a coma, her body jerked forward. Nana broke down crying and I just about crapped myself! The doctors said that it happens but she was still in a coma and would not recover. After we left, they removed life support and it was not long before she passed.

January 28

I went to Vancouver for my appointment with Dr. Night. I made sure to arrive early so I did not have to stress out worrying about being on time. I parked in the parkade and pulled out my wheelchair. I made my way inside the mall where his office was located and I came to an escalator. There was no elevator. How was someone in a wheelchair supposed to get up an escalator? I just parked in handicapped parking! What did this mean? You could park at our mall but you could not come in.

I wheeled back to my car and grabbed my crutches. I had no idea how I was going to crutch through the mall to find out how to get in with my wheelchair. I approached the escalator and did not know how I was going to get on. It was going so fast. My leg was not made for this! I crutched on and almost wiped out in the process. Great! Now I had to get off without wiping out and then do it all over again to get back to my car!

Thank god the information booth was not too far from the escalator and they explained to me how to get inside the mall with a wheelchair. I went back to my car to get my wheelchair. Thankfully I arrived on time to my appointment. I was so tired of this crippled shit!

Basically, Dr. Night said that I was screwed. He advised that I get an MRI, which I had been asking for since my accident. If the doctors had listened to me in the first place, I would have had the appointment already. I would probably need to wait for another six months just for that.

Dr. Night explained that most people do not recover from such a rare injury. They did not know much on how to heal such an injury because not too many people had experienced them. Most surgeons would never see such a case in their practice. He told me that it would take at least a year before I could expect any significant improvement and that I may never regain full extension of my knee joint.

I could handle walking funny but it was the pain that was killing me. I still could not touch my knee with a feather without screaming. It was ultra sensitive! I left the doctor's in a numb state of mind. I did not have time to deal with my problems because I had Amber's dad's wake to attend. I needed to pull myself together for her and her family.

I stayed in Surrey as my aunt's funeral was the following day. There was a lot of food left over so my cousin Christopher, his wife Chloe and I filled up trays of food to bring to the homeless drop in center down the street. A large dump of snow dropped during the night and it was difficult driving down the side streets. Chloe did not think we would make it. Christopher told her, "You don't know my cousin," with a mischievous grin.

The people at the drop in center were on a very different planet. I had done many drugs in my day and I could not imagine how much it would take to get in the state that those people were in. I really felt sorry for them because they were so lost. I honestly felt that there was no hope for them as they were that far gone. Nobody gets up one day and decides they want to be a junkie. Somewhere along the line, they slipped through the cracks. Let us not forget that they are still human.

I left Surrey after the funeral and made my way back home. I was hoping that I would get there in one piece because I did not have winter tires. There was quite the dump of snow and it was not letting up either. It would be a real good idea that I not get in an accident or stuck along the way. Actually, I could not get stuck in it because I could not walk in it!

Once I was on the highway, the roads were not too bad. I managed to drive between sixty to eighty kilometers an hour until I entered Chilliwack. The rest of the drive home I white knuckled it. Driving thirty kilometers an hour was enough to make my nice white underwear, brown. All I wanted to do was get home unharmed.

By the time I approached the weigh scale by exit 160, it was as though I entered a different world. It was the most bizarre feeling. I was so close to home yet that stretch of road was eerily empty. Honestly, I was sure that I was still driving on the road because I would have felt if I had left the road. It was so white out that I could hardly tell that I was on the road. A part of me did not want to continue but I was only a few exits from home.

There was so much snow in town that I could hardly drive past thirty kilometers an hour even if I wanted to. I was glad to be home safe and sound.

Mystical Puzzle

I wished that I could go out tobogganing but I could not walk in snow. My leg could not handle the motion of falling through the snow and if I slipped and fell, I was going to end up in shock from the pain!

It continued to snow over the next couple of days and I was unable to leave my apartment. Over two feet of snow came down. The road crews never cleared my alley so I was unable to get my car out of the garage. My landlord never cleared the sidewalk in the front of our building, which meant that I could not leave if someone picked me up.

February 5

Natasha won hockey tickets at work to see the Chilliwack Bruins and brought Lorne and I. Lorne was embarrassed that I was bringing my wheelchair. He said that he was going to walk a few feet in front of us and pretend that he did not know us. He was such an ass sometimes!

After the game, it did not take Lorne long to figure out how fun it could be, pushing someone in a wheelchair. He ended up going so fast that we wiped out going around a corner. Lorne fell to the ground and my wheelchair flipped on to its side as I fell out of it. We were so lucky that it landed on the side that it did. I was able to save my leg so that I did not injure it any further.

As soon as Lorne realized that I was not hurt, we both laughed our heads off while lying on the floor. Security was watching and must have just about had a bird when they saw me flying out of my wheelchair. Lorne helped me off the floor and we got the hell out of there!

We grabbed some more beers and went to Lorne's after the hockey game. A Johnny Cash song was playing and it reminded me of horseback riding. Lorne got on all fours and told me to get on. He walked around his pool table a few times like a horse while I rode his back. I had so much fun! Who would have thought that riding your friend like a horse around the pool table could be so much fun? Maybe all the beers we had to drink had something to do with that.

It was not long after that event that I told Natasha that I thought that I was going to die soon and maybe even this year. I told her that no doubt, I was having a tough go at life but I did not want to commit suicide or anything like that. I just felt like I would be dying soon. Maybe it was just because Molly, Mick, and my Aunt Chandal all died within a week and I was tripping out on death.

I ended up buying some cocaine. I did not know why, but I did. I only bought a couple of grams and I never cooked it up. I just snorted little lines and stayed up for hours playing guitar hero. I kept on dying on a song that I could normally play.

In between snorts of coke, I continued to try to beat one particular song that was stumping me while I was high. It was driving me nuts to keep failing at the beginning of the song, so I kept on trying. In fact, I kept on trying for over twelve hours straight. My guitar crapped out while I was playing because it was not meant to play for such long periods without rest.

I tried to borrow Lorne's guitar because mine no longer worked but he would not lend me his. He told me that his sister was borrowing it but really he knew that I was high and that if he lent me his, I would break it too.

~ ~ ~

I found out that the first surgeon who saw me a week after my accident, you know the one that told me to find someone else to figure my leg out because he was going on vacation. Well, he told my doctor that nothing was wrong with me. He told her that I was fine and to put me on the wait list.

Nothing wrong with me?! It had been almost eight months since my accident and I was still screaming in pain! I used a wheelchair for fuck sakes! If the doctors listened to me when I told them that there was a serious problem, and got to the injury right away, I was sure that I would not be in this predicament. All because that surgeon had vacation on his mind, and not helping patients, I was crippled.

February 21

My baby nephew Ayden was born. I guess I would never have to worry about dropping him because unless my leg healed, I would never be able to hold him while I walked. I did not realize how much was taken away from me until I tried to do something. Then I was faced with the ugly truth that I could not and may never ever be able to do it again.

February 25

I saw my surgeon Dr. Cholt. He had flat out refused to order an MRI for me. I told him that I would no longer need his services. He collected money each time I saw him every month to tell me, "Gee Tanya, I don't know why you are in so much pain and can't move your leg." He could not fix my leg the first time so I was sure the hells not letting him open me up again!

By mid March, my doctor had finally prescribed Morphine, Toradol and a muscle relaxer to help with the pain. I could not believe I had suffered for nine months before I was finally getting something other than Advil and Tylenol. I was on those drugs around the clock. I also started to take an anti-depressant. I had tried to get by without them but I was really starting to fall apart.

It had been a week since I had been on the drugs. I really did not notice any difference in the pain. My physio therapist asked if I was sure that I was taking the drugs. I asked my doctor if she prescribed me placebo's because the drugs were not helping the pain. She explained to me that I was on heavy duty narcotics and that I should be feeling some relief. As I thought she was giving me placebos and the Morphine was not working, she increased the dosage.

~ ~ ~

The weather was starting to get nice so I thought that I would use my wheelchair to run some errands that were only a few blocks away. How hard could it be? I whipped around the malls in my chair so I should be able to go a few blocks in town.

Famous last words, how hard could it be? I did not get half a block away when the tears started to stream down my face. My wheelchair kept on trying to steer me off the sidewalk and on to the street. I watched as everyone gracefully walked by and I struggled in that stupid chair! Why did this have to happen to me? I just wanted to be back to normal! I wanted to be able to cross a street without it feeling like I just climbed Mount Everest. I did not want every second of my life to be a struggle. Sometimes I felt like I was born just to see how much abuse and trauma I could take before cracking. Well I had had enough! I was cracking! Therefore, if anyone was listening out there, I am done!

~ ~ ~

I decided to stop taking Morphine and Toradol. It was useless for the pain. All it did was made me stupid in the head and made me feel like I was drunk all the time. I had been on it for three months and it had not done a damn thing! I stopped taking the drugs cold turkey.

I did not know if I was supposed to wean myself off as my doctor never said anything, and knew that I was stopping the drugs. Something was happening and I did not know if it was because I stopped the Morphine or not. I had become so suicidal that I was crying myself into a frenzy while holding a bottle of pills.

The battle had begun. Take the pills and end this misery for the last time or fight to stay alive so I could see my niece and nephews grow up. *Not this again!* I almost lost the battle the last time I tried this. In fact, I was in a coma and on life support.

I paced my apartment, crying and confused. I did not want to die! I was all screwed up, and I could not sit still! I did not trust myself! I phoned Amber and asked her to pick me up to take me to her house for the night. I never told her that I was afraid I might kill myself. I just told her that I was not feeling good and wanted to stay with her.

May 23

I met my new surgeon, Dr. Ernie. He wanted to wait until I received my MRI until he made a decision on how to fix my leg. For the time being he told me to stop all physio and exercises as my knee was hypersensitive and the exercises seemed to be aggravating it, rather than helping it to get better.

My nephew Jake came up for his birthday date weekend. I could not do a whole lot with the kids anymore because of my leg, but I did manage to bring him to the lake. It worked out well because I had an appointment in Vancouver to get my MRI done the day after I took Jake back home.

I almost did not get it done because I could not straighten my leg enough for them to slide me through the machine. The whole reason I was getting the MRI in the first place was because my leg was literally stuck. I could not straighten it and it was stuck in a slightly bent state. The technicians maneuvered me around enough to finally get me inside the machine.

I stayed in Surrey for a few days because I had an appointment in Chilliwack on June 19th with a shrink. I figured that I might as well stay in Surrey and go home on the day of my appointment.

During that time, I went to the mall by myself to shop. There was such an incline at the entrance I went in, that my wheelchair almost flipped. I was struggling trying to get up the hill and a man came and pushed me. I graciously thanked him. Hills and wheelchairs do not mix!

I was in one of the department stores and needed to get down to the bottom floor. I approached the escalator and as I was looking down at the steep ramp. I was starting to think that maybe those things were not meant for wheelchairs. I did not know if my brakes would hold me on such a steep ramp. I loitered around the escalator trying to figure out how I was going to get down.

I looked up and I saw Duncan. I have known him since elementary school. He has been handicapped all his life. He used to be able to walk but now he was in a motorized scooter. His girlfriend used a scooter as well. The two of them showed me where the elevator was in the mall to get to the bottom floor. They thought I was crazy for thinking that I could take my wheelchair down the escalator. I did not know. I was just learning how to be handicapped. I did not know all the ins and outs yet.

It was fun cruising through the mall with them. I felt like I had my own little convoy. The three of us cruised through the mall in our wheelchairs as if we were on a mission. We stopped in one of the restaurants for a beer. I paid as they were on a very limited budget.

All my life I had periodically ran into Duncan. It was usually at the malls in Surrey when I would see him. He had been disabled and handicapped all his life but he always had a smile on his face and he never gave up. When we were kids he could not walk that well and he lagged behind but no matter how far we were going, he wanted to come with us. He did not get the greatest hand when the cards were dealt for him, but to watch him was very inspiring.

On the way back home from Surrey, I stopped in Chilliwack for my appointment with a shrink. Her name was Dr. Thornwick. When I first asked to be put on her wait list, I was told that there was no wait list and that I should be called right away. If that was the case, why did it take over four months to get my first appointment with her? It was a short appointment. She asked for a little bit of background information and she prescribed some anti depressants. I made another appointment to see her in a couple of weeks.

June 27

In the early hours just past midnight, Lorne and I were drinking and listening to music. He had phoned Amber to invite her over even though I told him not to because she was in bed sleeping. She never did answer her phone when he phoned.

We were about to put another song on when I noticed my phone flashing. That was weird because someone must have just called but we never heard the phone ring. We thought that it must have been Amber to give us heck for waking her. When we listened to it, it was only a couple of seconds long and we could not make out the message.

Lorne wanted to know where it came from so he dialed star sixty-nine. I told him not to because it costs money, but he would not listen to me. His eyes went big as he discovered that it was his phone that just called my phone. That was impossible because he was sitting right in front of me. We both walked down the hall to his suite to see if anyone was there.

No one was there and nothing had been touched. Lorne started to freak out because he said that phones could not just phone phones on their own. I told him that maybe it was the ghost that I had sent over to his apartment.

A couple days prior, I felt a strong presence in my apartment. I told the ghost that I did not know what it wanted or how to help it. I also told it to go down the hall and hang out with Lorne because he did not believe in ghosts. "Why don't you show him a thing or two," I said.

The next day we showed our other neighbor Rod the message. Right away he said, "This place has ghosts!" We tried to slow the message down to see if we could pick up something but we could not decipher the message. Both the guys were freaking out and could not figure out why I was not. There was nothing to freak out about because I knew that the presence was not in my apartment, so I had nothing to fear.

I received the results of my MRI and it did not look good. There was so much scar tissue in my knee and surrounding area that they could not tell if I had a high grade partial ACL tear or a complete ACL tear. They were unable to assess the injury due to the *arthrofibrosis*. The arthrofibrosis had been causing all the pain. Since it had taken so long for them to discover the problem, it now may be permanent. It was without a doubt confirmed that I had a serious painful problem that may never go away.

July 2

I had an appointment with my shrink. I proceeded to tell her how I was feeling and she told me that she was not there to listen to my problems and that she only gave out prescriptions. Then what was I doing there?! I did not want to mask it! I wanted to get to the root of the problem and heal once and for all! She suggested that I go to the psychiatric day program at the local hospital. She said that they could teach me the same in a few weeks that it would take her over a year.

I was really falling apart and each minute of life was a struggle. All I did was cry. I could not do this stupid life anymore! With every minute that passed, I felt more and more shattered. I was having a difficult time doing anything or going anywhere because I could not stop crying. The only thing that was on my mind was to die. There was no way that I could continue in this state. I was a mess!

July 4

I saw my new surgeon Dr. Ernie. Surgery had been scheduled for September 26th. He explained that I had a tough year ahead of me and that I may never heal my leg. He told me to not look at the bright side and prepare for the worse. He was planning several surgeries over the next year. He also told me that most people never heal from such injuries because the pain was too great. This completely numbed me. I was slowly deteriorating and felt like there was going to be nothing left of me but a physical body.

July 9

I went to the psychiatric day program for the first time. I felt better about my own situation in the presence with other people that were emotionally messed up. It made me feel like I was not so alone. Each of our problems was very different, but we shared one thing. We were all in deep emotional pain.

I felt good throughout the program but as soon as I drove the half hour home through the mountains, I would start to cry uncontrollably. I would cry the entire way home. *I hated my stupid leg! I just wanted to be normal!* When I got home and started to back my car into the garage, it took all my might not to completely floor my car into my dirt bike and through the garage wall. "Stupid piece of shit bike! I hate my leg! I hate that bike! And I hate my life!" I did not smash anything and went to my apartment to cry myself to sleep.

Mystical Puzzle

July 14

I went to the psychiatric day program for the second time. I really did not know how they were going to help me. Everything they had showed me, and the handouts that they had given me, I already knew about. I was very well aware of how the mind worked, and the reasons that had caused the depression. I felt as though no amount of information was going to snap me out of the hole that I was in. Again, I felt good while I was at the program but cried myself all the way home.

I had to pull myself together because I would be spending the next five days camping at Silver Lake with Amber, Kate, and Gayle. While I was at the day program, Amber came to my place to pick up all my camping gear. It had now been a year since my accident, and I still could not carry things up and down the stairs on my own. I was still very dependant on my friends and family to help me get through the day. I tried to do as much as I could. Even if it did take me ten times longer. There were some things that I just could not do.

We were camping at the lake that I had my dirt bike accident at. Amber and I shared my tent on the first night. Kate slept in her own and Amber's mom and her friend slept in another tent. I was ready to shoot Gayle and her friend because they were yapping all night like a bunch of school girls and kept us up. You would think that being in their sixties that they were tired and would just go to sleep. Oh no! They giggled and yapped all night.

I had a night terror. I always had them when I did not sleep with a night light. It was embarrassing when it happened while camping with friends. Actually, it was embarrassing regardless of when and where it happened. Amber told me to shut the fuck up, and that there was nobody out there and slapped me in the head. Good god! I hope she did not say that to the foster kids she planned on having.

The next morning, Kate, who was the quietest of all of us, said that she was ready to kill us because she never slept a wink. Between Gayle and her friend yapping, my night terror and everyone snoring, she could not sleep.

Amber made fun of me and my night terror and everyone was miserable in the morning. We were up just after 6am. I woke up soaked in sweat and Amber was freezing. I swore to god as usual that I did not sleep and Amber said, "Well you were snoring all night so I would like to see what it looks like when you are really sleeping!" We had not been there for twenty-four hours and Amber had discovered that she did not want to camp with us for the next four days.

Amber was not a barrel of laughs in the morning. She was picking on me so I told her how comfortable sleeping on my air mattress was. I did not feel any of the rocks underneath us and Amber's paper plate of a mattress was so thin, that she felt every rock. Her sleeping bag was so small that it barely came past her ass. *It sucks to be you Amber.*

After I had a nap, I got up and built myself a camp bathroom. I could not walk to the outhouse and back every time that I needed to go to the bathroom, so I used tarps and trees to block off an area, and placed my camp toilet inside of it. I also had a camp shower. I filled it with water and set it in the sun to heat up. Once it was heated, I hung it up in a tree and had a shower. I gave everyone a tour of my bathroom and they were afraid that I was going to smell our campsite up.

Grant, Wanda and their kids came to visit us at our campsite. Grant made fun of my camp bathroom because he said I should be able to walk no problem to the outhouse and back. No one got it! No one understood the torture and pain that I lived through day in and day out. The pain was so great that sometimes I could not think straight. The pain consumed me!

I got in my car and left crying. I found a forest service road that I knew my car could go up at least a couple of kilometers. I could not understand why no one understood what I was going through. They thought that I was over exaggerating and faking it. The comment I heard most was it must be nice to sit on your ass and be paid for it. Who would want to be a cripple for any amount of money?!

I cried until I could not cry no more. I felt so alone. Bit by bit everything inside of me was shattering. It did not feel like there was much left to take away. I felt so numb and zombish. Soon there was going to be nothing left of me. I almost felt non existent. It was starting to get dark so I made my way back to the campsite hoping that Grant was not there.

Grant was gone by the time I arrived back at the site. This camping trip was supposed to be relaxing, and it had turned out to be emotional and stressful. I never knew at the time, but I had just finished watching the video footage from that camping trip on March 20, 2010. I found out that when I left crying, Amber pulled out my video camera and they all pretty much made fun of me and thought that my feelings and emotions were just one big joke!

The thing that hurt the most was I was always there for Amber when she had her breakdowns and never made fun of her. She could not drive to Chilliwack without being accompanied because she thought the mountain was going to fall on her. Yet I was in constant pain and facing being permanently crippled and she told me to shut the fuck up and stop my crying! Amber was so insensitive. It was ok when she fell apart but no one else could.

In the end, the camping trip was not at all that I was hoping it would be. The dogs drove me nuts too. There were four of them and every time someone walked by our campsite they would all start to bark and would not stop. Our campsite was along the path to the lake so people were constantly walking by. I was glad to go home.

July 21

I went to the psychiatric day program. This would be my third day in the program. It went pretty much the same as the last two times. I was ok when I was at the hospital but cried all the way home again. Reality kicked in when my leg was throbbing with pain.

July 25

I went for my fourth session at the psychiatric day program. One of the activities we did was relaxation. We lay on mats on the floor, and we had pillows and blankets. The instructor led us through relaxing our entire body. We did that for an hour. At one point I was wondering why my bed felt so hard and then I had realized that I was not at home. I was at the hospital lying on the floor. It was somewhat trippy because it was as if I had gone somewhere. Some people actually fell asleep and were snoring.

I did not cry on the way home this time but as I was driving through the mountains, the words *mountain*, *sky* and *falling* kept popping into my head. I wondered what that meant. Was a mountain going to fall down on me? Amber, Kate, and I were planning on going to the family cabin. Was a mountain slide going to happen on the way? On the other hand, was it like Chicken Little saying, the sky is falling? I had no clue what it meant.

For the next few days the words, mountain, sky, falling, kept haunting my thoughts. One afternoon while I was sleeping, I was awoken to loud crashing sounds. I phoned Amber dazed, confused, and asked her what all that noise was. I asked her if one of the mountains just fell down. She replied with, "No you fucking idiot! That was thunder. What do you think the sky is falling or something?"

Hey! She just said sky is falling. Was that it? Was that the reason the words had been haunting me? Was I predicting words that Amber was going to say? No. I did not think so because it had not stopped. The words haunted me everyday.

July 29

I went to my fifth session at the psychiatric day program. There was a man there that I could tell did not really want to be there. He just looked down the entire time and did not say a word. I started to mention to the group about the fact that I did not feel as though I slept and I had been waking up soaked in my bed. The man that never said a word suggested that I was checked for sleep apnea.

I did not cry on the way home this time but I decided that I was not going to go to the program anymore. I did not feel like I was learning anything new. Everything they had talked about, I already knew. I just did not think that they could help me.

July 30

My friend Sam came over for a visit. She had mentioned that there was a landslide on the sea to sky highway. It was not until a couple of hours after she had left that the light bulb turned on. *Mountain, sky, falling; mountain falling* on the sea to *sky* highway. Wow! I think I was predicting the land slide but did not know it. I was no longer haunted by those words.

Maybe there was a connection somewhere there. I was in a completely relaxed state before I was haunted with those words. Maybe if I relax more, my sixth sense would be more active. I did not know what the purpose of predicting something like that would be.

A bunch of family and friends came to Hope from Surrey and Saskatchewan for the August long weekend. Despite the depressed state I was in, it was nice to see them all. Good times were had by all.

As the days passed after everyone left, I found myself completely shattered. I felt empty and hollow. There was nothing left of me but the shell of a body. I could not live like this anymore. I refused to live like this. If I did not like the progress my leg was in by the end of the year, I was killing myself.

How was I going to get through more surgeries and pain when all I wanted to do was die? I was losing it. I was completely falling apart. Every ugly trauma I had ever lived had been resurfacing. I would wake up crying and I went to sleep crying. Every night I found myself crying and rocking back and forth pleading for help. Only I did not know whom I was asking because no one was there but me.

I knew what I needed to do. I needed to go away. Maybe I could go on an African safari. I had the money. I had enough money to go away for a very long time if I wanted to. That was why I saved the money in the first place, to go on a trip around the world. My leg put a stop to that!

Whom was I kidding? Somehow, I did not think Africa and the jungle was wheelchair accessible. I guess I could scratch that off my list. Maybe I could hire a helicopter to bring me to the top of a mountain and then pick me up in a week. That was not going to work! I was petrified of the dark and the boogeyman in the forest. Not to mention the animals that would want to eat me. I guess I could scratch that off my list too.

I did not know what I was going to do. I really needed help but I did not know where to go for it. There was no way I was going to survive the surgery next month with this kind of mind frame. I really did not want to die, but I felt like I had no choice.

Nobody understood the pain that I went through each day. Not only the physical pain, but also the mental and emotional pain as well. I was not exactly a couch potato. I was thirty-six years old and I still wanted to jump a ditch if I so desired. I wanted to walk across the street without feeling pain. I wanted to live! This body was not living!

I was on the internet and I came across an ad for a place located in Sedona, Arizona. I had a strong feeling to click on the link. It was some kind of spiritual retreat only it was one on one and not a group setting. Maybe that was the place that could help me. I did not really know about spiritual stuff but I had a deep urge to call them.

CHAPTER 3

A Chance to Get My Life Back

August 13

As I hung up the phone, my shoulders released. A smile that was a mile wide began to grow across my face, and the tears began to pour. Those were not tears of sadness. Those were tears of joy. I had the feeling that I was going to be ok. That somehow I was going to make it. Could it really be? Was this the answer I had been seeking all my life?

Honestly, I could not imagine being revived of the death that I had been living. Sedona had to be the answer. I did not want to die, but I could not live like this either. I had been depressed and suicidal before, but this time, it was different. It was as though I was really dying inside.

I had exhausted my being with so much trauma and pain that it could no longer feel, so it had shutdown. It could no longer cry. It was empty. It was dead. My spirit was dead and my soul was lost. What the hell did that mean? I was not religious or spiritual by any means. I do not know where those words just came from.

In fact, I did not use the word God. It was always the "g" word. I never believed in God. There was no way there could be a God. If there was, why had I lived the life of trauma and torture? What did I do to deserve all this pain?

All my thirty-six years of life, my heart had slowly cried tears of blood. Something told me that this was the book that I was to write. Everything that had been happening to me had been happening with purpose, and for a reason. Something big was about to happen. *I knew it!* I just knew it! I had started to record everything that was happening.

Forget the *Four Wheeling Trails for Dummies* book. I was losing valuable research time because I could not drive my manual transmission four wheel drive. If I were to break down, I could no longer walk myself out. Believe me; break downs do happen. Long hikes out of the back forty were sure to happen!

I had three and a half weeks to organize and prepare for the trip. I was spending five days touring Arizona and seven days with some of the best spiritual practioners in Sedona. I strategically booked my spiritual retreat so that I would be home for one week prior to my surgery.

Mystical Puzzle

I knew deep within me that if I did not get a handle on my mental health, my physical health was doomed! Once I awoken from surgery, I had a hellish year awaiting me full of unspeakable pain and challenges. I needed the best possible head to get me through that. Not one that wanted to give up and call it quits.

I had given myself until the end of the year to see some progress with my leg or else my only option was suicide. I could not live with this head and I could not live with this leg. If that ended up being the case, well then I was going to go on a little mini rampage before I ended my life. I thought about driving into Dr. Sukai's legs so that he could feel and struggle as I did. I might as well go out with a bang.

I really hoped this Sedona thing would work. I did not know how and I did not know why, but something deep within me, was telling me that it would.

I saw my shrink at the end of August. She gave me a prescription and told me that I needed to make an appointment with her two weeks in advance before I ran out to get another prescription. I did not really like her because she was nothing but a pill pusher.

When I was going to the psychiatric program, I over heard a staff member say that most of the people that went to the program were my shrink's patients. My guess was she did not want to do any real work and actually help people; she just wanted to write out prescriptions.

I pretty much had everything booked for my trip. The only thing left to do was figure out exactly what I would like to check out while I was there. The more I researched about Arizona, the more I wanted to see and do. I could only imagine what kind of an adventure that I could have had. With a functioning body, the sky is the limit.

Houston, we have a problem. When did you plan on sleeping? Once I figured out all the places that I wanted to visit, I discovered that there was a whole lot of driving and no time for sleep. Somehow, in my head I had forgotten that I was handicapped and thought that I could just drive for seven hours. Visit a site for an hour. Hop back in the car and drive for another six hours. Visit another site for a half hour. Back in the car I go and drive for another four hours. Whoa sista! Slow down! There was no way that I could sit for that long. Back to the drawing board I went.

I eliminated some of the places that I wanted to visit and came up with a decent itinerary. Now for the tricky part, did I mention that I have absolutely no sense of direction? Seriously, I am not kidding you. I was surprised that I did not get lost in my one bedroom apartment. I literally planned each turn I had to make from the time I left my place in Canada, until I returned back home.

Now that I use a wheelchair, I could not just leave my apartment and hope that everything worked out for the best. It took careful and precise planning on my part or I could get myself into trouble, especially if I was on my own. There was no one to depend on but myself.

First, I needed to figure out where exactly I was going. Then, was there handicap parking? Were there any hills? How far was the entrance from the parking lot? Was the place I was going to wheelchair accessible?

You know, I knew it was coming seven months ago. I had mentioned to a couple of friends at the beginning of the year that I had the bizarre feeling that I would be dying soon. I also reassured them that I was not planning to commit suicide, I just had a strange feeling that my time was up.

At the time, I really believed that the death that would have taken me would not be from suicide. As the year progressed, the feeling of death just around the corner had become stronger and stronger.

I started to create a music video to be played at my funeral. I thought it would be a nice little something to leave behind for my friends and family. I also wrote out instructions for what to do when I die.

That reminded me of a list of experiences that I had written down and had tucked away in one of my safes. My whole intention with the list was to write every traumatizing event that had ever happened to me, go to the top of a mountain, read it, scream, cry my little eyes out, then burn it. By burning it, I was hoping that those traumas would then leave me.

I started the list in 2001 when I was backpacking in Asia. It was now 2008 and the list was no where complete. I could not leave it for my family to find, so I had decided to go to the mountains and burn it before I left for my trip. It would be hard enough for them to deal with my death, never mind knowing my deepest, darkest traumas.

I could not go to the top of a mountain so I settled for a forest service road part way up a mountain. I knew how far I could go up this particular road due to the last time I tried. Those roads were not meant for cars. They were meant for four wheel drive trucks. There was a perfect spot that I could turn around before climbing a hill that would rip my muffler off.

At that spot was a wooden bridge that crossed a creek. I brought a couple of beers, a joint, and some deep dark secrets. I sat in my car at first because I was a little apprehensive being there by myself. With the creek roaring below, I would not hear if a bear was approaching.

I drank my first beer and then lit my joint. I left my car to go sit on the ledge of the bridge while I read the list of experiences. As I read the six pages of writing that I had, I let the tears flow in hopes that this would be the last time

I cried for the reasons written. I burned all the pages and back to my car, I went. I drank my second beer as I was driving back down the mountain and back to civilization. It did not really feel as though I released the trauma from those written pages but at least I got rid of it so my family would never find it.

September 7

I went to my moms for the night because she was taking me to the airport in the wee hours of the morning. She was worried that we were not going to get any sleep and then she made me yap for two hours.

September 8

Two and a half hours of restless sleep was not nearly enough. I only had four hours of sleep the night before. Screw the shower! Besides, I had just dyed my hair and I could not wash it until the evening. I did brush my hair and teeth and changed my underwear and socks. Just incase you were wondering.

On the way to the airport, I smoked my last joint for twelve whole days. We made it to the airport without any troubles. I smoked for as long as I could before checking in and going through security. I waited in the handicap zone to wait for my airport buddy to wheel me around.

The flight was uneventful. I had two and a half hours to kill before my next flight. During the security check at the airport, I had to go through a ten minute pat down. Tits and ass too! She asked if I wanted to go somewhere private for her to pat me down. *Hell no!* I thought she wanted to pat a little more if you know what I mean. I will take the patting right in front of everyone, thank you very much! That flight was uneventful as well and I tried to sleep most of the way. Upon landing, I took a shuttle bus to the car rental.

It was a good thing that I was wearing shorts because it was one hundred and ten degree's outside! I was so excited! It was not the year long backpacking trip around the world that I had originally planned. However, I was out there, in a wheelchair, by myself, and I was going to have a great adventure!

I wheeled myself to the counter, ready to rock and roll and gave the agent my booking number. I proceeded to give him my bank card and he told me that it could not be used for payment. He asked if I had a credit card. I did and I proceeded to tell him that it was a prepaid credit card. I had phoned two times prior to arriving in Arizona to ensure that I could use my bank card for payment as I was informed that my prepaid credit card was not good enough. I also offered to give him one thousand dollars cash that he could give back to me when I returned the car.

The agent refused to rent me a car. I could not believe what was happening! I had spent the last three and a half weeks preparing for the trip. I made sure that I crossed all my T's and dotted all of my I's.

Travelling was not new to me and I was handicapped for christ sake! I did not have the privilege of just walking out my door and going about my day without careful planning. All I could think was I had just spent thousands of dollars on this trip in hopes of getting my life back and I could not get myself from the airport to Sedona.

I burst into tears and just about threw up on the spot. I left my luggage at the car rental place and looked for a washroom. All I could think of was that this could not be happening! I just got there! I knew I was meant to be there. Why was this happening? Had I not had a screwed up leg and did not have a wheelchair to worry about, I would have just hitch hiked to where I needed to go. Given my situation, I really did not have that option anymore.

I was so distraught that my face was beat red and my eyes were almost swollen shut. I felt like crawling under the ground to be swallowed up. I cleaned the runny snot, splashed water on my face, and wheeled back to the car rental.

I had asked to speak to the manager. The agent insisted that this would not help me any. I asked again to speak to the manager. The agent left and went inside an office just behind the counter. He came out and said that the manager would not see me and there was nothing he could do. However, he could do something. He could rectify the situation by renting me a car and allowing me to pay with my bank card as previous agents told me two times prior.

He chose not to rectify a situation that was caused by misinformation related to myself from two agents. You could bet that I would never attempt to rent a car at that rental company for the rest of my duration on this earth. Why could I not just pay with cash? That is what I had. I did not need credit cards because I paid everything with cash.

So there I was stuck at the airport and had no friggen idea what I was going to do. The agent mentioned that there was one place in all of Phoenix, Arizona that would rent me a car for cash. Of course, there was a catch. The rental was three hundred and fifty dollars more and I would not have unlimited miles.

I did not have a choice. I was there and I already invested thousands of dollars on the trip. I was picked up by someone from the hotel who rented the cars. Oh no! My itinerary was from the airport to my first stop, not from that hotel. Oh, double no! How was I going to find that hotel when it was time to drop off the car and catch my plane home? I really was not exaggerating, when I said that I did not have a sense of direction.

Ok. Things were starting to pick up. Off to Flagstaff I went. I caught myself going one hundred miles an hour a few times. Yes miles, not kilometers. I just missed being nailed for doing twenty-five miles over the limit. Not sure I wanted to get a speeding ticket or have any trouble with law for that matter.

Mystical Puzzle

I arrived at my hotel in Flagstaff just after 8pm. I was so exhausted that I called it a night. It was a long stressful day and I had a big day tomorrow at the Grand Canyon! Yeah, baby, yeah!

September 9

It was hard getting my butt out of bed due to lack of sleep and the stress and anxiety from the previous day. I went to the lobby for my free breakfast and found a loaf of bread, butter, jam, donuts and coffee. It was definitely something to write home about. My plan was to be on the road by 7:30am but I was too exhausted so I ended up on the road by 10am.

I excitedly arrived at the east entrance of the Grand Canyon and paid my park admission fee. As I used a wheelchair for any kind of distance, I requested an accessibility pass. The park attendant refused to issue me a pass because my handicap parking permit stated temporary not permanent. She also mentioned that I must be a U.S. citizen.

It was only day two of my trip and I have to say that it had been more than challenging. Because I had left Flagstaff so late, I could not stop at too many view points because I had to get my fluorescent white ass to the Grand Canyon airport for my helicopter tour.

I made it to the airport just in time. Honestly, the helicopter ride was not as great as I thought it would be. I did not know if I still had a bad taste in my mouth due to the episode at the entrance. I was at the friggen Grand Canyon, one of the wonders of the world and I was just not feeling it. After the helicopter ride, I went to Grandview Point to watch the sunset.

As I made my way to Page, the closer I got, I knew there would be a surprise waiting for me at day break. I arrived around 9:30pm and the motel was much nicer than the one I stayed at in Flagstaff. I pretty much went to bed right away, as I was not feeling well at all. I had a sick feeling in the pit of my stomach all day long. It was so bad that it took me half an hour to eat half of a sandwich. I hoped that it was just anxiety and not something bad happened to someone I love.

September 10

I had nightmares all night long! My leg was not damaged at all during my dream. It was as though I never had the accident. My dad (but it was not what my real dad looked like) had kidnapped me. He raped me and beat me. I tried so hard to get away but he kept on finding me.

Finally, somehow I managed to escape and I found myself naked running through the streets. I ran into an office. There were people of Asian descent all talking on phones. I was standing there naked shaking in fear, asking for help and not one of them gave me a second glance.

I did not know what to do. My dad was going to find me and no one would help me. I climbed under a desk and just cried and rocked myself. I kept wondering why no one would help me and it was as if they did not know that I was there. I thought at least if I were hidden, he would not find me.

It was horrible! It felt as though I had dreamt from the time I went to bed until I woke up. Maybe I should have brought my dream catcher in from my car. My head was pounding while I was sleeping so I got up at 6:30am to take some Advil and then went back to sleep.

Perhaps I had a headache because of the change in altitude. I went from five hundred feet above sea level to eight thousand feet. I slept until 10am and I woke up very confused and distraught from the nightmares. My mood quickly changed when I made my way outside.

The landscape was beyond words, amazing to say the least. I actually think I liked it better than the Grand Canyon. I mean the history of the making of the canyon was amazing but I lived in the Fraser Canyon in British Columbia. I have always been surrounded by mountains and go four wheel driving and hiking, so that did not really enthrall me as I see it everyday.

I made my way to Wal-Mart as I had two hours to kill before my tour. My legs were killing me! I was probably more active yesterday than I was in a normal week. I used an electric wheelchair while shopping. It was much easier to use than the manual chair.

Ok, were people just plain stupid or ignorant and rude? I could not tell you how many times people had blocked me from getting by. They would stand in the middle of an aisle and stare right at me as I was approaching them with a wheelchair that clearly would not get by unless they moved over. They would not move unless I had asked them to. Sometimes, I really do not understand people!

I motored over to the alcohol section and just about jumped out of the wheelchair, a sixty ounce bottle of whiskey for fifteen dollars! In Canada, a sixty ounce bottle would cost fifty-five dollars!

It was a good thing I took that Imodium the other day, because that very well could have made me crap my pants. For someone who liked alcohol, I had just found a gold mine. Too bad I could only bring one bottle back.

I could not believe my little eyes, another jump out of the wheelchair moment. At the deli, they had little baby fifty-three milliliter bottles of mayonnaise and mustard to go with the baby ketchup bottle that I already had at home. Now I would have a family of baby bottle condiments. They were way too cute to use. Some of the simplest things really amused me!

I checked in at 1pm for my Antelope Canyon tour. We left a half hour later in the back of a big ass truck. It was a fun ride on the way to the canyon. Once we had arrived, we proceeded to walk inside. Our guide immediately called us back to the truck.

Mystical Puzzle

A lightening storm had just started and flash floods happened frequently at the canyon. The guide had told us that one year, eleven people had died due to a flash flood so they did not take any chances. It was disappointing but I guess it was better to be safe than sorry. As I really wanted to go for a tour in Antelope Canyon, I re-booked for the next morning.

I drove to Lake Powell to check in at the condominium that I rented. My original plan was to hang at the lake for the rest of the day but once I saw how amazingly beautiful the landscape was, screw the beach! I drove around to all the nearby scenic views. I watched the tail end of the sunset and then went back to my condominium for the night.

September 11

May peace be with those who lost their lives and to all their loved ones.

I did not sleep well again. It felt as though an entity of some sort grabbed one of my legs using two hands and started to drag me to the end of the bed. I felt the hands and I felt myself being dragged, but I had just ignored it, as I was too tired. When I woke up, I was at the end of the bed. It was somewhat freaky!

When I left the condominium, thank god I looked over to where I was parked. Standing there was one of my suitcases. That would have been so uncool if I had forgotten it!

The Antelope Canyon tour was amazing! The tour guide explained that two million years ago it was solid and over time, rain and wind, carved out what it was today. Apparently a young Navajo girl found it by accident looking for her sheep in 1931. Due to the risk of sudden flooding, entry into the slot canyon was only permissible with a guide.

By 10am, I started to make my way towards Sedona. My first stop was Tuba City to see the dinosaur tracks. A man there guided me to the tracks for a fee. At the native arts and jewelry stand, I found a juniper bracelet that I liked. All I had was twenties so the man gave it to me, as he did not have change. I certainly appreciated the kind gesture.

My next stop was the Wupatki Pueblo and Sunset Crater Volcano. I loved checking out the ruins. There was a blow hole coming from a crack in the earth's crust that blew air. I had never seen anything like that before. The air blowing out was cool and refreshing for such a smoking hot day.

My next stop was the Sunset Crater. I could not actually see the crater; I did however walk a short trail where pieces of hardened lava were all over the place. An information board along the walkway stated that the volcano erupted between 1040 and 1100.

I also checked out the first meteor crater that was discovered on our planet. Apparently it struck approximately fifty thousand years ago. What an amazing site! It was astounding to see the huge crater it had left on impact.

I finally arrived in Sedona at 7pm. There were bats everywhere and bugs called cicada's that made a whole lot of loud chirping. I could not wait for day break to check this gorgeous place out.

September 12

I drove to the head office of the spiritual retreat to meet my Sedona guide, Megan at 9am. She gave me my welcome package and gave me a run down of how the week would go. Within ten minutes of being in the office, I started to sob. I felt like a scared little five year old not knowing why I was crying in the first place, why was I there and how did I get there.

Megan assured me that I was right where I was supposed to be. I hoped that the week would go well as I was not getting a good vibe from Megan or the owners and founders of the retreat. The woman owner screamed phoniness. The male owner did not seem to have any warmth what so ever within him. I could only guess that I met him on an off day. It seemed as though their first objective was the all mighty dollar and their second objective was helping humanity.

My Sedona guide Megan and I left the head office and toured Sedona in my rental car. She pointed out the streets of where my practioners were located. Our next stop was the airport vortex. As my leg was unable to do the climb, we continued to drive to the giant cross above the vortex to meditate.

I was disappointed with the meditation as it was maximum seven minutes long. When I was advised to dress accordingly, I had thought that the meditation would have been much longer than it was. I was not connecting with my guide. I was trying to but it was as if she would not give me the time of day. I was finding her very uncomfortable to be around and was not looking forward to connecting with her on a daily basis.

I took Megan back to the head office and then I drove back to my condominium to rest up before my next session. Most of the practioners were five to fifteen minutes away from my condominium. It was nice that everything was central.

My first session was with Kylee, an intuitive reader. We hit it off right away. She was my kind of person. I shuffled the cards and put my energies into them. We said a prayer before she proceeded with the reading. This was some of what she shared with me.

(Please Note: *Throughout the book, I typed word for word what the practioner / intuitives told me.*)

"The first card is death. It has to do with your inner personal being. How you see yourself? What you think about yourself. Something has had to die in the recent past to shift you around and you can now get the rewards that you are starting to recognize about yourself and things about yourself that you couldn't see before or really get before. You didn't have the availability to see it because you weren't in a position to have to receive it or look at it."

Tanya – "I did feel like I died recently. That is why I am here. My whole inside is dead!"

"The other card is all about rewards, all about great things. So it literally had to be that the old part of Tanya had to die because it was built on a false foundation. A bunch of stuff that wasn't good programming for you. Now you have the opportunity to open up to something much greater. Something much bigger than yourself.

"Even though you have felt very set back, you have accepted it and you have learned to just accept the set back and the things that have challenged you and the things that have forced you to have to connect into a different part of who you are. Your family, your home, your foundation, everything has just kind have been challenged for you to make this change in your life. What sign are you?"

Tanya – "Gemini."

"Oh, especially that Gemini, so full of idea's and visions. Its been a good change for you and I see as far as partnerships, I feel like its really brought in a new balance into partnership into your life that needed rebalancing or maybe relationships that were in your life weren't balanced are coming into a whole new level of balancing.

"You know when we see distortion when we look at it inside of us looking out and creating the distortion. So we have to own and heal that part of us that created the distortion through our unconscious mind. It wasn't anything happening to you, it was what you pulled in. It's what you created out of your unconsciousness, your fear, or your unconscious thoughts or whatever.

"Its all about forgiveness and release and it's a big piece of healing. When we forgive ourselves and really get that we create everything and we really, you know, that's huge. I mean how is that possible that I create everything in the world. I mean it's just overwhelming, that concept.

"But when we look back on our lives we realize that we did create everything and instead of being a victim to any of it, we are like, why did I need to create that experience? What in me, did I judge that? What in me polarized myself to this? It is a very powerful time for you to wake up.

"Get focused on your feminine side. It seems that you are more balanced on your male side and it's your male side that seems to get you into trouble, maybe being over aggressive."

Tanya – "My male side got me into my accident. I had a dirt bike accident last summer and now they don't know if I am permanently disabled. I go for surgery on the 26th and then repeats for an entire year and brutal physical therapy."

"What area is it that hurts?"

Tanya – "My knee. My knee is stuck."

"Do you want to hear something so weird? I have been in pain in my knee for awhile now. This is all forcing you to slow down.

"Did you have issues in a relationship or are you married?"

Tanya – "I have been single for almost ten years because I am so scared of trusting someone. I don't really have a dad. I mean I do but he just chose not to be a part of my life. I have abandonment issues and I am terrified to open up and let someone come close to me."

"Do you like woman at all?"

Tanya – "As in like sexually? No."

"There is nothing wrong with that."

Tanya – "I'm maybe curious but I definitely like males. I am hoping through this week here that I can release some stuff and now with my accident, I don't know if I am disabled. Who wants to be with a cripple?"

"Don't even go there! Don't focus on the disabledness. You focus on getting healed. It's up to you what you want to create right now. You created yourself up to this point. You created the doctors to not get it. You created it so maybe there will be this incredible benefit come to you that is going to allow you to get to some new place. Just visualize yourself getting healed. Don't feed any energy into the not because what do you get, more not.

"This is your time to really nurture yourself and change some habits. This is about you learning about you and what you can create. And realizing that you don't have to break your dreams, maybe this is a part of making your dreams come true.

"I feel like you are going to develop some new strength about yourself and feel good about yourself, feel more confident about yourself. You can't say that there is something wrong with me and nobody will like me. You are a nurturing person, you are sensitive, and funny, you are beautiful. It has nothing to do with minor little glitches like that. I've seen people in relationships where one person is in a wheelchair and the other is not but it works for them."

Tanya – "Do I have to forgive someone for sexually molesting me?"

"Absolutely, because somehow you needed that experience to wake yourself up and we don't know what you did in your past. I know it's hard to believe but you have to forgive the killers. You need to trust that for whatever reason you had these horrible experiences, and as you come to heal yourself and see your power and do forgive the people that have hurt you and to know that on some level you needed to have those experiences. If you are a healer, than how do you get to that? You need to get free from things and then you can help others to get free. What a beautiful thing that is. Once you embrace everything that has been done to you and hurt you, then you are neutralized. Then you get to create from a new place.

"I highly recommend that when you are going through these kinds of transitions that you change your diet. That is no alcohol, no sugar, and no coffee. I suggest a lot of greens and grains.

"You're here to live now because you have already died. So now, you just have to choose to really do it differently and get on a lot of greens, a lot of salads. You want to really clean up your system to get in an alkaline state. Alkaline is balanced, acidic is off. That is what all the sugar and alcohol does; it just throws us in an acidic state.

"I feel like you are balancing from the past. You need to not be the victim. You need to break all agreements with being a victim. I know I created all this. I don't know why. I don't know what I have done in the past but I have to own that I created it. Then start making your way back to a positive journey.

"I feel like where you live is an excellent community and there is a lot to be gained there for you. But this negative stuff you really need to clear out. Your mind is just full of it. It is full of so much negativity and you really need it flushed out.

"With your health I feel like you need to get off of this addictive stuff like cigarettes. You need to clear your lungs out. You need to do a cleanse. The lungs is covering your heart chakra and keeping you from feeling the pain. Sometimes you have to take that band aid off. Be willing to go to a whole new level. Be willing to die for the life you have known. It was a horrible life. It was a scary life.

"The death card again. I don't know. Are you happy where you are living? Maybe it's not getting you where you need to go."

Tanya – "Death. I don't know. I have been thinking about it a lot lately for some reason. It's almost like I need to prepare myself because it might be happening soon. But it's not because I want to kill myself. Yeah sure I feel sometimes like it is never gonna work and I don't want to be here anymore but I have already tried it once and I don't want to do it again."

"Death to me is transformation or completion of a cycle. So you may need to make a move. You may need to move from the world that is not working for you. You need to find people that you can connect with, that you can feel at home with.

"I do see a spiritual man coming into your world who has information for you and is going to help you plant new seeds and help you connect into gear. I do see someone influencing you that you will get some good new movement from and get yourself into a new gear. Almost like a fatherly figure that you didn't have. Someone that you can feel safe with and will support you in getting free in a more clear view.

"What is your first question?"

Tanya – "I feel like I have a sixth sense. Things come to me but I can't control it. Where is my psychic developing going?"

"You are definitely coming into your psychic time. It has to do with feeling safe inside yourself and loving yourself. You are holding the love back from yourself because you never knew to love yourself because you weren't made valuable and if anything you were made to feel shameful and a lot of weird guilt.

"So this is what you need to clear out and then your psyche is ready to open up more and more because you are an intuitive, you are a psychic and it may be a part of the work that you do in the future. It has a lot to do with you learning and having compassion for humanity and your accident and your horrible experiences growing up are all a part of you having compassion for the human experience.

"The death card again. The death is the limited part of you; the part that is played very small. Plays on that linear that a + b = c. That is dying for you. You have been opened up to a multidimensional part of life and it got you here. Spirit got you here because it is time for you to have a new beginning and you have to go with it.

"Do a cleanse, clean out your lungs, your kidneys, your liver, your colon and clean it out. Then you can say you are ready for this new way. There will be a lot of sadness released. Let it go. Do the crying.

"You have this whole artistic side that wants to express itself. I definitely see you doing this creative side.

"You are finishing a cycle. So many people die at thirty-six like John F Kennedy Jr, Marilyn Monroe, and Princess Diana. You are entering a new cycle; they didn't come for the next cycle. They finished what they came to do.

"What is your next question?"

Tanya – "I don't know if you can answer this but do I have any bad entities attached to me."

"Ok, I am sure you do."

Tanya – "The reason I am asking is because I played around with an Ouija board when I was a teenager and some really bad things happened to the point that I will never touch anything like that again! I am scared of the boogeyman! I am petrified of the dark and I sleep with a night light!"

"You need to get on a cleanse because boogies do not like a clean diet. No sugar, no meat, no dairy.

"What is your next question?"

Mystical Puzzle

Tanya – "Was my cat mentally ill or was she being bugged by spirit entities?"

"You need to start smudging your house to clear your house of anything that is not of the light. You have to start doing your shaman work is what I am getting at here because that is who you are. Even though you don't remember who you are from your past yet but hopefully you will get some inclination as to why you are getting all these things to work with right now. Because otherwise you wouldn't even know that they were happening. You have a lot of powerful sessions ahead of you.

"I definitely think that your cat had some weird spirits around her, a lot of illusions, a lot of things were happening because you have a lot of psychic energy in your environment. I feel like she took a lot of inner karma when she left.

"I do see someone coming into your world. You are opening to having a relationship. First with yourself and then a connection with God where you really feel like there is a force working through you and that you are awake and you go whoa, I'm not asleep anymore, after all these sessions that you are going to be going through because that is a lot. You are going to be, it is intense work.

"You need to be patient. You are moving into the shamanistic era where you are definitely here to do Goddess work and spiritual work and you need to help to wake up the Goddesses in your area.

"So you are being woken up. You came here for your training. I feel like your direction is moving into the spiritual realm and the healing realm and doing Goddess work. I feel like you have done it in other lifetimes and it will be something that you will remember. You are not here to learn. You are here to wake up and remember who you are.

"This is why when you know when you get beat up it's because they want you. You look at a person down the street and nothing is happening to them and they are just living their life and then you're like, what's that about. Ignorance is bliss.

"You came here for a purpose. I feel like your cat was just a part of pushing you out the door of where you kept safe. Soon you are going to be healed enough to want to be connected with the world and want to do things for people and be part of something.

"You are here to plant new visions, plant new seeds. You need to trust, it's like you paid forward the first thirty-five years of your life by going through the horrible times, going through the darkness, going through all of this.

"Now you are going to have the other side of this but if you don't accept it, then you're like, what is going to trip me up now? Eventually we stop looking behind. Trust me; I had to go through this.

"You have to die to be reborn and you are definitely being rebirthed right now and you must develop a trust that you just need to trust yourself that you are not going to create any more crap because you are going to keep your eyes wide open and be conscious of what you are putting out. Conscious of thanking God for the great life you have even if you don't know you have it yet.

"What is your next question?"

Tanya – "What is my future going to look like after this week?"

"You are here to birth yourself. Everyone here is a midwife for you. You are going to have an incredible transformation. It is going to be grateful. I think you have done a lot of the pain and hard work it's just about opening up and releasing now and just letting it out of yourself. I see a big change from the path for when you go home. I see you going home with wisdom and knowledge and feeling like its ok to be alone, its ok to use my time now.

"I see someone from your past coming into your life in a relationship that is going to help you to move forward; someone that you have known in another lifetime. Or someone that you have met earlier in this lifetime, but didn't connect on that level.

"I see you release a lot of control that you felt from your mother and woman that have controlled you and how you have controlled yourself. You are definitely going to move through some adjustments and some of these people may even be reflections of your mother or reflections of your, maybe helping you move through some things.

"If someone shows up and they really activate you because of however they are, they are really there to serve you into letting it go so be open to it even more to that experience instead of going oh this is bringing, say oh, ok, I get what this is.

"I definitely see you finding this new path and birthing your new way. You are going to do really well. This is the beginning of a whole new life for you and a life that is going to be filled with creativity, fun and it's about what ever you are going to program.

"We have time for one more question?"

Tanya – "This probably isn't appropriate but will my leg heal?"

"Are you going to heal your leg so that you are comfortably walking on this Earth? I am getting such a big yes! I get this yes like you can't believe and once you heal yourself, you are going to help other people heal because that's just who you are.

"It's you. When you get fierce about something, look out people because you get what you want. This is really where you need to get it. Don't listen to those people. Don't give them the power and release the fear that is sitting in that knee.

Mystical Puzzle

"You are carrying fear from your mother's life time, your grandmothers, your lineages, your genes; you are carrying the fear in the energy because that is what I am getting in what I am doing from the feminine side. This is about you getting rid of all the scars and the pain and the healing and everything you are doing, you are doing for your lineage.

"I'm definitely getting you cleared and you get fierce and strong and don't let the outer world program you. You are just going to program your own. You are going to plant the visions and do the work."

Before leaving, I purchased a meditation cd on forgiveness. I had one hour to kill until my next session so I went back to the condominium for a snack. My next session was with Brenda for an hour and half nurturing massage and energy work. I thought she was in her early forties and she had told me that she was sixty-five!

She had given me the idea to get a picture of what a normal functioning knee looked like inside and to ask the highest power of light to help heal my knee to a normal state. She said to use the power of intention. She also taught me some meditation techniques to bring in the light and remove negativity.

By 4:30pm, my sessions were done for the day, so I went to a place that sold crystals. What an amazing store! It was so overwhelming that I needed to spend the evening studying crystals to see which ones I should buy.

I wanted to start getting into rock hounding. I did not know where that had all of a sudden come about. I had never really thought or knew about gems and crystals besides in the jewelry format and I was finding myself mesmerized by them. I did not buy any crystals, but I would tomorrow. It was too expensive to eat out, so off to the condominium I went to make some dinner.

September 13

My first session was a two hour session with Bianca on emotional clearing. Her big lesson for me was I did not need my mom or dad to take care of five year old Tanya anymore. I was capable of doing that myself. I did not know that the session included a massage so that was an added bonus. After my session with Bianca, I went back to the condominium for lunch before my second and last session of the day.

After lunch, I met with Sal for an hour and half of Shamanic Astrology. I have to admit that when I first met him, it looked as though I had woken him up and he seemed a bit scatterbrained. However, once we got started, holy cow! This man would be partly responsible for my new direction. He blew me away! I now understood a lot of my confusion of why I had certain thoughts and ideas. I could truly say that I loved that guy! He was the shit! He knew me better than I knew me. Here was some of what he shared with me.

"Tanya, we are all on this journey to wholeness. We are seeking to become whole beings. The way we become whole, lets not think of this as twelve signs, Aries, Taurus, Gemini, etc. Let's think of these as what they truly are, symbols of real cosmic energy. The way we become whole is to live many, many, many, many, many lifetimes working with these twelve energies.

"In a given lifetime, there are usually three or four of the twelve that are really powerfully activated in us. These are universal cosmic energies that we are literally made of. When we speak of your souls past or your souls purpose or what we call the true intent of your soul in this lifetime, we are talking about which three or four energies has your soul incarnated into this body we call Tanya. Which energies is your soul really seeking to experience in this lifetime on its journey to wholeness? And when you have lived enough lifetimes that you have experienced all twelve of these sufficiently to have all twelve energies to be perfectly integrated and perfectly balanced in your being, that's when you become whole.

"It is a journey. It can be many lifetimes. It can be hundreds of lifetimes. It just depends. It is not the same for everybody. It just depends on basically three things Tanya. Courage, will, desire. We go as far as the courage, the will, and the desire to go.

"Most people give up. Most people are not engaged in these at all. Most people are like, I don't know all about that. I don't know if its true or its just way too hard and I didn't know it was going to be this hard so I think I will just drink beer and watch American Idol.

"Most people are not engaging their soul at all! It is like their soul has become that machine they call the television. Don't wait on everybody else around you to get it because you can be waiting a long, long time. In fact, a lot of those around may be waiting on you to give a certain thing so that you go and teach them. That is very possible for you.

"Of these twelve energies, the strongest in you is Gemini and Scorpio. These constitute past life experiences for you. Now this is not all of your past lives. This is just a certain portion that your soul sort of brought the memory of having lived these two energies into this life with you so that these two sort of constitute your base, your foundation.

"So the way you would have lived the first part of this life up until now because they are easy for you. You have already done them. You might not be finished with them. You might come back in some other lifetimes and pick up some more Gemini and Scorpio. But you have done enough of it so that you could what I like to call soul level memory of having worked with these two energies or sometimes you hear the phrase cellular memory.

"Our cells carry memories of past lives and they do. These two are not exactly constituting challenges for you. These are the two that you already know well and it's like a comfort zone for you to stay into these two energies rather than moving out and exploring the unknown.

"We have this built in fear of the unknown. So all of us; you, me, all of us; tend to move to these two past life energies because they are familiar. The soul goes I don't know; it's wild out there. I don't know if I want to go exploring out there. It's scary out there. The soul then goes; I think I will just keep doing this Gemini Scorpio thing because I know how to do that.

"Ok, Gemini. That is a big one for you in a past life experience. Gemini is the twins. The key word or phrase for Gemini is seeking freedom. Gemini's want to be free! Like a bumblebee.

"When we say that Gemini seeks freedom, it implies that they are somehow in bondage. Well what are they in bondage to? They are in bondage to the perception of duality. If all of us just entered our hearts, we just have the feeling of somehow, we know it is all one and if we could just love one another, everything will be unified. The heart knows that.

"But then you go into the mind and the mind goes, no it's not heart. It's not all one, it's two. I like the music or I don't. I like the food or I don't. It's dual heart, it's not one. There's good and there's evil. It is right or it is wrong.

"You have spent multiple lifetimes working with the Scorpio Gemini energies. You have spent a lot of lifetimes like a bumblebee. Let's call one twin curiosity and one twin restlessness. Think of a bumblebee that comes across a field with five thousand flowers and is curious about the nectar like the mind going and investigating something.

"The curious twin flies over like a bumblebee and pops right down into the nectar for about two or three seconds and then the restless twin goes ok that's enough lets go. Let's move along here. Gemini is like a Robin Williams kind of energy just wild and crazy and free and all over the place!

"You can say one twin is dribble and the other twin is drabble. A little bit of this and a little bit of that. A little bit of this and a little bit of that. In this jack of all trades and master of none sort of thing. They are great communicators and networkers and can just about talk about anything.

"Ultimately the mind is a gatherer and dissimulator of information. That's basically all our minds do. Books and travel are Gemini's best buddies. They love, love, books and short journeys. That is how they gather information about duality. They are trying to get free of the minds perception of duality that this is good and this is bad, etc.

"You have come into this lifetime with a more neutral point of view and nonjudgmental. That is a strength for you. You ought to utilize that. Keep reading and keep exploring duality.

"If we add this Scorpio energy to this, Gemini is an air sign, the mind. Dear you might want to study shamanic astrology. Ok, Scorpio, the water sign.

Water represents feelings and emotions and Scorpio represents the deepest feelings and emotions that humans experience.

"What some people call going into the dark shadow aspect of ourselves and explore Pluto and the underworld. So a chart like this could easily be, oh yeah, wow, can be fascinated with the dark because you have already looked at dark and light. You don't have the judgment about it that most people have.

"Most people who saw Evil Knevil jump the Grand Canyon thinks he is crazy, but this kind of chart might go wow, maybe I should do that. I don't know about jumping the Grand Canyon, but maybe a few cars. There is fascination with the dark and with danger; the firewalker, edgewalker kind of living.

"One Tanya might go to church on Sunday morning all dressed up just sitting there thinking about Jesus and then you leave church and go out and hang with the Hell's Angels.

"What you were doing in those past lives was doing the duality dance of looking at life and death. You were curious. You really wanted to know life but you also really wanted to know death. I want to learn both. Not die, I want to study and explore.

"You like confronting death and say come on death; you think you can take me. You have been playing in dangerous situations for the thrill; for the thrill in a sense; the thrill of feeling actually. When we live in these lifetimes, we don't actually realize why we do these things. It is the thrill of feeling all of our feelings. Not just the ones that feels good.

"So Evil Knevil jumping the Grand Canyon. He is doing that to challenge death and he is saying catch me if you can. And if he makes it across there he goes, wow, what a rush! If he doesn't and breaks one hundred and twenty-one bones in his body, believe it or not, he would be lying in that hospital bed, moaning and groaning and still says, wow, what a rush!

"Ok, so you come into this life with more of a connection to the feeling feminine element. And I mean feeling the real power of that. Like a witch and I mean that in a good way. Like the medicine woman in the Amazon, the real strange one that throws the bones, talks to spirits and can heal a broken leg in an hour, not six months in a cast. She knows all of life; life and death.

"So she can do things with energy that other people can't do. Sort of like the witch, the shaman, the sorcerer, the medicine woman. Scorpio is that kind of energy. You have had a period of between November of 2007 to November of 2008 where life is like saying to you, hey Tanya; you are here to be a different kind of woman in this lifetime. You are here to be a different expression of woman.

"What you want to do in this lifetime is take that neutrality where you are not nearly as judgmental in the mind because it is the mind that does all this judging.

Mystical Puzzle

The heart only knows love. You are really done your exploration of the dark and you want to take that strong mind you have, you have a powerful mind.

"Gemini and Sagittarius, which we will talk about in a minute, those two are the most resilient energies in the circle. They bounce back quickly. What you want to do with your strong mind, our lives are like spirals, Tanya. So we really just go round and round in circles and do the same thing over and over and over and over. But each time we were going around the circle, the spiral is a little higher up and a little wider and then you go around again and by the time you get back here, you get a little higher and a little wider and that is what you want to do with your mind in this lifetime.

"You're living the Scorpio Gemini daredevil counter energies because it is easy. It is easier for you to do that and break your legs and what not, it is actually easier for you to do that than to go forward and take on the challenges, in other words to change into something else and grow and expand and evolve and move forward in this lifetime.

"Next we are going to talk about the true intent of your soul for this lifetime. What your soul has incarnated in this body we call Tanya, to have new experiences, to grow and to evolve in this lifetime. And the big experience your soul wants to have in this lifetime is Sagittarius. Your rising sign is Sagittarius.

"You have a big dose of Gemini though. You have the moon, sun, Saturn and Mercury in Gemini. The moon aspect is the past life part. Gemini and Sagittarius are one hundred and eighty degree's from each other. They complete a pole. Instead of looking at it as two ends of a pole, you want to start looking at it as one pole. You can dance anywhere along the pole and be ok.

"You have looked at duality real strong in past lives and you have said ok, I have done pretty well with that Gemini thing but now I am going over here and checking out that Sagittarius tribe to complete a pole. Here is what that pole is. Gemini is polarity.

"You have gathered a bunch of information on polarity in past lives and it is like you have come into this lifetime with a suitcase full of post it notes about duality. You have come to move from your human mind to your higher mind. You want to work with all your information to come up with one cohesive truth that works for you; your personal truth. That is what Sagittarius is; your personal truth.

"It doesn't matter what Buddha's truth is, not to Sagittarius. Here is the key phrase for Sagittarius. This is the focus you want to have in this lifetime. This is the big focus that you will get plenty of mileage out of and it is this phrase right here, to *always* Tanya, in this lifetime, to be expanding the horizons of your personal truth. That is what the Sagittarius tribe does.

"So the Gemini is a piece of you. Scorpio is a piece of you. You have to honor those but you don't want to get lost in those tribes or you will end up with more broken bones. That experience was to break you of living the old Gemini. The wild, crazy, Robin Williams Gemini and to realize and nothing is wrong with it, but all of us tend to cling to the past life energies because it is fun, easy and no challenge.

"I have a Gemini moon too like you. When I was in my twenties, I was shooting heroine and cocaine. I was super crazy honey! I mean I can sit and tell you, we could sit and probably trade war stories and have a good time, you know what I'm saying.

"So I know. At some point, you need to say that I am not that bouncing bumblebee anymore. I am going to be good at being a bumblebee but to do something with my ability to move around like that. For you, this would sort of constitute the ability to communicate with all kinds of people. That is very important for you.

"Like the kind of person, say you invented something; there is invention energy about you too. Let's say you came up with an invention and you got invited to the White House. You're sitting at the long table with the President and the First Lady and everyone else is all tight and nervous because they are in the White House and they are going oh shit, fifteen forks and twelve knives, oh god what if I pick up the wrong fork, right?

"And you might be just kind of like, wow, damn; I'm in the White House! And then you leave there, take off your evening gown, put your jeans on and go sit on the curb with the drunks and just shoot the shit. That is one strength of the Gemini energy in this life time. Your neutral, the president isn't any better than the drunks.

"If I am with the President, I will talk about Bosnia or some shit. If you're talking with the drunks, you'll talk about, hey, I got some money, and I will buy us some beer. Sagittarius. To always be expanding the horizons of your personal truth. Like pushing Tanya, for the next vision and the next version of truth.

"No matter where you are in this lifetime right now it is at thirty-six. You have one version of truth. Whatever that is, it doesn't make any difference. Whatever it is to you! That's fine. You are probably kind of worn out on that truth, ok.

"Now it is time to refill and get onto that next truth, which you're doing. Here you are in Sedona. I'm ready for some new truth. I'm ready to expand the horizons of my personal truth. Because this truth I was isn't working to well anymore. Big accident! No accidents here really. Big jolt is how you should look at that.

"Life is saying, ok Tanya, you can keep on in this direction but you will end up dead or in prison. So if you want to die and go to prison, keep doing what you're doing. And if you don't, boom! Well then Tanya might say oh fuck it!

Mystical Puzzle

Maybe I will just die and go to prison. Your mind says that, but your little soul says, no Tanya, no. I don't want to spend fifteen years in a prison some damn where. Then boom! Let's break Tanya of that habit and pattern of that version of Gemini.

"Now you want to use that, your mind is strong Tanya! It is very Strong! It might be stronger than you know! And now what you want to do is use that strong mind because you got Mercury in Gemini. Mercury rules Gemini. I mean that makes your mind really strong! You want to use your little mind sweetie. I mean go Tanya!

"What are you doing now? What's the next horizon and truth? What's the next plateau? And you might spend two or three years getting information from Sedona, doing this, and doing that and then suddenly in two or three years, maybe you find yourself and you say, I did it! I got to a whole new plateau here.

"And the Sagittarius part of you wants to just take a moment, buy a hammock and relax and just savor every moment of this new horizon of truth that I have reached. And you should do that, just kind of chill.

"And then shit! You go nothing is happening anymore. Ut-oh, where is the next plateau? No ends for the search for truth. That is what Sagittarius is about. It is not about being a Christian and oh, we have the truth and all these other people are wrong and Jesus is the only way to God and blah, blah, blah. That is right for those people to do that.

"And then you got the Muslims and Allah and blah, blah, blah. That is right for them. Or then you have some other group like the Wiccans or the this and the that. Sagittarius's job is to kind of say to the other eleven tribes, see; these other eleven tribes get into this fundamentalist truth thing because it makes them feel secure. And it's ok. It is not wrong for them to do that. It's not wrong.

"It's alright for them to say that Christianity makes me feel secure. Believe in the Pope and what the Pope tells me how to do sex, even though he has admitted that he and his buddies are peda fucking philes. It might be crazy but it is right for them in this lifetime.

"Sagittarius's job is to say, ok you other eleven tribes, I understand. You all go along with your right and everybody else is wrong, blah, blah, blah and I am going to go out and expand the horizons of my truth and then I will come back, ultimately Tanya, the guru, the wise woman. Tanya, that's what you want to go for!

"You got to quit jumping barrels and shit on the motorcycle honey! I'm telling you, that's not your path in this lifetime. You already did that. You have the courage and Scorpio is will power and ooh, that Scorpion, that powerful little teeny weenie little thing can fucking kill you! You understand.

"When you see a scorpion, you wonder where it came from but you don't play with it. It is powerful. So you don't play with it is what I am saying. So you got that ability to do that and dance with the dark so to speak. So since you have come in pretty comfortable with light and dark, so then your thing is you got those twins in collaboration here.

"So now the thing is to go on and discover a new truth that encompasses everything! Not just Christians or just Muslims or just the men or just the woman or just the republic or just the democrat. You're here to say I already explored duality. You guys are still trying to figure out duality. I already did that.

"So now let me put all that together and come up with a more expansive, all inclusive truth based on a great degree of, Tanya, compassion. And that is what Gemini has a tough time with. Barack Obama has a Gemini moon. The Aries Gemini moon in you, in him, in me, has a really tough time allowing itself to feel the compassion.

"You don't have any trouble feeling danger and craziness and wildness, having sex with fifteen people, whatever it might be. What your soul wants to do is explore and go and investigate, let's call it, the truth, and the power of compassion. That is a big thing right there for you. Explore that and be real about it.

"Look at how much compassion Jesus and Buddha and all the great saints and masters, all the great teachers and all the great prophets; they said hey humanity, five things, love, compassion, tolerance, mercy, and forgiveness. All the great saints, all the great prophets, all the great teachers, all the great masters, *all* of them Tanya, said hey humanity, you follow these and you will have a pretty good life but they end up killing each other and blaming each other for everything and try love, try compassion, try tolerance, try mercy, try forgiveness. See what happens, just see what happens. Try them!

"But we don't do that. We talk about doing it, but most people don't do the stuff they were talking about. You are here to explore that. To explore what's the truth here. Jesus and Buddha and all them, they said that these are way more powerful in the long run than bombs and the electric chairs and shit. What is the truth there?

"Always be pushing the boundaries. And once Sagittarius gets kind of rooted in a solid truth, take your fifty thousand post-it notes and mold it into a truth that works for you Tanya. It doesn't matter what I think of your truth or anybody else. All that matters is what you think and if it works for you that is what matters.

"Once you do that, there is going to be some folk out there that thinks that Tanya seems to have it more together than a lot of other people. If nothing else, she sure seems comfortable with herself. Something is working for her. And then you invite them to come over and sit down and then they start listening.

Mystical Puzzle

"They listen. They might not follow you right to the letter but they listen because they know she is a little more expansive and inclusive than these other truths. The Catholics say we are right and the rest of you are all going to hell. None of that shit is true by the way.

"So people start listening and gradually over time when you're fifty-five, fifty-six, fifty-seven years old, you will find yourself in the position of the wise woman. Why? Because these other people get lost in Scorpio and the underworld, daredevil, fire walker, edge walker. They get lost in that. They have got to deal with that at some point. How they really feel.

"You have the ability right now to be a guide for souls Tanya who have not explored the dark like you have. So these little souls that are lost in the dark will begin to gravitate to you and you will say oh darling, I've already been there. Let me tell you how to get out of that. Boom! And then you lay a little bit of information and then like that little bird, you're gone.

"It is that Gemini Scorpio ability. You know Hermes in mythology, the messenger for the Gods, who can just like a bird get down there in the underworld, save some lost soul and say hey, get on out of there quick and then you're out of there. You don't get stuck in that swamp with them, but you can pop in there and say, go that way, say this, read this and then you're gone. You hear what I mean? That is the way you want to use your Gemini but in order to really do that, you've got to develop compassion for pretty much everybody out there.

"Democrat, Obama, me, black people, white people, stupid people, smart people, rich people, poor people, the more you can get in the truth about compassion, then the more they are going to realize, oh she doesn't judge me. She understands why I was a Republican all those years or why I was a democrat. She understands. She really doesn't care whether I was Republican or Democrat. And she doesn't care that I am feeling lost and insane and confused right now. She doesn't judge me. She doesn't care that I raped somebody and spent ten years in prison. Tanya doesn't judge me. She has compassion.

"It is the truth and power of that. That is what you have to work on. I promise you Tanya, it is possible for you. To get to the place where every Monday so to speak, all the little disciples and all the guys gathered at your feet, to hear your newest vision or newest version of truth. And Tanya says alright, here is what it looks like to me and they go, oh thank you, and scamper off.

"They come back next Monday and Tanya might go, oh babies, you know that truth I gave you all last Monday, scrap that. I have discovered something else here. You are a guide for souls, leading people along. That is the journey for you in this life time.

"Oh interesting. The secondary thing for you in this lifetime is Taurus. So just like you were Gemini Scorpio in past lives, it is Sagittarius and Taurus in this lifetime. Taurus is opposite Scorpio.

"Scorpio represents emotionality, those deep feelings, and emotions. Taurus represents physicality. Taurus is an earth sign. Here is what it is for you. When you were doing that Gemini Scorpio thing in past life times, believe it or not, what you were trying to do was get your masculine mind connected to that deep powerful feeling feminine energy.

"You were trying to say, come on mind, let's go explore Scorpio so that you can get more comfortable with the feminine energy. Now you are saying, ok, I've got that part in down pact in past lives and now I am going to gather all of this information in one cohesive truth by going to explore the other end of this pole also, physicality; the other part of the feminine energy.

"Fire and Air, spirit and mind, those are the masculine energies. Earth and water, feelings and emotions and physicality, those are feminine energies. The great idea's from spirit and mind are worthless, worthless and are of no importance what so ever unless they take form.

"You can have great ideas but unless you get them to form what the fuck good is that idea. It's no good. You are really seeking truth in exploring the feminine energy over a number of lifetimes. You did that in Gemini Scorpio, you explored that adrenaline rush, that emotional feeling, defying death that is the word that I was trying to find.

"And now you are saying you want to become equally comfortable with physicality as I am with feelings and emotions. But Tanya, Gemini has a terrible time, terrible time realizing it has a body and the importance of the body and loving and respecting the body. It has a terrible time! Believe me; I had surgery four years ago just the same as you.

"I couldn't get that Gemini moon, that Gemini mind to say ok, I have a body here and I have to take care of it. You keep reading about duality. Don't go jumping barrels, start reading about duality. We understand the power of the mind but we don't understand the power of feelings. That is the big problem with American culture; because feeling is caring.

"When we feel for something or someone, we care about that person and we care for them. If we don't feel, we don't care about them or care for them. And the mind doesn't feel. It is not supposed to, it only thinks. We have created a world void of deep feeling, which means void of deep caring and look at the world we have created. Not working to well and it is getting worse by the day and its going to keep getting worse until we get into feeling.

"The more we feel personally ourselves, the more we will feel for others and the more we will care for others. That's the bottom line. That is what you are working on for your personal growth and evolution. You say let me take my strong mind and go exploring Scorpio to feel your emotional energy and now explore Taurus the physical energy.

"Get the book, *Goddesses in Every Woman* and in that book read about Aphrodite's wisdom and that version and vision of women. That's what you've got to work with. That's what will change the planet for men and women to get out of just the masculine part, the mind and really get into our feelings. That's what you are really here to work with and become a wise woman eventually.

"Google *body wisdom* and see what you come up with. Body wisdom is like paying attention to your body. The body has its own language. The mind does. The soul does. And language of body when we really start paying attention to it, you might think. Hmm, I'm hungry what am I going to eat? I'm going to be watching a movie so I will just eat a big tub of popcorn. Fine and go watch the movies but grab a sandwich or something.

"Learn to listen to the body wisdom and the wisdom of the earth. The earth is telling us there are fifteen fucking hurricanes every weekend, floods, tornados, and volcanos. The earth is saying, hey man, I am in pain here. I am a living organism; whether you idiots think I am or not.

"You all can't keep taking all the oil out of me and all the iron. If we took all the iron out of your body, we wouldn't be able to sit up straight and you would flop over. If somebody picked you up, you would flop right back over. Explore physicality as an expression of our heavenly mother, all physicality.

"Ok so Taurus; Taurus, the pleasure principle. That's really, what Taurus is. That is the key little phrase for Taurus. And what we mean by that is the pleasure pain polarity. Even more specific than that, see you have explored all these polarities.

"Scorpio, you went in playing with pain. You're like take a match and burn my arm so I can see what that feels like. You see what I mean? Really! So you explored all that. Taurus is an earth sign and that is what are planet is. So it symbolizes that that tribe is trying to help us understand how to live here in physicality and creating more pleasure than pain.

"We create more physical pain on this planet than we do physical pleasure. And it doesn't have to be like that. We can change that. Eighteen thousand people starve to death everyday. Everyday! It saddens you because you feel compassion. You might have never called it that. You might have just looked at it like, that saddens me and could make me cry.

"That's the Mother Teresa spirit in you that you are here to develop in this life time. What would America look like if Tanya could get people to live like Mother Teresa did? Not just she was a great soul and I could never be that way. Yes, you could! But everyone wants to believe that they can't.

"We want to change the ninety-eight percent physical pain and two percent pleasure and flip that and learn how to live on this planet where we create ninety-eight percent physical pleasure and two percent pain. That is what you want to be kind of devoting your life to. Bring in the wisdom of compassion, the wisdom of woman. Try and ask yourself Tanya.

"A good meditation for you and a good prayer partner for you and that sort of thing is our Heavenly Mother and Archangel Michael. He can take on anything that is brought his way. That is like you. That is your buddy, Michael. You hear? And talk to him like we are talking right now. They don't care about all that down on your knee shit. Say, hey mom and Michael, Sal says I am here to help you all. I'm with you now; let's go. Guide me along. You hear?

"If Bush and them could feel they couldn't fucking bomb Iraq off the face of the earth. There are other ways to work that out but they don't look for other ways. The ticket for you in this lifetime is you are trying to get to Sagittarius Boulevard and Taurus Road. That is the big intent for your soul. That is the destination.

"Let's say when you are seventy or eighty years old, if you get there. You're a wild woman but you can get there if you want to. You want to be sitting on the porch thinking, I did it! I engaged that Sagittarius Taurus energy, woman wisdom and the wisdom of the heavenly mother and I made some progress. I did it! This is a destination that could take you a lifetime to fulfill.

"Then the next question becomes, who is trying to get to that intersection? Who is it? It's her, Venus. That's the woman here sitting at the table. Venus shows us which out of the twelve possible expressions of woman or the Goddess that you have come here to explore.

"You have Venus in Cancer; the tribe of the mother. The mother. That's what Cancer is all about. You have Mars and Venus in there. Venus is the woman sitting here at the table. Mars is your inner masculine. The key phrase here is the responsible nurturer. You're here to develop that aspect of yourself.

"There is a mother spirit in you. It is defiantly in there and you want to develop that. It is going from a Gemini type woman to a Cancer type woman. Wild Robin Williams type woman to say more of an Oprah. It is that kind of shift.

"Gemini Scorpio is like the Robin Williams Hells Angels Gang. Gemini's are funny and they can be comedians because they look at both sides. What makes this twin happy makes this twin sad. Gemini's have the ability to make things funny that other people don't necessarily think is funny but Gemini will come along and make them laugh about it.

"You are to work on being the mother spirit but not necessarily with a family and kids. It could be that. I'm not saying that you can't do that but whether you do that or not, this is like everybody. All these babies are mine and if I can get the energy of the feminine and the mother more empowered on earth then all babies will be better cared for.

Mystical Puzzle

"It is not necessarily that you want to have a bunch of babies yourself as that could drive you a little crazy. It really could. Be careful with that. You really love all of them. The more you dig into yourself you are going to find that the real spirit of you is like, you might almost have a feeling Tanya, that all seven billion people on earth are all your little babies. Just a feeling in you.

"You love other people's children but you love the seventy, eighty, and ninety year olds too. They just need a mother to nurture them. What you want to do is promote growth and empowerment of the spirit of woman on earth, even in men. Help make men more nurturing because the more the spirit of the mother grows in us, and we really begin to consider Mother God as much as we consider Father God.

"They are different vibrations. Father God is sort of like the architect. The one sitting by and thinking, I think I will do a creation here. Mother God gives form to them. Mother God gives birth to Father God's ideas. They work together that way. But we don't respect mother God. It is changing, but we have a long way to go before we have those two really balanced.

"And that's what you are going to do. Get connected to the wisdom of woman. Most women don't know what that is. Most women only know that they are not men and that they are pissed off at men. But they don't know what woman is, not really. So you really need to go out exploring that. Use your courage and your daredevil energy to have the courage to go and explore love and compassion and tolerance and mercy and forgiveness.

"Now look what happens if you actually try and live like Jesus. These are the people that worship him but if you try and act like Jesus, people will think that you are weird. So it takes courage, to step away from what is popular and from what is going to get you accepted from the in crowd.

"Those people need a new truth. They haven't discovered what works for them they just know that the ones their parents gave them don't work. There is more to the mother spirit than cooking, cleaning, and the baby maker, picking the kids up from school and taking them to soccer practice. That is one aspect of the feminine.

"But there is also that Joan of Arc aspect. There is also that tsunami powerful witch medicine woman, real scary thing. You are here to say that we are way more than that. The major thing you are here to say is we are feelers. We feel more than men. We feel deeper than men. And that is what is needed on earth.

"If we stay in our minds much longer, we are going to nuke ourselves. You are going to help us out of all that Tanya. My favorite bumper sticker is, if you're not outraged, you're not paying attention.

"You are a powerful woman! You are a powerful woman! Quit playing with that power. Quit letting it just flop all over the place because next time you might get someone else hurt. That's another thing. Next time you might go, oh shit! I don't mind having five broken arms and now I have this other person paraplegic for life.

"Use that powerful mind of yours to help develop the feminine energy on earth. And the Capricorn in you here, the mother, father, look new rules. That is the phrase you want to think about.

"There is a certain group of people on the planet who make the rules and like you said awhile ago, it is the wealthy. The wealthier you are, the more power you have over the rules that we live by. Man made rules; I am not talking about cosmic laws. Everybody has to stop at the stop sign. Everybody has to have twelve years of education; anti-abortion and pro-abortion.

"You have to go and change all of those rules by doing all what I have talked about here. Look at yourself as the messenger for the Gods. You are a messenger for our Heavenly Mother. That is exactly what you are. You are a messenger for her. You want to gather woman and men who can relate what I am talking about and form Aquarian partnerships.

"The spirit of Aquarius, the days that we are moving into, that is real. The spirit of Aquarius is equalitarianism. You have capitalism and socialism. Equalitarianism is fairness and equality for all. That is going to happen on this planet. A lot of people think that it is not, but it is going to happen. Because it is just time, it is the cosmic timing. Nothing can stop it.

"That is why things are going so crazy out there. We are in a big shift. Real big! From now until the next sixteen years until 2024, all these greedy ass corporate people, they are going to fall. One of the richest banks on the earth just collapsed. You can turn on the news and I bet there is something on there about that. Their stock went down around seventy-seven percent within two days. The whole corporate structure is getting ready to collapse.

"And because we need new rules Tanya. We need new rules and the new rules we need are we need moms to have equal presence in every boardroom on the planet. Not woman acting like men, women being women. But before they can do that, they need to discover the true feminine essence and have the courage to live it and express it.

"And that is where you come in, little ole courageous Tanya. You want to use that to help women fight for their babies. Tell the president, we will send our babies to Iraq as soon as you send yours! As soon as you send your daughters and children over there, I will send mine. And not sending your daughters to work in the office, send them in with all the land mines.

"All four hundred and thirty-five of you congress people, the next war you all start, and our children don't go until yours go. And if you don't have any children, then you go yourself. If they had to go or send their own, your damn right they will find another way. And as soon as women come together and say, enough is enough!

Mystical Puzzle

"You know what all women have to do? Close their legs and say you don't get no more until you stop killing my children! And I promise you that would get their attention. Not only should you read about Aphrodite, you should also read about Athena and Artemis.

"Aphrodite is like the spirit of pleasure but Athena and Artemis are more the warriors, the Joan of Arc. And you are kind of a combination of those. You also kind of have a bone to pick with these religious people. So it's really both the corporate people and the religious people who are in power on earth and it is not about blaming them it's about saying, look, you folks are making the rules here.

"The corporate people are making the social, political, and economic rules we live by and the religious folk are making the religious rules. It is not about blaming them or fighting them, it is about it is not working well! Someone is responsible for the way this planet is. It doesn't just happen. Those rules are not working well! Let's change the rules.

"About twenty years ago, hurricanes were named only after women. After the women's lib, every other hurricane was named after a man. So now, we need woman to say, we need to make every other pope a woman. I can't even believe that women are into Catholicism myself.

"Do you want to burn some energy off? Go an organize a million women to march to the Vatican and say, Mr. Pope, tell us one more time why can't women become bishops and arch bishops and popes and things. Now why is that Mr. Pope? It would be a different world if every other Pope was a woman.

"It's ok that there is men but we need a different perspective and we need new rules. We need woman on the Vatican council. We need women everywhere. Not just women, it needs to be balanced, fair, and equitable distribution of resources. That is what you want to fight for.

"Just take a step at a time. You know you don't need to see the whole staircase to climb to the top Tanya. All you need to see is the next step and just take it. Don't worry about the whole staircase because you might fight yourself and say oh shit I got to go way up there.

"Just look at the next step. For you, you asked spirit what would be your next step. Spirit said, go to Sedona that will be your next step and you took it and so now you get the next step and take it. Yeah, you get out there and fight for these children honey. What are you planning on doing in the next few months?"

Tanya – "Umm, mostly it is going to be my surgery on September 26th and if my rehab is anything like my last surgery, for every waking hour and half, I have to work on my leg. But in the time in between that, I am going to be studying all the stuff that I am learning here and bring myself closer to my purpose."

"Ok, look, Tanya. Oh man, look at this! Whoa! Between now through June 2010, you focus on what we talked about here in a real serious way. Don't rush your rehab, just read, study and talk a lot with Michael and the Mother. Call them M and M; Michael and the Mother. Tell them I'm going to call you all M and M, they like that kind of stuff. Just say when I say M and M, I am talking to you two.

"Say, hey Michael, Sal said for you to grab one arm and Mom you grab the other one and the three of us, you, Michael and the Mother will move through the rest of the remainder of your days on earth, Tanya like the three musketeers. These two invisible radiant powerful beings on either side of you will walk with you for the remainder of your days on earth. Say to them, I am at your service, you want to fire up some people to take care of these babies; I will fire their asses up.

"Now until October of 2009, you just focus on everything that you have learnt in Sedona. Then come October of 2009, you kick into that window of magic. If you really work on this and what you get from Sedona and just generate momentum and use the knowledge that you get from here, just kind of build, build, build a bit, then comes that window of magic honey, you could find yourself really surprised at the life you are living."

After my session with Sal, I bought a couple of crystals. I had to finish crystal shopping the following day because I closed the place down. Once I got back to the condominium, I finally unpacked and organized my belongings.

September 14

My first session was with Carter for Investigating Core Pain for two and a half hours. That had been by far the hardest session. In fact, it was so hard that I was going to walk right out of it without finishing. It is not as though I had to be in that session. I paid for it; therefore, I could choose to just walk out.

I toughed it out and ended up staying. It was not that I did not like Carter or that I could not connect with him, it was the simple fact that the session was painful. The root of my pain comes from feelings of abandonment; particularly that I did not have a dad.

I tried to explain to Carter that the reason I did not have a dad was that he chose not to be a part of my life; he did not want me and he did not love me. He has chosen that everyday for the past thirty-six years. I had never felt the warmth, love, and security from my dad; and I never would. There was not a day that had not gone by that I was reminded that I would never have a dad.

Carter would not buy that. By the end of the session, my tears turned to laughter. We had a good laugh over how I was going to walk out, and that I am sure I had been one of his most challenging patients. Carter said that I was a great bullshit detector and he was glad that he met me.

Mystical Puzzle

As that session was two and a half hours and very painful, I did not attempt to listen to the recording of it until March 31, 2010.

I went back to the condominium to prepare and eat lunch before heading to my last session. An hour and a half rock and rain massage with Carla. During the massage, I had relaxed so deeply that I had forgotten where I was. The massage was very soothing.

At the end of the session, I had felt like I was emotionally beaten. It was as if I had been crying for days on end. I could hardly drive back to the condominium. I needed to rest so I went to my meditation room and I ended up falling asleep for a couple of hours.

The phone awoke me during lucid dreaming. Thank god because I had two awful dreams. The difference between those two and normal type of dreaming was, I was able to recall in detail both dreams. With normal type of dreaming, I forgot as soon as I woke up what I was dreaming about.

The first dream was about me being stocked by someone whose intention was to hurt and rape me. The dream started with me being in the apartment hallway that I currently lived at and I was talking to my neighbor across the hall. Only it was not my friend Lorne who normally lived in that apartment. It was someone that I did not know.

I did not know him by his looks but by the way we were talking, I was guessing that we had chatted before maybe even hung out. There was not closeness as if I knew him well, but well enough to chat with him.

Although the circumstances leading up to me knowing that someone was wanting to hurt and rape me did not play out in that dream, I did however know it. Just as we were saying our goodbyes and going back to our own apartments, he dropped a piece of paper. I picked it up and looked at it. As I glanced back over at him, I said, "It's you!"

I screamed for help and was yelling, "It's him! It's him!" The apartment door next to his opened and all my friends came out. There was no way he could hurt me now. The strange thing was, all of my friends were friends that I hung out with in the present time, and they all looked like they did presently. I find that that rarely happened in dreams. It ended with me knowing that the person would not be able to hurt me in any way.

The second dream was me driving through the current town I lived in. I was on my way to my place of work to pick up some of my friends that were getting off shift. The car I was driving was not my own and I did not recognize it. I felt like I was drunk, although I did not consume any alcohol during the dream.

I picked up my friends and proceeded to drive down the curvy mountain road as I usually did. I like to nickname it my Indy five hundred road.

Of course, everyone in the car was giving me crap for my excessive speed, and what they would call erratic driving.

Just as we were driving down the hill and approaching the bridge, the engine came out from under the hood and flew over the car. It happened so fast that at first I did not know what it was. The next thing I knew, my steering wheel had come off and we were approaching the narrow little bridge with oncoming traffic.

I could not let that happen, as too many people were going to get hurt. As I no longer had a steering wheel to steer the car, I leaned from side to side to get it to steer where I wanted it to go, away from all the oncoming traffic. What a miracle! The car that I was driving did not smash into anyone and we all came out of it unscathed. I was not sure what those lucid dreams meant but it was the fourth one I had since I had been in Arizona.

I still felt like a bag of poo! It could be from a number of many things. I was about to get my period any day, my session with Carter was extremely emotional, Carla released a lot of negative energy, I had forgotten to take my anti-depressant and it was a full moon to boot.

I dragged myself out of the condominium and drove to the giant cross on top of the airport vortex. I went there to meditate and to try to remove some more negative energy. Unbelievably, I actually felt much better afterwards.

I also watched the sunset and full moon from there. Lucky me as I had the place to myself. Just a couple of blocks down the road there were hundreds of people watching the sunset from a popular lookout. After meditating and enjoying the views of the sunset and full moon, I went crystal shopping. I ended up closing the store down again. I was not finished so I would have to go back another day.

The phone at the condominium rang in the late evening. I guess the only way I was going to find out whom and why they were calling was by answering it. It happened to be one of my best friends, Amber. She phoned me because she said that she missed me and that she drove by my apartment every day and honked her horn pretending that I was at home.

When I left for my trip, I made specific rules that *no one* was to contact me for any reason. I gave examples of things that may happen, but still asked not to be contacted. They were:

* If my apartment burns down and I lose everything, do not contact me.
* If your male dog miraculously becomes pregnant and has babies, do not contact me.
* If you become pregnant and give birth within one week's time, do not contact me.

Mystical Puzzle

So could someone please explain to me why Amber called me when I made specific requests to only contact me if there was an emergency? I was not going to leave a phone number of where I could be reached just incase someone would actually phone it. Death was an emergency. I miss you, *giggle, giggle,* was not! I had only been gone for one week.

September 15

Another dear friend Rod sent me a text to my cell phone of something so ridiculous it could have waited until I got home. He wanted to let me know that he wanted me to pick him up some pot when I got home. That was not the way I wanted to wake up. What was wrong with people? Why did they feel that they were excluded from the do not contact me while I was away list. Because the last time I had checked, there was no such list!

By 9:30am, I still felt like crap! My first session was at 11am with Amanda for an hour and a half nurturing massage and energy work. I could not wait because I really needed the energy! If it was anything like the session with Brenda, I should leave revitalized and glowing.

Upon arrival of my session, I got the feeling that the practioner had other things on her mind. She apologized for being late, and had mentioned that she had just received a phone call from a friend that she had not spoken to in awhile. It was clear that I was an inconvenience and that she would rather continue her phone conversation.

I did not really connect with Amanda but her home was incredible. It was a compound sanctuary of peace and love. Even the indoor rooms had waterfall like ponds. Amanda showed me the reflexology point on my foot to help heal my knee. It is the spot between my ankle and the side of my heal. I call it the river. I was advised to massage that area on both feet everyday.

She also taught me to breathe like the ocean without stopping; in through the nose and out of the mouth to flow energy. After my massage, I went back to my condominium for lunch. A baby lizard and a humming bird joined me on the patio. The sun chairs looked inviting so I went over to one and proceeded to sit down.

The chair ripped in half right away. That could have seriously injured my already screwed up knee. Forget the sun tanning. I watched a DVD on places of peace and power instead. I had already been or was planning to go to quite a few of them. In fact, I discovered that the year long backpacking trip that I had planned to go on before my accident consisted of different world power spots. Up until now, I had no idea that world power spots existed.

My next session was with my angel guide Marlene. It was a two and a half hour session of inner journey with breath and sound. I had no idea what that session was going to be about, but I guess I was about to find out.

I felt that I had a strong connection with Marlene. I started to confide to her that I had always felt that I have had a sixth sense of some sort but I did not know how to control it. Things would just come to me when they felt like coming. It seemed the more I relaxed and meditated, the more stuff just came to me. I also discussed my lucid dreams with her and the fact that I could feel when spirits were around me. Sometimes they are good and sometimes they are bad. Either way, I did not know what they wanted or why I knew when they were around and other people did not. Frankly, they scared the poop right out of me!

I told her about the time that I had sent a ghost to Lorne's apartment and then his phone phoned my phone. Marlene advised me that I do not sent spirits to other peoples places. She told me that it was obvious that I was gifted and intuitive and that I was in a time frame for whatever reason, to wake up.

I was not exactly sure what she meant by wake up. I was awake. Could she not see that my eyes were open? She said that somehow spirit had sent me to Sedona with people that could support me in the waking up. I really did not know what she was talking about.

I continued to talk about how spirits were attracted to me. It had been like that all my life and I never knew what it was or who to talk to or what to say. Anytime I would try to talk about my experiences, I would be told to stop being a glue bag and it was all in my head.

Marlene proceeded to tell me that even though I may not be aware, I probably carried a lot of light and was very gifted with abilities that I had not yet discovered. She was telling me that I have a very deep deep connection to spirit. When disincarnate beings are lost and cannot find their way, they will see a light like me and come to me.

One of my jobs may be to help send them on their way. She explained that it was very scary at first but it would become a very beautiful thing to be able to help spirit to move on. She explained that there was an obvious calling on my life and I had been brought to Sedona to unfold what I really came here to be.

Marlene explained that she would be teaching me a form of breathing to bring me to expanded states of awareness and she let me know that I may feel the following:

* Chi energy moving through the body
* Might see color, hear sounds, feel numbing and tingling, vibration
* Sometimes old injuries may act up producing pain or aching
* Dry throat

Mystical Puzzle

Rare but may happen:

* Dizziness
* Tingling in the lips
* Spasms in hands and feet

Some of the things that could happen are:

* May go back and live the birth process
* May go back and live an experience from birth to present day
* May go back and see a future experience or past life experience
* If you get to transpersonal band of consciousness, anything goes, anything is possible, other planets, dimensions, be a tree, etc

   (One of her clients was cured of a herniated disc after one breath session.)

Resistance will show up in many different ways such as:

* Mental chatter
* Intense fear
* Starts to feel like a lot of work

Ok, so I believe in spirit, no doubt. However, she was trying to tell me that my hands or feet might start to spasm. Yeah right. I mean, I believe in a lot of weird stuff, but spasms, vibration, tingling, etc. Go to space or back through the birth canal? I did not know about all of that.

She explained that my higher self would take me into the experience that was most needed for that day. You never knew what kind of experience you would receive until afterwards. Each time it was different.

She taught me the breathing technique and we both went to the bathroom before starting the session. After the bathroom break, I got comfortable on the meditation bed covered with blankets and an eye mask. Marlene started the music and I started to breath in the way that she had taught me.

I am not sure if I am going to be able to explain in words what happened, but holy sheep shit! About ten minutes into the breath and sound session, my hands started to spasm and started to curl towards my wrist. I did not understand how that was happening! I was trying with everything that I had to uncurl my hand and straighten my fingers, but I could not do it! Why could I not control my own hands? Marlene had warned me that this could happen, but I have to admit, my thoughts were, yeah right!

I believed in many things, but come on. She had noticed that I was struggling to free my hands and they were spasming so bad that it was quite painful. I wanted to release the spasm myself but for some reason, I just could not do it. Marlene brought her hands and waved them above mine. Just like magic, the spasm released and I could straighten my fingers and hands.

During all of that, I just continued to breath. I remembered Marlene telling me, just breath. About twenty minutes into the session and my body started to tingle. My mouth was tingling, vibrating, and making sounds. I was not speaking. The sounds were sort of like when you are being shaken and travelling at extreme speeds and you are trying to keep your mouth shut, but the force was popping it open and strange sounds were coming from it.

All of a sudden, it was as if electrical prongs were plugged into the bottom of my feet. There was so much forceful energy emanating from the prongs into my feet, that it felt as though my body was levitated, and was being violently shaken, although I was in no pain. Even though I had an eye mask on, I was travelling at warp speed through a dark tunnel with sparks of energetic light everywhere.

Again, during all of this, I was just breathing away. And then *bang*! I was at ground level. So low that I was wondering if I was the ground? I proceeded to look up and could see the Great Pyramid of Giza. Oh my god, I had to stop! I had to pee so bad that I just could not hold it anymore. I did not want to stop though. Why was I there? In Egypt? With another hour to go, I had to have a pee break. I let Marlene know that I needed to go to the washroom and she put the music on pause.

As I got out of the meditation bed and proceeded to walk to the washroom, I just about fell over. Actually, I just about fell over several times. I was walking as though I was completely intoxicated. I did not know what was going on. Marlene helped me to the washroom and I could not believe how much pee came out of me! Where did it come from? I just went thirty minutes ago. I had never in my entire life had that much pee come out of me at one time! So much was coming out that I did not think it was going to stop. I was actually sitting on the toilet wondering, was it going to stop? That had never happened before.

Of course, it eventually stopped, and Marlene helped me to get back into the meditation bed. She started the music again while I started to get back into the breathing rhythm. It was hard to get back to the state that I was just in. I honestly did not really recall much of the last hour of the session and did not think anything profound happened like during the first half hour.

Once the last song was over, I removed my eye mask, and the first words out of my mouth were, "What the heck was that and can I do it on my own?" I had to go to the washroom again, and again I released so much pee that I did not know where it was coming from.

Marlene and I discussed what happened during the session. She had mentioned that my hands curled the way they did because I did not get enough oxygen when I was breathing. I needed to breathe more deeply. She

Mystical Puzzle

mentioned that the reason I had to go to the washroom so much and so much was released was because during the session, my metabolism had speeded up enormously.

Marlene gave me a CD of the music that was played during the session and off I went. I left the session in pretty much a daze and completely wiped out! I still could not find the words to really explain what happened during that session. If someone had tried to tell me they experienced what I had experienced, I would have thought they were on crack!

All that I can say was all the stuff I had been scared to talk about was very real! There was a completely different world out there that so very few know exists. I would have to tread lightly when I got back home because if I said too much, either I would scare people or they may think that I was off my rocker. What I had experienced with Marlene was truly magical!

I went back to my condominium and crashed for three hours. Once I got up, I went crystal shopping and closed the place down again. Instead of closing bars down, I was closing crystal shops down. I had started quite the collection and was going to continue collecting them when I got back home. I did not know where I was going to find crystals back home. I must be able to find them in Vancouver.

Ok, this was weird, but I could now say the "G" word. God! I now understand why I hated God before. No life would go perfect for anyone. Along with the hurt and pain, there were lessons and growth. We all have lessons to be learned; the good, and the bad. Due to free will, God could not intervene. I now know why I had my accident. It brought me here to a new understanding of the spirit life.

September 16

I only had one session today called Heart and Soul with Raina. I felt as though the three hours spent on that session, not to mention the money, was a waste. At one point during the session, I had asked Raina to move it along because I could not continue with what we were doing. It was not my thing. Raina was a wonderful woman. It was not that I did not like her; the session was just not right for me.

I stopped off at the jeep tour company to confirm my booking and they said that no one else was going, so I could not go. I was a little pissed as I was looking forward to the tour and had booked a couple of weeks in advance. My choices were a two hour tour or no tour. I guess something was better than nothing was.

I pretty much finished my crystal shopping. I would have loved to buy more of course, but I could only buy so much due to the duty taxes, plus the extra weight in my suitcase. My plan for the evening was to make dinner and then continue to watch the Magical Egypt DVD's.

While I was watching the DVD's, Sal phoned and said that the MP3 of our session was ready. I put the DVD on pause as I was just going to whip over to his place and come right back. After leaving Sal's, I approached the highway. Right took me to my condominium and left took me to uptown Sedona.

I turned left. I turned left! Why did I go left? My condominium was the other way. What was I doing? I had a strange urge to go to the crystal store in uptown, but I was already done crystal shopping. Whatever it was, I guess I would just follow along.

I ended up yapping to Pamela who worked there for two hours. During that time, a retired woman named Gina was shopping for crystals and yapped with the both of us for an hour. She was full of spunk and life.

She was just a customer but for one reason or another, my intuition brought me to the store. Once Gina had left the store, Pamela and I looked at each other with a dumbfounded look. Pamela said, "Do you ever get the feeling that you are suppose to be at certain places at certain times or meet certain people?" Ah, yeah! Like I did not know how I ended up there.

We both agreed that that just happened. For whatever reason, the three of us were supposed to be there at that time. Perhaps it was the words of wisdom from Gina. I did not know but I was definitely called there.

Pamela and I continued to talk as she was closing up the store. Holy crap it was late! The DVD had been on pause all that time. Once I returned to the condominium, I continued to watch the Magical Egypt DVD's as I found them quite interesting. I have always had a deep drawing to Egypt.

September 17

Today my only session was with Rhonda for an hour Intuitive Integration. I really did not get anything out of this session either. Again, there was nothing wrong with the practioner, I just felt like the session was not useful.

I found out Rhonda did past life regression so I booked a session with her for the end of the day, as that was not included in my package. Back at the condominium, I received a phone call from Deirdra, one of the owners of the retreat telling me not to worry about the chair that broke and proceeded to start laughing.

No kidding! The chair was faulty and could have seriously injured my already painful disabled leg. I really did not find it funny at all! She was phonier than a phone. I did not particularly like her husband either. On the website, he was portrayed as someone warm and friendly. I did not get that from him at all from the second I met him.

I am sure there were many people out there that felt the complete opposite of what I did, but I stick by my guns. I feel that they were in it for the business side more than helping people. I was shocked that they had charged me eighty-five dollars for doing nothing but charge my credit card for the past life regression session that I had booked on my own with the practioner. I believe that everyone had to make money in order to live but charging me eighty-five dollars to swipe my credit card did not seem so white light to me.

I went for my jeep tour from 2pm to 4pm. The scenery was amazing and it was fun to get out in a four wheel drive, but been there, done that. For people who had never been, it would be very exciting. The best part was watching the old fuddy duddy's getting a kick out of it. I am guessing they probably did not go four wheeling much.

After the jeep tour, I went for my past life regression session with Rhonda. I am not sure what to think. Were the memories actually from past lives or did my head somehow make up what I saw. I did not know. They were quick glimpses of scenes. I could not hold on to what was coming.

Some of the things I saw were I was a male wearing a sari and blue, pointy curl up shoes. I was at a palace of some sort and the furniture was all white. My name was Gabatrar.

Another scene was I was a young boy between seven and nine years old. I was in the forest with another boy that looked exactly like me. We were fighting with sticks and I accidently killed the boy. I was crying and shaking the boy to wake up.

Another scene was I was in a cave and I was petrified because there was evil in there. There was a demonic being with his ugly gray demonic dog laughing at me.

On the last scene, it was in an era of horses, wagons, bonnets, and dresses. I felt as though I was in a court house and the judge was wearing a white wig. Abraham Lincoln was there beaming proudly that justice be done and to make sure the person was punished for stealing cattle. The person being convicted was putting up a fuss as he was being dragged from the court room.

I did not know what to make of any of it. I was not sure that I found that session useful. I want to try to train myself on how to dig into my past lives to see what I could find out. I want to learn if past life experiences were affecting me today.

After the session, I went back to the condominium for dinner. I watched some more Magical Egypt DVD's. During one of my smoke breaks on the patio, I saw a baby scorpion walking around. Yikes! Those creepy crawlies had better not come into the condominium! I was paranoid after that.

September 18

Today I left Sedona and Arizona. I got up at 8am and started my day off with bacon, eggs, and toast. Next, the three S's; shit, shower and shave. I would hate the poor person sitting beside me on the plane to have to rub up against my prickly legs. I took an Imodium as well incase my nervous stomach / diarrhea started acting up.

The housekeeper was there at 8:30am. Why did people do that? Check out was 11am and my car was in the driveway. Then she told me sorry for waking me up. She did not know that I was up a half hour ago. Common sense says do not disturb!

For some reason my luggage felt way heavier. I stopped by the retreat head office to say good bye. Again, Deirdra was so phony and her husband was less than warm and fuzzy. Surely, I was not the only one who saw this.

Off to Phoenix I went. I could not believe that I (Miss Absolutely No Sense of Direction) travelled all over the state without problems. Usually even with directions, I would get lost. I made it back to the hotel to drop off the rental car without messing up. I was so proud of myself as normally I could not find my way out of a paper bag.

I arrived at the airport and my luggage was twenty pounds overweight. Ut-oh! Wait a minute. I had a back pack in my suitcase. Since we were allowed two carry on luggage bags, I just might be able to pull it off.

The next dilemma was fitting twenty pounds worth of stuff in my back pack. There I was at the airport check in with my suitcase open and trying to find the heaviest items to put on my carry on. It was quite funny because one of the airport attendants was helping me too. "You got any jeans or books in there?" He said. "Because those weigh a lot." I did not know how I managed to get all that stuff in my back pack, but I did.

I have to say being handicapped, sometimes had its advantages. I was pushed in my wheelchair through the airport, and I was privileged to go to the front of the line at security. They did not give me any grief what so ever. As an added bonus, I did not get body searched that time.

Everyone was on the plane ready for take off when we were told that there was going to be a delay, and to just sit tight. Of course, I wanted to know what the delay was about. A steward informed me that the ground crew discovered something wrong with the landing wheels and that they needed to be changed.

Basically, they would have popped on landing. Good thing they caught it because we were about to leave the bay and get ready for take off. I said to the steward, "You do know what would have happened had we landed with tires on the verge of popping." He assured me that we would have all been fine.

"Umm, have you ever been driving down the highway at speeds over one hundred kilometers and had a tire pop on you?" "No." He says. "Well I have. Trust me buddy, it wouldn't have been pretty." I said with a matter of fact smile. I think he knew; he just wanted to shut me up so that the other passengers did not panic.

The delay took a little longer than the crew anticipated, so everyone de-boarded the airplane. Well everyone except a few of us that were handicapped. We asked if we could just stay on the plane, as it was a pain for us to get on and off.

That reminded me. Every flight that I had been on during this trip, they had me sitting at the back of the plane, knowing that I was handicapped. Logically, the handicapped people should be near the front of the plane.

I found out the delay was going to be one and a half hours, so I decided to get off the plane and hang out in the airport. What a sight! Everyone was flipping out on an airport attendant whom was frantically trying to switch their flights because they were no longer going to make their original connection.

"Great! Now what am I going to do? I don't have anyone to pick me up at the new arrival time!" screamed one woman. "This is ridiculous! I'm going to miss my connecting flight!" yelled a man. "What about my connecting flight?" and so on and so on.

I admired how that attendant was handling himself. Everyone was yelling and screaming at him and he kept his cool the entire time and stayed focused on the task; getting those passengers on new connecting flights. I mentioned to him that he impressed me with his calm attitude. He replied with, "This is nothing. I use to be a cop in Miami and got shot at."

What was wrong with all of those people? Did they not get it?! They should be thankful that they were going to be late. Had the flight not been delayed, there was a good chance that none of us would have had to worry about making our connecting flights, because we would not be alive to do so.

Hey. When I booked my flight, I had the option of booking a flight that wouldn't leave me too much time in between connections or wait at the airport for a couple of hours before the connecting flight took off. Something told me to pick the later flight and now I knew why.

I sat patiently and smiled away as everyone around me was in a complete uproar. Well you know, getting pissed off would definitely help in making your connecting flight. Normally waiting around like that would piss me off too! For some reason, I could care less. I actually found the whole ordeal quite comical. People were pissed off because they got to live.

After the long hour and a half delay, we finally re-boarded the plane. As I entered the plane, I mentioned to a flight attendant that we should all get a complimentary drink. She kindly told me that she did not have authority to do that, only the captain did. "Where is the captain? I will ask him." I said with a smile. She assured me that that was not necessary and that she would ask him. The door to the cockpit was open and surely, he heard our conversation.

During the first flight, I watched the movie *What Happens in Vegas*. I am sure the entire plane had wished that I not did that. I was laughing in hysterics throughout the movie. Those that know me know that I am not the quietest person. I do not try to be loud; I just am.

The drink cart came by and I decided that I would have a beer since I had not had one for over a month. I proceeded to pay and the steward said it was on the captain. Of course, they never announced that there was a free beverage on the house or my guess was more people would have taken up the offer.

Right when a good part of the movie was on, the plane crew shut it off because we were starting to descend. What?! Why did they do that? Play a movie that they knew we would not be able to finish watching. I am so going to have to rent that movie now to see what happened in the last twenty minutes.

I did not have as much time to kill as originally planned, but I had enough time to get a bite to eat. I could not quite put my finger on it, but something was different. I had been noticing that certain people would pick me out of a crowd. Not literally pick me out of the crowd, but gave me a look of knowingness. It was as though certain people saw something that no one else did. What did they see?

Like pretty much everyone at the airport in a hurry, they were mindlessly moving forward and then they were almost startled like as though they were seeing something that they had not seen for a long time. They would look over at me and smile as they continued on their way. I knew they knew something, but what was it?

I sent a text to my sister asking her to bring me two rolled joints with her when she picked me up with my car at the airport. She did not know how to roll, so I told her to get mom to do it. Well I guess they were thinking ahead and knew that after not smoking any weed for eleven days, I was going to want some. My sis text me back and said they were already rolled and ready to go.

The flight from San Francisco to Vancouver was uneventful. I discovered that duty free went up to seven hundred and fifty dollars. Had I known that, I would have bought more crystals. I thought I was only allowed to bring back two hundred and fifty dollars worth of duty free goods. By the time I went through customs and arrived at my sister's house, it was around midnight. We stayed up and yapped for a few hours and then off to sleep I went.

Mystical Puzzle

September 19

It did not feel as though I had slept that long and I heard the sounds of little feet. I was sure that it was my nephew Jake as I was sleeping in his bed. I waited until he was real close and then, "Rarrrrrrrrrr!" as I jumped up. Ok, so I did not really jump up. I went from laying down to sitting up.

"Auntie Tanya, you scared me!" he said with his piss and vinegar grin. I did not get much sleep but got up with the kids anyways. As we live an hour and half away from each other, I did not get to see them often. I accompanied my sister and the kids to drop them off at school.

I was planning to go back to bed after the kids went to school. I ended up on the computer looking up *crystal children*. What were crystal children and why was I looking it up? Surely, I could do this another time. I was so tired and all I wanted to do was go to bed, but I felt compelled to look it up. I found out that there was such a thing called crystal children. I was not exactly sure why that term came to my head to look up, but it did.

The Crystal Children began to appear on the planet from about 2000, although some date them slightly earlier. These are extremely powerful children, whose main purpose is to take us to the next level in our evolution, and reveal to us our inner power and divinity. They function as a group consciousness rather than as individuals, and they live by the "Law of One" or Unity Consciousness. They are a powerful force for love and peace on the planet. Many people believe that these kids are signs of the next evolutionary step for us humans. (*Fenn*, n.d.)

I discovered while I was on the computer that my oldest nephew Michael was sending an instant message to his mom. Hey! I thought he was supposed to be in school. Apparently, he had a professional development day. Cool! I did not think I was going to be able to visit him because by the time he was home from school, I would already be on my way back home.

Normally, I would just stay to visit, but I had an appointment at a sleep disorder clinic an hour away from their house. Since my appointment was only half hour away from my house, I would have just continued on home and not gone back to my family's house. I told him that I had to sleep for a bit before I picked him up as I have only had about three or four hours of sleep.

I was so beat that I ended up sleeping longer than I should have. If I wanted to make my appointment at the sleep disorder clinic, I would not be able to see my nephew. As I normally did not come to the city often, I decided to skip the appointment and hang with my nephew.

It was not an important appointment. All I was doing was picking up some sort of machine to test for sleep apnea. I could just as easily pick up the machine next week. Although it would be an hour of driving once I was home, rather than picking it up on the way home, hanging with my nephew was more important.

As he lived with his dad, I drove there to pick him up. When I got to the front door, his little yappy dog was barking away at me. He told me it was ok to come in and not to worry about the dog because he hated everyone.

I made my way upstairs and sat down on the couch while Michael got his things together. His dog jumped up on my lap and started to lick me repeatedly. I thought that this dog hated people, yet he would not stop licking me. I was there for about ten minutes and the dog was all over me and licked me the entire time. Thank god he was just a little lap dog as that could have been a problem.

Michael and I left his house and we went over to my moms for a visit. I showed him all the crystals I had bought while I was in Sedona. He took an immediate liking to them, almost in an addictive type of way. Whoa, buddy! Slow down! I was not sure if he was interested in the crystals or if he was just interested in them because I was.

Mom and I went into her bedroom for a smoke. She was supposed to smoke outside but sometimes she sneaks them in her bedroom. Unexpectedly she said, "There was something different about Ayden's birth." "What do you mean?" I questioned her. "I don't know, just something different." She said with a puzzled look on her face.

I really did not know what she was talking about and why she would bring that up out of the blue. We were not talking about babies or giving birth. Not to mention, Ayden was seven months old already.

A light bulb just came on. Crystal children. Did Ayden have something to do with crystal children? I started to question my mom more about Ayden's birth to try to see if she could tell me anything that she remembered, and to see if it matched with what others have said. She could not give me anything other than his birth was different.

Hmm. Perhaps I should keep an eye on him. On the same day, I looked up crystal children on the internet not knowing why, or if such a thing existed, and then my mom unexpectedly started to talk about how different Ayden's birth was. It seemed somewhat strange.

After visiting with my family, I made my way back home. It was so nice to be home and to sleep in my own bed for a change. I was glad I did the trip to Sedona. Even though it cost seven thousand dollars, I felt good. I no longer wanted to kill myself and I felt like no matter what life threw at me, I would get through it.

While I was unpacking, I came across the booze that I had bought for such a great price. The first thing that came to me was what was I supposed to do with it? And, what was I supposed to do with the other fifteen bottles of

Mystical Puzzle

booze in my cupboard? Not long ago, any time one of the bottles was half empty, I use to go to the liquor store and buy another one, just in case I ran out!

CHAPTER 4

The Transformation – Tanya Who?

September 25

I drove to Langley to see a pain specialist. There had to be something other than Morphine and Toradol to help me over the next year. According to the specialist, there was nothing else that I could try. He told me that if I were having difficulties already, the next year would be hell. Well that was a waste of a drive. He could not offer me any help to alleviate the pain that I experienced.

When I returned home from my appointment, there was a message on my machine stating that my surgery was canceled. It was as though someone had phoned me and said, sorry; I cannot meet with you today but how about tomorrow.

Only it was more like, your surgery has been canceled, and we did not know when you would be getting it. You are at the top of the list and we might be able to get you in for the beginning of the year.

Why did this not have me enraged, and phoning every single person I knew to share how the doctors had screwed up again! This would have normally consumed me for weeks; maybe even months and it did not matter. Why did this not matter to me? I was not pissed off. I was truly ok with it and I did not know why. I should not be ok with it. I just saw my surgeon yesterday for a pre-op consultation and he never mentioned anything to me then. I started to smile thinking that everything happened for a reason.

Ok, so I had been home for a week. I really did not know what was happening, but I was in a complete state of bliss for no apparent reason. Everything could be falling apart around me and it did not matter. I was still content and happy. In fact, I have never felt like this before. I did not really know what "this" was. I no longer cried myself to sleep and woke up already crying. Instead, I went to sleep blissfully happy and woke up blissfully happy.

I felt as though I was being guided, but who was guiding me? I felt like I was Noah as in Noah's Ark. I did not really know the story of Noah's Ark so I did not know how I had come to that conclusion. It was in my head, but I did not know how it got there. I did things and I went places because I was being guided to do such, but I did not know where it was coming from.

Mystical Puzzle

I had decided that I needed to turn my apartment into a peaceful sanctuary. Most people are sound asleep at 1am, but that was my prime working time. I love being up in the middle of the night and sleeping in the day. I call it the hamster effect. I proceeded to rip apart my bedroom and took everything out except for the bed. Since being handicapped, those kinds of tasks take huge amounts of time; but that was something that I had.

I might not be able to do everything I use to or do things as quick as I use to, but I was starting to become stubborn in a toughening up kind of way to try to do things for myself. I hated always having to ask for help.

I went on the internet to pick out some paint colors. I was hoping my mom felt like painting as she was coming over in a few hours and I had just decided that I was painting my bedroom. As I had not gone to sleep, I thought I had better get a few hours before she arrived.

September 26

Mom arrived with Michael and could not believe the mess I had going on. I had only been home for a week. I informed her that I was painting and rearranging my bedroom. "Have you ever painted before?" she asked with a smirk. "Not really. How hard can it be?" I said as I gave her the, do not worry mom, it will be fine look.

Mom being mom knew that look, and said that I could do the cutting while she did the painting. In all honesty, we both knew what would have happened had I painted my room by myself. An enormous mess! In some ways, I was still like a five year old. Besides, it would have taken forever for me to paint it due to my leg.

She painted my entire room in the same amount of time it took me to do the cutting. I guess it was a good thing she was helping me, as it probably would have taken me a week at this rate to paint one little room. The colors I chose for the bedroom were indigo and violet. It looked good. I just needed to add a peaceful touch to it. Mom and Michael went to bed around 2am. I stayed up and tinkered around.

September 28

I had not gone to bed and at around 5am, I heard a voice telling me to go to the bedroom window. Huh? Where was that voice coming from? It was not mine, but I could hear it in my head. I was not afraid of it; I was just not exactly sure where it was coming from. I kept hearing it. It did not stop until I went to my bedroom window.

I lifted up the blinds and oh my heavens! I have never seen stars that looked like that in my life! It was so incredible! It was so incredible and bizarre at the same time that I wondered if anyone else saw what I saw. It was as though they were bright yellow, larger than usual and hanging down ever so low. I was so awe struck that I found myself staring at the stars for over a half hour and not wanting to stop.

It was as though they were trying to tell me something. What was it? What are you trying to tell me? I did not understand the language but they were definitely trying to communicate something to me. Somehow, I had a feeling that a part of what they were telling me, was to go to Rona in the morning and buy the outdoor gazebo tent that I had my eye on.

What was this?! Why were stars calling me to the window and trying to communicate with me?! This was totally fucked up! This did not happen! Why was I cool with it and did not feel fear or wonder who told me to go to the bedroom window? I was content but I did not know why. I would never forget what those stars looked like, for the rest of my life. I had better get to bed because before I knew it, my mom and Michael would be up.

Once I had some sleep, Michael and Alex accompanied me in town as I had a few different errands to run. Mom hung out at my apartment. I had so many errands that I wrote out a list and put them in order of where I would be stopping. Rona was last on the list.

As we left my apartment, something told me that I must go to Rona immediately! As Rona was located near me, I was there lickety split. I could not believe it! The tent that I wanted to buy went on sale from four hundred to two hundred dollars and it was scratch and save day to save an additional percentage.

I immediately went up to the cashier and asked her if she could save the tent for about twenty minutes as I had to go home to transfer money from one account to another, and then go to the bank machine to withdraw the money. The cashier hummed, hawed, and informed me that someone might want to buy it. Yeah, that someone was me! I pleaded her to wait for twenty minutes. Thankfully, she agreed to hold it.

I made my way back to my car where Michael and Alex were waiting for me. I must have been glowing from head to toe because Michael said, "Holy auntie. What happened to you?" I explained that the tent that I had wanted to buy was on sale and that we needed to move quickly before someone else bought it. I raced back to my house to transfer the money. Then we went to the bank machine, and back to Rona we went. Michael's curiosity was piqued so he came into Rona with me to see what the tent thing was all about.

I went back to the same cashier and proudly told her that I would like to purchase the tent. She went outside to grab the price tag. While she was out there, a customer approached her and asked what she was doing with the tag. The cashier explained that the tent was sold. The customer said that she had come to buy the tent.

Mystical Puzzle

Wow! Had I waited and came to Rona last as originally planned; that customer would have already bought the tent. Not to mention I received two hundred dollars off plus an additional six percent off. As we were leaving Rona, Michael looked at me and said, "You're kidding me! Right?"

"No buddy! That tent is the coolest thing and it's going in my living room!"

"What?! Auntie no! You are never going to be able to have anyone over. You are scaring me! What is happening to you?"

I explained to him that I honestly did not know what was happening to me. I did know that there was going to be many changes, and I did know that I was *soooo* happy! His look of fright turned into a smile. He looked over at me as I was beaming and said, "You really are happy. It's as though your life is a puzzle and it's just starting to come together."

"Yes!" I screamed with delight. I could not have said it better myself. That was exactly what it was like. My life was a puzzle in a whole bunch of pieces and I was finally finding the pieces that connect. Man, kids could be so smart! We really need to give them more credit.

I reassured Michael that yes, there were many changes happening, but they were all for the good and I was so very happy! His next question was, "Does this mean you aren't going to get drunk anymore and have loud parties? It is so much fun when you are drunk and have parties." "Buddy, I do not know. One day at a time." I assured him.

Once we finished all the errands, I dropped Alex off at home and proceeded back to my place. Michael packed up his belongings, and he and my mom made their way back home.

I talked to a couple of friends and asked if they happened to be up and outside at 5am. Two of them said yes and confirmed the bizarre stars. They too, had never seen anything like it. Well at least I knew that I was not seeing things. Not that I thought that I was, it was just that they were so unreal looking.

The paint on my bedroom walls was good and dry so I rearranged it and removed all the clutter. I did not have a whole lot to decorate it with at this point, but enough to give it a start. I spent a half hour moving candles around in different formations on the table behind my bed.

It felt important. It felt like it must be just so. I looked at one of the formations I created and thought I must use that formation, but not at the present time. I would know when it was time. I pretty much spent the whole day and night in my bedroom until I was satisfied with the arrangement. Now all I needed was a couple of end tables, curtains, mosquito net, plants, waterfall, and letters to spell the words, Love, Peace, Unity, and World.

The Transformation – Tanya Who?

I had been spending quite a bit of time reading and researching history. Right about now I was thinking why did I not pay attention in school? I knew the answer to that. Because I was too cool for school and getting high and ditching class was much more interesting.

If only I had this head, back then. I was browsing some history websites when, you have to be kidding me! Staring back at me was the *Kabbalah Tree Of Life!* I had never heard of such a thing or saw how it was formed.

The Tree Of Life was the exact formation I put the candles in a few nights ago. How and why and what exactly did that mean? It was strange how information just found its way staring back at me from my computer screen.

During one of my days of researching, I came across an advertisement for the University of Metaphysical Sciences. Something was driving me to look at the website. It stated that Sedona was the metaphysical mecca of the world. I just came from Sedona. There must be a connection of some sort there.

I entered the website and proceeded to see what the University was all about. I could not believe it! Had I only known such a school had existed? That was exactly what I needed. Not only would it help me to learn and understand about this sixth sense that I always believed I have had, but I believed it would help me to understand what was happening to me.

Not only could I continue to learn and grow for myself, but also it would give me a chance to help so many others! I could actually see myself loving this job! I would love it so much that it would not feel like a job. It would simply be a way of life. I could obtain a Doctorate Degree on line. That would be perfect! Due to my leg, I could never sit long enough to enroll in classes, but doing it that way, I could lay down while I was learning and studying.

The funniest thing was I could establish a church. *Me!* Any of my friends, colleagues, teachers, family, etc would think that was the biggest joke they had ever heard. Many years ago, I use to joke about starting my own religion and church and call it the Church of Tanya.

At the end of the teaching, for those who wished to participate, would light up a joint and smoke it. Again, I use to joke about this many years ago. It disturbs me at how religion separates people instead of unifying. My biggest belief is we are *all* equals and we *all* deserve to be treated with love and respect.

I agree with many of the different teachings in all the religions, but would never agree or follow a religion to the "T" so to speak. I do not believe that people should be looked down upon because they did not follow a specific religion. There were many things that I believe and do not believe about religion, which I do not wish to get into. To each their own.

Mystical Puzzle

But wait. How much was this going to cost? University was so expensive. It was normally so expensive that so many never have the opportunity to go without going into debt for the rest of their lives. I questioned whether I should even bother to check. I guess it could not hurt.

To my surprise, not only was it affordable but it was a non profit corporation. Which must mean the person that has founded the University was genuine, and was not out there to make a million. That really appealed to me. I could not believe it, but I was going to enroll.

A Doctorate Degree? Me? Hell yeah! I did not know why, but that was not frightening me in the least. It felt right. Since 2002, I had been saving for a trip around the world. I certainly had the money. By paying for the course in full, it reduced tuition costs.

I had no doubts in my mind that this was the right thing to do. I was so excited! A few weeks ago, I was dead and ready to give up on life and here I was enrolling in a Doctorate Degree program. I felt like I was on top of the world!

~ ~ ~

I confessed for the first time what was going on to my aunt and cousin. Or at least what I thought was going on. Since they lived in the same town as me, and we see each other frequently, I thought I had better give them a heads up. I needed to talk to someone or I was going to burst! I was living some kind of, I did not know! I wished someone would just tell me!

I was starting to wonder if I was some kind of a human angel. I really did not know what they were thinking when I told them that. Did they think I was really going crazy? Actually, come to think about it, it must be ok that I told them because M and M would stop me in my tracks, or give me some kind of warning to shut my hole.

In case you had forgotten, M and M stands for Archangel Michael and Heavenly Mother.

My aunt had astral travelled before. I remember her telling me that when I was a teenager. I asked her back then to teach me and she said, "No Way! It's been a long time since I have done it and it is scary!" She was aware of other dimensions so I believed she was safe.

She was the person I usually confessed all my troubles. She always had the right words of advice and wisdom. However, telling them I thought that I might be a human angel. That might land me in the loony bin!

My cousin looked very interested in what I was saying to the point that it looked as though she was holding back tears of sincerity. I was sure she had no idea what I was talking about, but she somehow trusted whatever it was that I had been telling them.

Lorne started to hang around again. There was no way he was going to be able to handle my new self. In fact, I was scared that he was going to look me right in the eye, laugh his face off, point his finger at me, and say, "Fruit fucking loop!"

I had tried a couple of times to tell him that we should not be friends because he would not understand me. I could not handle the thought of being ridiculed by him. He kept telling me that he was not going anywhere and that I would find out whom my real friends were. I guess only time would tell.

~~~

Holy! For someone who hated to shop, I had been doing it almost everyday. I had been picking up stuff here and there to decorate my apartment into a peaceful sanctuary. I could not say that it had been particularly easy, as when I shop, I needed to use my wheelchair. I could only grab as much as I could stick in one basket.

I used one hand to hold the basket while the other wheels the chair. I also used my good leg to push along the floor to get more speed. I could cruise with my chair pretty good but it could get tiring quite quickly. There always seemed to be obstacles and challenges. However, when you want something done, you just do it!

At the end of each day, I would call Lorne to unload my car. Each day he wondered what was I going to do with all that stuff. My response was always, "You'll see. Sometimes you have to wait for the good things in life," as I cackled my wicked laugh.

Oh dear! What have I done! Ok, so I knew I had been at my apartment everyday and I had just took notice of the tornado that had ripped through my home. What was going on? That was not me! There was stuff everywhere! There was hardly a clear path to walk through the apartment.

There was food in a pot on my stove with mold in it! Mold! I do not do mold! I had not been to my mailbox. I had not been to my mailbox! That meant that I had bills that needed to be paid. I do not know how I slept at night.

It would usually bother me if nothing were in its place. Nothing was in its place! I had never been late paying a bill in my life. And guess what? I really did not care. Why was it that I did not care? Why was I quite proud of myself for the mess I had made?

To you, that may sound terrible. To me, it was amazing! I let food go moldy and made such a mess out of my apartment that I could hardly walk through it. Could it really be? Was my obsessive compulsive disorder (OCD) gone?

It must be because I really did not care that I had unpaid bills, moldy food and a mess so big, it was going to take me a week to clean. I felt so free! I did not know how it happened. In fact, I did not need to know how or why. All that mattered was I was free from OCD! It had controlled so much of my life and now I was finally free!

One of my obsessions was making sure everything was in its place. I would start my day scanning each room to ensure everything was in place. When I mean in place, I meant in place, to the millimeter! If something were out of place, I would fix it to my liking. Sometimes that meant moving an object only a millimeter to the right or left.

I had to do it or it would drive my mind crazy! If I so much as got up to go to the bathroom, I would have to re-check and ensure everything was still in place. You know, just in case it moved all by itself.

Even though I knew it would be impossible for anything to move on its own, as no one was there to move it, I still had to check. Ugh! It was so ridiculous! I knew it was ridiculous but I could not stop. That was just one example of my OCD. There were many more. It had been going on since childhood and suddenly it was gone!

Lorne and I were on our way to the place where we were employed, when I received an urge to stop at the second hand shop in town. "What the hell are you stopping here for? It stinks in there!" he said. "I don't know. It is just a feeling. I will figure it out once I am in the store for awhile. Either there is something here that I must buy, or there is a person who is already in there, or will be soon that I need to talk to. Suck it up Lorne, let's go!" I rambled on as we were heading inside the store. I scanned each aisle of the used items to see if anything called out to me. Perhaps I was there to talk to someone.

I was walking through the last possible aisle and nothing had jumped out at me. Ah huh! That was it, an antique looking brass balance! I was not sure why it needed to go home with me but I was sure that I would figure it out eventually.

"Why are you buying that thing?"

"I don't know."

"Then why the hell are you buying something you don't even know why you are buying it?"

"It is just one of those things. I do not know why now, but I will later. Just trust me Lorne. When I get urges to stop suddenly at unscheduled places, there is a reason for that. If you happen to be with me, we have to stop." He giggled; shook his head and back to the car, we went.

Later on, I sat down in my heap of a mess of an apartment, and decided to make a list of what I needed to buy to get my sanctuary started. I went through each room and decided what colors I would like the walls painted, and what needed removing and or added.

I knew it was not going to happen overnight and it may take me several months to build it, but it was going to be the coolest set up. I was sure people's initial reaction would be what is the matter with you? However, I was also sure that once they really looked at it and felt its vibe and energy, how could they not like it. I had not really told anyone my plans to change my apartment other than be prepared to see many changes.

~~~

Nelson had stopped by my place with Alex one night to return some money that I had lent him. They were only there for a few minutes and he realized that his wallet must have been in the van as it was not in his pocket. He went to go grab it and came back frantic. He could not find his wallet anywhere! He had cashed his entire check as he had just been paid, and needed it for rent.

I suggested to him that he retrace his steps to where he last remembered having his wallet in his hand. He just had it at the gas station before coming to my place so hopefully someone found it. He came back disappointed, as he did not find his wallet. Ok, it was more like he was freaking out because that was his rent money.

I tried to encourage him to think positive and to pray that someone decent found it and returned it with all his money. I told him that I would pray as well. After Nelson and Alex left, I said a prayer to my angels asking that the wallet find its way back to Nelson. They were a young family and that money was their rent money.

Six hours later, I was sitting at the kitchen table and noticed a wallet sticking out between the blankets. No way! That was impossible! Number one, Nelson never took one step into the living room. Number two, I had sat in that very spot several times over the last six hours and looked over where the wallet was now, and it was not there earlier.

It was sticking out like a sore thumb! It was creepily cool! I did not know how the wallet got there, and I am not so sure I wanted to know how it got there. All that I knew was it was there, and Nelson and Melissa could rest assured that their rent money was found. I thanked the angels for whatever part they had in the return of the wallet. It was 1am and I knew they were sleeping but I just had to phone them so that their minds could be at ease.

Mystical Puzzle

Over the course of the week, I continued to buy the items on my list. I could not find the wooden letters for the words I wanted to put on my walls but I did find the perfect sized wooden plaques. I could just stencil the letters on and add stickers to decorate them. Did I just say that? I am going to make my own decorations and hang them up for all to see.

Was I sick or something? I did not do crafts! Anything I made was ugly and I had absolutely no creativity. A five year old had more creativity than I did. However, for some reason, I wanted to do this. I could do this. Instead of spelling out the word "World," I had decided to place my world wall map in its place.

I wanted to buy curtains but Amber said she could make me some for cheap when she made covers for my floor pillows. Quite often Amber comes up with brilliant ideas and offered to do things or make things for me but rarely followed through.

Most times, I did not ask her to make me things, she offered, I would say yes and then I never did receive what she intended to make. Alternatively, she would gladly volunteer someone else to do what she said she was going to do without asking them. She was so funny that way.

We drove into Chilliwack to pick up all the fabric and ran whatever other errands we had to do. In hindsight, I spent more money on material than I would have if I just bought the curtains. Amber never did end up making the curtains. I still have all the fabric that I bought that day. She was kind enough to get her mom to make the pillow covers though.

~ ~ ~

Looking at my apartment, I wondered how I was going to paint it. I could not stand for long and my leg ached all the time. I would have to stand on something to reach the walls toward the ceiling. If I fell, I would end up in a coma or shock from the pain.

In conclusion, it would take me until the rest of the year to get my place painted. Oh, Lorrrrrne. Lorne had lots of time on his hands since he was laid off. I asked him if he wanted to paint my apartment. His reply was, "Not a fucking chance! Maybe I want to paint my own apartment." "Bullshit! You are not going to paint your apartment." I said laughing my head off.

He did not budge but I would give him a couple of days. Eventually he was going to get bored and would want something to do. A couple of days later, Lorne asked me if I had any joints that I could sell him. "No way man! I hardly have any and I am not going to the city for a couple of days."

The light bulb came on. With my, I am up to something evil little grin, I said, "Lets make a deal. You paint my apartment, I will give you a couple of joints now, and when you finish the job, I will give you the sixty ounce of whiskey I bought in Arizona and all the other bottles of booze that I have. There is an equivalent of another twenty-six ounces."

"Done! But first, you better clean this shit hole up. I can't paint in this mess!" He said in excitement. That was too cool! Now I would get my apartment painted in a day instead of a year. This would also be a good way to get rid of my alcohol because I did not have the urge to drink. Prior to today, I had already got rid of a few of the bottles that had not been opened.

Since I did not need furniture anymore, I asked Lorne to move my couch and rocking chair into the main hallway of the apartment. I would just leave it there until I could find a new home for them. Once all the big furniture was out, I could clean my carpets. My place was getting a scrub down from top to bottom!

~~~

It was just after 6:30pm and it was still daylight out. I heard a voice telling me to go to the bedroom window. That same voice as before when I saw the most amazing stars. I remember what they showed me last time they called me to the window, so I went without hesitation and I proceeded to the bedroom window. The sky was clear without a cloud in sight.

I saw a bright ball of white light travelling across the sky. I could not help but follow it. I have not the foggiest idea of what it was. It was travelling the speed of a plane but it was clearly not a plane, only a very bright ball of light. As my eyes were following the bright light, I started to see sparkles of light in the air. Was I starting to see energy? I had seen sparkles before, but not like that. They were everywhere and so mesmerizing!

I took my gaze off the bright light to look at all the other sparkles for a second. When I looked to where the bright light was, it was gone! All I could think was, where did it go and how did it disappear like that? Whoa! What the heck was that?!

Wait a minute! I remember that voice. I am not just talking about when I was called to my window last week. I am talking about when I was about eleven years old. My friend Misty and I had decided to have a sleepover in my tent in the back yard. My little sister Corrina was three at the time.

Corrina was sitting at the fire that we had built, while Misty and I were running around in the back yard like a bunch of yard apes. As we were running around, I heard a voice telling me to go to my sister before she fell in the fire. I immediately ran towards the fire. Just as I was approaching my sister, she had fallen out of the rocking chair and into the fire. I grabbed her by the back of her shirt and yanked her out! She started to cry.

Oh no! We could not tell mom that she fell in the fire. I tried to get her to shut up before mom heard but it was too late. I warned her not to tell mom or we would all be in trouble! As it was dark out and we had a huge back yard and a field that was approximately one and a half acres, mom could not see what was going on, she could only hear Corrina crying and Misty and I trying to shush her up.

"What's going on out there?"

"Nnnnothhhing!"

"Then why is Corrina crying?"

"Don't worry mom, she is ok."

I told Corrina that she had to stop crying! I yelled across the yard to mom while I whispered to my sister to be quiet. Mom was not convinced that everything was ok and continued to ask what was going on and why was Corrina crying. I was forced to fess up.

"Corrina fell in the fire!" I yelled across the yard. "Jesus Christ! Bring her in here!" Mom yelled back! It turned out that her burns were not that bad. She did not need to go to the hospital or anything. Thank god I got to her when I did! It could have been much worse! I never did tell Misty or my mom about the voice that told me to go to her. The weird thing was, looking back; I never questioned the voice and never hesitated. I just did what it said and I immediately ran to my sister. I also never talked to anyone about it.

~ ~ ~

I went over to Amber's and confided in her that something really weird was going on. I asked her what she would do if I were different. She asked me if I was gay. If only that were it because at this point it would seem so much easier if I were just gay. I think people would accept me more.

"No I am not gay dumbass! What if, like, my DNA was different from yours? Ok, like I am not crazy but there is just really weird stuff going on. Not bad stuff, good stuff. Someone or something has been calling me to my window, and I have been seeing amazing or unexplainable things. I think I am some sort of earth angel or an indigo." Trust me. I felt silly searching *human angel* on the internet and was shocked to find that there was a whole world of information on such.

I watched for a reaction and she was calm. She looked at me like whatever Tanya; everything was going to be all right, even if you were an earth angel. What?! That was it. She did not freak out and think I was crazy. Hmm. That was not so bad. She did not seem freaked at all. I just told her that I thought that I may be a fricken earth angel and I hardly got a reaction from her.

I also let her know that there were going to be big changes in my life and my apartment and that she may not see me that often over the next year. I explained to her that I needed time to myself to get use to the new skin I was wearing. I hoped that I could count on her, as she was my best friend in town. I did not plan to share what was going on with anyone else; well at least not any time soon.

I went to bed early for a change. There was a beautiful rainbow on my wall. I have lived in this apartment for four years and there had never been a rainbow on my wall. I knew it was coming from the motel sign beside my apartment, but why had it never done that in the previous four years? It was amazing! If only all of my walls could have looked like that.

I asked for guidance before I went to sleep as to what was going on with me. I woke up several times talking in my sleep. At one point I yelled, "NO!" While I jolted to a sitting position. I was confused, looked around and went back to sleep.

~~~

I went to the post office to pick up my mail. As I lived in a small town, my mail was delivered to a box at the post office. After returning home, I proceeded to open my mail. One of the pieces of mail that I received had red colored letters in one of the sentences.

Wow! Those letters were really sticking out of the page as though they were 3D. I moved the paper around and no matter what angle I looked at it; the red colored letters were 3D. They were sticking out of the paper about a quarter inch. Could everyone see it this way or was I the only one? It was weird!

While looking on the internet for places to buy crystals, I found a woman who lived close to me. Not only did she sell crystals, but she was also a reiki energy healer. I had phoned her and made an appointment for an energy session.

October 5

I went to my first energy session with Becca. I felt all kinds of sensations and energy going through me. I had felt a painful burning sensation in my lower back and volts of energy shooting through my leg. At one time, I felt like I was going to throw up. When it was time for me to open my eyes, I could not open them. It was too bright. I kept seeing indigo and violet. It took a few minutes before I could fully open my eyes.

At the end of the session, Becca discussed with me what she saw. She had started to become extremely emotional and apologized. She explained that her crystal singing bowls played in a way that she had never heard before. She also said that she saw the Garden of Eden and Jesus was by my side.

She saw my body extremely tall, twenty feet tall, and mentioned that she did not know how it was possible, but I was made of pure crystal. She mentioned that she removed an energy blockage below my right knee. That was where I felt the volt of energy shooting through my leg.

There was also a strong hold of an attachment hooked into my sacral chakra that she had removed. That must be why I felt like throwing up and my lower back was burning. She left me with I was a walk-in.

A walk-in is a soul that bypasses the usual process of being born. The original soul leaves the physical body and the new soul steps into the body that was left. So in essence, walk-in's are:

* wake up one day and feel like their life has been a bad dream, or one they don't recognize
* don't remember their childhood, or significant chunks of their life
* have a history of suicidal fantasies or attempts
* have heard from friends and family "your not the same anymore"
* make sudden and drastic changes, such as changing first name, moving, divorcing, switching careers, adopting different religious beliefs, and so on (*Virtue*, 2002, p. 99)

Well that would certainly explain why I had been behaving the way I had. When I left the session, I felt relaxed and knew that when the time was right, everything would appear, as it should. I stopped off at the post office on the way home and was confused as to why it was not open. I did not think it was a holiday.

I had asked a woman that was leaving and she said it was after 5pm. What! I just about fell over! I just lost two hours of time that I could not explain. I phoned Becca when I got home to see if she realized how long the session took. She was well aware of the time that it took. I was flabbergasted that I was at her place for three hours and could have sworn it was only an hour.

So much was starting to make sense. Like why I kept thinking I was going to die at the beginning of this year, and that I should make a video of myself so that it could be played at my funeral. Before I went to Sedona, I wrote an in case I die letter giving instructions what to do.

That also explained why I was doing, feeling and thinking everything different from the last Tanya. Because I was a walk-in that was going to kick some global ass! I knew when she died. My close friends felt something too. I remember telling Amber that I was dead inside. There was nothing but emptiness and blackness.

That must be why I had the dirt bike accident. So that the old Tanya could leave the physical body and the new Tanya would emerge, a much higher frequency Tanya. When the first soul leaves, it takes with them the emotional, mental, and spiritual bodies and new ones from the incoming soul are infused. That would explain why all my old hurts and pains have magically disappeared.

Like I did not cry anymore or felt saddened by my dad and his abandonment. I felt that I was lucky that my mom stuck it out with us because god knows the first Tanya would have committed suicide had she walked the shoes her mom did. That explained why the sudden urge to re-do my apartment, to make it a peaceful sanctuary. I would have loved to have a sand carpet. Perhaps sometime in the future I could have that arranged.

I wondered if my walk-in was fully integrated the second I hung up the phone when booking my Sedona trip! That was when the blackness started to lift away. I wondered how many walk-ins I have had. Have I had more than one? I had a big personality change after trying to commit suicide when I was twenty-two. I turned into Polly Anna for a little while. Thank god it did not last that long. That was so not me!

After my session with Becca, I bled lightly for a couple of days. I am not sure why as it was not time for my period and I was not irregular. Perhaps it was because of the attachment that was released from my sacral chakra.

~ ~ ~

I had tried to make an appointment with my shrink for more meds but she said she could not see me for six weeks. She had previously told me that I needed to give her two weeks notice and I did as I was going to run out of meds. I asked if she could phone in a prescription and she said that she needed to see me.

I told her I would run out by the time six weeks came up; as she was the one that told me, I needed to give her two weeks notice. Her response was that it was not her concern. I knew there was something flaky about that woman. I was not going to see her anymore. She was useless. Most of the time, her own secretary did not know where she was or what day she would be back.

I had an appointment with my doctor to ask her about getting off the anti depressant. She took one look at me with her head cocked to the side and a big smile and asked what happened to me. I simply told her that she had been trained to think a certain way and that if she was interested on where I went, she would have to research it on the internet. I told her that I went on a spiritual retreat in Sedona, Arizona that was known for its powerful vortex energy spots. She had convinced me to stay on the Effexor because it was just a matter of time before my next surgery. With all the pain and challenges that I would be facing, it would help.

~ ~ ~

It was a beautiful fall day and school had just been let out so I phoned Alex to see if he wanted to go to Sucker's Creek to build sand castles. Of course, he was in. What ten year old boy would turn down getting dirty by the river?

I decided to make a huge tree of life symbol. I found a nice clear spot to start building it. I took off my shoes and socks to feel the sand beneath me and through all my toes. That was very abnormal for me, as I usually did not like my bare feet touching anything but socks!

I used a star shaped sand mold to build the tree of life symbol. Once that was done, I dug out a huge circle around the tree of life to symbolize unity. Unbelievable! I had sand under my nails and I did not care!

I stood back to have a look at my creation and noticed the letter "T" imprinted within the unity circle. I asked Alex if he had drawn the "T," because it was not there the entire time that I was working on my sand creation. He assured me that he did not.

I asked him repeatedly if he did because how else would it get there. He kept on telling me repeatedly that he did not draw a "T." I started to get agitated and threatened him that he would be grounded if he did not tell me the truth! He assured me that he was not lying and he never drew the "T."

He pointed about thirty feet away from my sand creation and showed me an "S" that he had drawn. I decided to stop wondering how the "T" got there and to just enjoy the beautiful day. I built the tree of life so that there was a rock for me to sit on at the top of the symbol. I meditated while Alex continued to build his sand castle.

~ ~ ~

My friend Rod, whom is also my neighbor, moved to the east coast and left most of his belongings behind. I noticed his furniture in the hallway and asked the landlord what he was going to do with it. He had told me that it was all going to the dump.

I asked if I could have the end tables and cool mirrors and he said I could take whatever I wanted. That worked out great! It saved the landlord money from having to pay the extra dump fee and it saved me some money from having to buy end tables. I did not want to keep any of my big furniture, but I did need little tables and what not to put plants, table top waterfalls, crystals, etc on.

~ ~ ~

My friend Lorne, who lived down the hall, came over one night while I was organizing my crystals in classification of chakra. He was jokingly telling me that he was going to mix them up. "Oh no you don't!"

I stood up to grab the bag of crystals out of his hand, and while he was trying to move them out of my reach, the crystals banged into the metal part of the chair. Oh my God! My eyes just about popped out of my head in shock! "What are you doing to my crystals!? You can't bang them around like that!" He really did not care that he banged them and said, nothing would happen, they were all right. I was a little pissed and told him never touch my crystals again!

Well, early the next morning, he came over to ask me to come over to his place because he wanted to show me something. The power in his apartment went crazy! When he turned his stove elements on, they would not heat up, but the oven fan would turn on. Each time he would turn on another stove element, the stove fan would go faster and his computer would lose power and shut down. A light that never worked before began to work and when he would try to turn one thing on something completely different would turn on.

I started to laugh my head off! "I told you not to mess with my crystals, now look what you've done!" Lorne was such a skeptic and always wanted to see a sign. I have tried to explain to him that just because you did not see it, did not mean that it was not there. If that was not a sign, then what was?

The building maintenance man was baffled and looked straight at me and said, "What did you do?" I told him that Lorne screwed with my energy, so my crystals were screwing with his. They ended up having to call BC Hydro to fix it because something was completely blown. That would teach him not to mess around with my crystals. He was not convinced that his screwed up electricity was due to him disrespecting my crystals. I was convinced otherwise.

~ ~ ~

Sal was right! One of my toughest lessons would be compassion for all. Do not get me wrong. I did not want people to be hurt in any way. I just get pissed off at the people who see it as their job to hurt others purposely and continually.

I saw a documentary on what happened to natives during the 1940's through 1960's in residential Catholic schools. I was sickened to my stomach! There are no words of how I felt and feel! These so called priests and nuns were brutally abusing and killing the children! I cannot fathom that!

They were so innocent and there are so many that live with the horror of remembering today. I know everything happens for a reason and for some reason it needed to happen, but it just ripped my heart into shreds!

Mystical Puzzle

Nana made the huge mistake of phoning me today! Let us just say the conversation was quick. Did I mention nana was Catholic? Bad, bad day to phone me nana!

I think I know why I may be afraid of water. I must have lived through a great flood in a previous lifetime. Like in Noah's Ark! That was how I felt like my life had been like recently! Like I was being guided and prepared for something. But what was it? What was it that I could not remember? What was going on here!?

But that is not all of it. I am also petrified of monsters in the water that will come and take me. Who had such fears? I cannot stand to dangle my hand or feet in the water! For some reason, I *know* there was a whole other world in the water that we were unaware of.

Perhaps it is not there now, in current times. It could simply be memories from a past life. However, why was I so adamant that there was something in the water? And it is not a good something. I have some bizarre fears!

Another bizarre fear was dead people and graveyards. I was afraid that dead people were going to come alive and pull me under the ground with them. I cannot walk through graveyards for that very reason. Why would I think such a thing?

I know that dead people did not come alive and pull people under the ground. However, in the same sense I also feared that. I have never gone to a graveyard site of a past loved one. I did not fully know why, I just knew that I could not go!

Ok, its mid October and I was feeling quite confused to say the least! I knew damn well that I was not the Tanya that was here a few months ago. This was not my skin! What the hell am I? Who am I? I looked up and started to yell, "What have you guys done to herrrrr! She is not strong, she is scared, and she is terrified of the dark! She cannot be by herself, and she needs help! She is dying. I need to know what the hell you guys did to her! Where is she!?"

I started to cry and frantically looked for Tanya in my own apartment. I looked under my bed and in my closets. What was going on and where was she!? I made it back to my bedroom and cried my eyes out. I mourned the old Tanya. I really hoped she was doing all right. I wished I could just talk to her to ensure that she was no longer in emotional pain and that she was safe.

I understood why she had to leave. She was so dead inside. She could not handle the fact that she may end up permanently crippled and that her adventurous life was gone, not to mention the pain. Maybe I would not feel the kind of pain as she did. Now that would be cool!

How on earth do I talk about this? Whom do I talk to about this? My friends? My family? They will think I am a whack job! I felt so alone and like there was no one else like me. I knew that there was but no one that I knew to talk to about it. I did not understand what was happening to me.

I was always happy and felt blissful and at peace with myself. Even when everything was falling apart around me, I was at peace. My heart did not bleed with all the built up emotional pain. How could it just disappear? This was not right! This did not happen!

Even though I felt so good, I was still confused as to what was going on. I was starting to see red in three dimensional on the computer screen and on paper articles that I was reading. So far, it was just the color red that I was seeing like that.

From the research that I had done, I know that I was a walk-in or a starseed or something; perhaps a mystical traveler? I did not know. All I did know was whatever the hell was going on, was not *NORMAL!*

I sent an email to my angel guide from the spiritual retreat I went on. I think something may have happened during my breath and sound session. Honestly, I still could not put into words what I had experienced during that session. I knew that she knew what was happening to me and I was ready for the truth.

I really hoped that she could enlighten me. I knew that I was not going crazy, but how did I convince my friends and family of that? And the rest of the world! Oh great! I am so going to be raked over the coals for this!

All my life I knew I was somehow different. I know my friends and family could attest to that! I have always believed that I have some kind of sixth sense. I cannot control it, but it was there. Here are some examples. Some call it mere coincidence. However, when it happened all the time, I believed it was more than that.

Mystical Puzzle

Flashback

More times than not, I knew who was on the phone when it rang. I am not talking about when I specifically ask someone to call me at a specific time. I am talking about random phone calls from friends and family.

I would be out and one of my friends would out of the blue pop into my head. Usually within one minute, I would go around a corner, and there they were. That also happened in such places that you would never imagine running into people that you knew. I was at a concert with thousands of other people. I happened to run into my cousin Christopher and my Uncle Brody. None of us had previously known that the others were at the same concert, yet we all ran into each other!

I have a built in police radar. Now that really comes in handy if you speed a lot. To me, I was not speeding. I was simply driving. Why do my friends and family think I am a maniac on wheels? I just did not see it that way at all.

I have driven to certain places and had a feeling that there would be a road block on my way back. Every time I got that feeling, it happened. It is a good thing I am such a law abiding citizen.

There was a time when I had felt that there was radar up ahead, but I had just bought a Mustang, and I wanted to crack it open on the highway. I had already told myself on the way back home, I was going to drive that car one hundred miles an hour down the highway and up the big long hill.

I said to myself, I am going for it. It turned out there was radar and it turned out I received a speeding ticket. I did find out though that the car could go at least one hundred miles an hour. The posted speed limit was seventy or eighty kilometers. One hundred miles an hour equaled one hundred and sixty kilometers an hour.

I guess I was lucky that I did not get my ass kicked considering I was only seventeen or eighteen and the cop was a chick to boot. They usually have bigger chips on their shoulders than the male cops. I was lucky though; the female cop that pulled me over was just doing her job and did not give me any lip or push her power around. I can appreciate cops like that but I have no time for the power trippers!

One day out of the blue, I started to open my windows and spray air freshener into all of my rooms. I did not understand why I was doing that because something was literally making me do it! My phone rang and it was a police officer asking if I could meet her at the apartment entrance so she could deliver some papers to me. I could now see why I was spraying my apartment down, to get rid of the pot smell. She did not come up to my apartment and I was not in any kind of trouble, but that just goes to show you how sensitive I am to certain energies.

I can detect bullshit a mile away! I guess you could say that I have a built in bullshit detector. I was born with this gift / curse. As I meet new people, I always warn them ahead of time not to bother to lie to me, because I know when people are lying and it really pissed me off when they did it right to my face!

I know when someone was playing "dirty." Sometimes I would actually get visuals of what someone was doing if it had to do with them being hurtful towards me. When it happened, I usually chalked it up as my head being way over imaginative. The only thing was, those over imaginative things always came true.

Other times I would watch others engage in conversations. Not only did I hear what they were verbally saying, but I would also hear their thoughts. It was hard watching people be two faced to each other. They would say one thing, but would think something very different.

I know if a person could be trusted or if they were creepola's! I did not intimidate easily. I have met people that appeared to be normal on the outside, but something about them made me want to crawl under a table and hide.

Even at five years old when I should not have known anything about sex, I knew what men I needed to stay away from because if I were not careful, they would touch me in places they should not have.

I feel the emotions and emotional pain of others, even strangers. I can see and feel right into people's souls. I do not know how to turn it off. That was why I cannot watch TV or movies without crying. Even though it was acting and I knew that, I still felt the emotions of what was happening in front of me as if they were happening to me. It is emotionally draining on me to feel all the pain of other people around me.

I have been sensing spirits / ghosts since I was a child. Very rarely, did I actually see them or hear them. They have moved things right in front of my very eyes. I am not particularly fond of that. I could never talk to anyone about that. When I try, I am laughed at, and told that there were no such things as ghosts. Usually, it was more of a feeling of knowing when they were around.

By far, I would have to say my scariest experience was when I was fourteen years old. One night one of us came up with an idea to try an Ouija board. I was not sure whom but we were at Hazel's house. We did not have one but we made one out of paper. As we did not believe in the Ouija, we asked to speak to the devil himself and evil spirits. We were asking all kinds of questions and the glass was moving all over the place answering them.

I started to think that someone was pushing the glass and that it had to be fake. I questioned my friends if they were pushing the glass and they claimed that they had not. I did not believe them. If they were not pushing the glass and I was not pushing the glass, then what was pushing the glass?

I decided to try something. I said if the Ouija was real; make the chocolate bar wrapper shake on the table. The wrapper started violently shaking on the table. Nobody was touching the table and the table was not moving, only the wrapper. Holy mother of my eyes!

I immediately turned the lights on and was freaking out! How could this be? None of us could produce an effect like that! We had not been doing any drugs, drinking, or anything of the sort. Not all three of us could have imagined that at the same time. As soon as I realized what we had tapped into, I flipped the lights off and began asking more questions.

When I went home, I took the rosary that my nana had given me and placed the cross upside down on my bedroom wall. I did not know why I did that as I was not a devil worshipper, but I also did not believe in God.

About a week after the Ouija board incident, I was in my bedroom playing Atari with my mom. I am sure some of you remember Atari. The only reason I had the Atari in the first place was that it was a hand me down from someone. My mom could never afford something like that. While we were playing, the phone rang and off she went to answer it.

She took forever to come back and my eyes were burning from staring at the TV and game for so long, so I decided to turn my lights off and rest my eyes. I heard a noise and looked towards my door. "Mom?" I called out. She did not respond. "Why aren't you talking to me? Turn on the lights, you are freaking me out!" She started to walk towards me but did not say a word, and that was really creeping me out.

All of a sudden, there were three demonic heads floating around in a circle in front of my face, the other thing in my room was getting closer and closer, and it was not my mom! I started screaming hysterically for my mom! She came rushing into my bedroom and turned on the lights and I started to cry and yell, "Auntie Bobbi Lee! Auntie Bobbi Lee! She was here! She was just in my bedroom! I saw her mom and I thought it was you!"

Of course, my mom thought it was all in my head and of course, I never told her about the demonic heads floating around me. I immediately removed the upside down cross from my wall. I did not know what the hell just happened but I was about ready to crap a load into my pants! I could not tell anyone about that! Who on earth was going to believe me?

I asked Hazel and Kara to try Ouija again. I was going to ask the Ouija board what happened without letting my friends know, so that they could not make up an answer. My question to the Ouija was why was my aunt in my room the other night? I never told my friends that the aunt that was in my room just happened to be dead.

The response that came back from Ouija was that she was there to protect me from the demons. My friends did not understand what that meant but I sure the hell did! I never did tell them what happened, and I was never touching one of those stupid boards ever again!

Something creepy happened in my new basement suite that I had lived in before moving to Hope. It was something that I would never forget! I was lying in bed when I heard a bunch of voices whispering. It was not regular kind of whispering; it was evil! I was so scared! I just wanted it to stop and I wanted it to go away! And god for bid I did not want it to materialize because I did not want to see it! Why did those things follow me around? It was one thing when I sensed spirits around me; it was a whole other thing when I saw and heard them!

I had to get out of my bedroom but I was scared to open my eyes. I did not want to see it! Please do not show yourselves and leave me alone! I was paralyzed with fear! I could not handle it anymore and bolted out of my bedroom! I ended up sleeping on the couch and I could not hear the spirits anymore and did not feel their presence. It only ever happened that one night and was never to happen again at that particular house.

I cannot count how many times someone has asked me, how did I know that? I simply told them; do not worry about how I know things. One of these days, you will get tired of asking me that and you will just go with it. Sometimes people get pissed off because I know things that I should not know.

Back in the late 1990's, Brady and I use to go to Cancun and area for a couple of weeks each spring. Less than a week before leaving on one of the trips, I kept telling my friend, Donna, that someone was going to die while I was on my trip. She told me to stop thinking so morbidly.

While we were on the trip, we came across an ancient Mayan ruin in the middle of no where. We were off the beaten path in a sense that we had not seen tourists or Mexicans for along time! We were on the only highway that runs from Tulum to Belize. We were somewhere in between the two places. The ruin was just off the main road.

When we arrived there, we noticed that there was no one in sight, no caretaker, and no nothing. We decided to check the place out. I did not think we were there for more than five minutes when I had the distinct feeling that we were not to be there and that we were to leave immediately!

I asked Brady if he had the same feeling because he also believed that he had some kind of sixth sense. He did and we got the heck out of there! Something did not feel right and we did not want to stick around to find out! Upon our return home, I learned that my nana Ebert had passed away. I knew it! I just did not know whom.

Mystical Puzzle

About three years ago, my nephew Michael was visiting during the summer break. On one of the days, I took him down the Silver Skagit Road to a creek across from one of the gravel pits. It was a smoking hot day! The creek was glacier fed, so it was ice cold, but also refreshing at the same time. It was a little bit of a walk to the creek from the main road but not too far. Probably no more than five to ten minutes away.

We found a nice spot to hang out and I spread out the beach blanket. We were there about ten minutes, when all of a sudden I literally jumped up, put my shoes on, frantically started to grab everything, and told Michael, "We have to go now!" "But auntie, we just got here! Noooo!" He begged.

"I'm not screwing around here! Grab your stuff *NOW!* We have to leave! I will leave without you!" I yelled. Of course, I would not leave him there, but I had to make him think that. I started to walk away from him. He soon got the hint and yelled for me to wait up.

We scurried out of there to the truck. He asked me what was going on. I told him that I did not know. I only knew that it was imperative that we leave! I know my instincts well enough that when they are that strong, it was for a reason! I for one did not need to know why. I just knew to get out of there!

We did not completely stop our day and go home. We did a little bit of four wheeling and went to a lake in town. A week later, campers or hikers found a body in the area that Michael and I were. Was that what I was sensing? Were we close to the body? Were the killers watching us? I would never know.

That was not the first time that I had those kinds of feelings and soon afterwards, a dead body was found. In January of 1995, my friend Leah and I went for a drive to Yale to visit Claire Clark. We were going for a walk along the Fraser River, and wandering away from Claire's house.

I had an eerie, strange, uncomfortable feeling that we best leave the area immediately! I did not know where those feelings were coming from, as it was not as if it was dark out. I told Leah that I did not feel good and we went back to the house.

No more than a week went by and I discovered why I was creeped out in an area that never creeped me out in the past. The body of a young woman was found near the area that we were walking. She was abducted from her place of work in Surrey on January 6th and found on January 26th in Yale. Claire knew the person who came across her body. I actually went to high school with the woman that was found.

It was horrible to learn of her ordeal. She was so young and innocent. I could not imagine being terrorized the way that she was. What was wrong with people?! How could something like that happen?! I cannot comprehend that horrendous act towards another! We live in such a sick, sick world!

Then it dawned on me. What was that creepy feeling that I felt when Leah and I were wandering around? Did I somehow sense Melody without knowing what I was sensing? All I could remember was that I wanted to leave the area immediately. I was scared but there was no reason to be. Not one that I could see, only sense.

The feeling was strong enough that it convinced me to get the hell out of there. I was glad that I listened to my feelings as I did not think either one of us could have handled finding a tortured young body of a woman that we knew. My heart pours out to her family!

I went on a day road trip in February of 2008. As I was driving, I had a sense that a section of the mountain of snow, was going to come down. Low and behold, on our way back a few hours later, the section that I was having a feeling about, did come down and they had road crew out trying clean it up and redirect traffic.

Something I noticed while going to the psychiatric day program in the summer of 2008 was meditation and relaxation strengthened my sixth sense. The first time I did the hour long relaxation in the program, I had become so relaxed and in a different state that I had forgotten that I was laying on the hospital floor on mats with a pillow and blankets along with everyone else in the group.

Another time, I was sitting on the toilet and the sense that Lorne and Natasha were in a car accident popped into my head. Ugh! Do not think that! What if it really happened!? Twelve hours later, Amber phoned me and said, "Guess who was in a car accident?"

Without hesitating, I said, "Lorne and Natasha." She wondered how I knew. I told her that it came to me twelve hours ago while I was sitting on the toilet. I found out that the accident happened before I had the thoughts of it happening. That in a sense was not a prediction, but I knew shortly after the accident happened that they were indeed in an accident.

I thought I would try something out. I wanted to see if I could will someone to phone me. It had to be someone other than Lorne or Amber as they phoned me everyday. I know, my mom. She just called me the other day, so there was no way she would call so soon. She knew the phone rules. I would give her heck if she called to often.

I put out an intention for my mom to call me within thirty-seven minutes. I kept that thought in my head while I was having my bath. Somewhere along the line while I was bathing, I completely forgot about willing my mom to phone me. I stepped out of the bath and proceeded with my usual out of bath routine.

Before I was done, the phone rang. It was my mom. Oh my god, it was my mom! I forgot all about that! It was too funny! I never did tell her

Mystical Puzzle

about me willing her to call. I never did give her heck for calling me. I just smiled during the whole conversation.

CHAPTER 5

Finally! I Now Know Why I am So Different.

October 24

Finally! The day had come that I would find out what was going on with me. I phoned Marlene to start our channeling session. She explained to me how the session would conduct and what would happen during the session. She also explained that her voice slightly changed when the guides were speaking through her. The following was the information that I learned:

> MG = Marlene's Guides
>
> TG = Tanya's Guides
>
> M = Marlene
>
> T = Tanya

MG – "You have always always always had many beings supporting you and working with you. At this time there is literally a quantum shift."

M – "They are showing me that your body is like electronic with a huge energy shift full of energy, like a transformer."

MG – "At this time there are now legions of energy collecting and moving with you in this transition."

M – "There is a tremendous activation in the first and second chakras. This is a wonderful event and wonderful happening for you. Tremendous amount of kundalini energy is moving in your body at this time. This is a huge part of what is going on with you."

At this point in the session, we are about six minutes in.

TG – "We are gathered here to make conscious contact with you at this time. You are in a process of consciously connecting in with us."

M – "These guides are not my regular group and your guides are coming in. Your guides are off world energies. They are an extra terrestrial group that is meeting with you at this time. They have activated all of your Chinese acupuncture points in the tips and corners of your nail beds on your fingers and toes along with your first and second chakra."

TG – "We are very much ready and aligned to make conscious contact. We are very much anxious in working with you in a conscious matter and that it is most certainly fine to make this contact through others such as Marlene at this time. However, you are aware you are opening very very rapidly and we are beginning to make conscious contact with you as well at this time."

M – "They are recommending you to do some writing through your left hand." (I am right handed.)

TG – "We are coming through to you in your dreams so it is very important for you at this time to begin recording."

M – "They awaken you between 3am and 4am to work with you in the deepest hours of the night. You can see them already as your sixth chakra is opening very dramatically. At night time when you turn the lights off, you can feel and sense them with you."

TG – "We are you; you are us. We are family. We are an integrated family. We are working as a group and this is an actual appointment. This is an appointed time."

At this point, they started to talk to Marlene and she made their two way conversation audible.

TG – "This one's soul is opening at a very very rapid rate. There is a very rapid acceleration of frequency shift. It is at a quantum level leap. As we move into these accelerated times, ones such as this will be shifting into gears that are quantum shifts that are exponentially exponentially driven."

M – "In compared to what I experienced when I went through the change, you are experiencing two to three leaps at a time in one chunk. All of your chakras are opening very rapidly and there is a very strong ET presence around you."

TG – "Your essence is as ours. Your essence is off world. Yes and no to your most burning question. It is as though your off world essence is now merging with your physical being. This is a merging with your other world self, your other dimensional self, your off world or extra terrestrial self. This is in fact that you are an off world origin, off world origin. However, it is not a walk-in, in the sense that one soul leaves and another enters in. It is as profound! It is as intense! However."

At this point Marlene let out a huge sigh and took a deep breath.

M – "They are saying that there is not a soul switch; there was not a soul change out. They are very emphatic about that. Your soul is an off world evolution."

TG – "So Tanya, the analogy that we would make at this time is that, you are no longer cut off from your origins, you are no longer asleep. You are no longer taken in by this culture, this society."

M – "Before you felt like you were all alone and that you were cut off and living in a box on your own and now there is this massive influx of extra terrestrial energy, but its home. It's home energy for you. There is going to be a sense of homeness that you have never felt before. The interesting thing about this as others that have come forward in previous times, including myself, this shift came in layers. It came in a process over a period of many years.

"With you, you just blew up the box! The box is gone! You are fully tapping into your off world essence. It's kind of a paradox. Your soul is still the same soul. You came in with this essence, however, it's like now you are plugged into your family, you are plugged in to your essence, to your origin. Massive, massive, massive amounts of energy are now fludding into you at this time. You are most definitely a transformer.

"We are mediators for you. This was an appointment. We are at the appointed time. Normally when this process happens, it's step by step by step. For myself, it took years and years and layers and layers to come off.

"They are showing me a very dramatic process that the box that was around you living within a human framework. You were cut off from this energy that is you, and you had accepted the cultural framework. The box that you were in has blown apart and disintegrated all at once.

"I keep finding this amazing so I keep having this internal conversation and asking them how is this possible as it is as though you just literally walked in and showed up as yourself. What has happened to you is highly unusual for it to happen in this manner."

TG – "And so Marlene, what we would say is the global planetary energetics have shifted now to the point that there is water here for Tanya to live in. There is water here for her to survive in her most noble expression in her highest expression."

M – "What they are saying is you use to be a fish out of water but you lived in this little tiny box. It was cut off from your essence and cut off from who you really are. Yet you survived in this little box that is our human framework.

"So I asked how can a person survive this when the box blows up all at once. They are showing me that over the last ten years, especially the last two years, we have been enveloped with massive rays of energy from the central sun, and the frequency is now high enough that it can support and sustain an individual such as yourself.

"In other words, fifteen, twenty years ago, or previous to that, you would have not survived it. If you came in this way, you also would have not survived it. Now the frequency on the planet can actually support you. You have tremendous support around you and you are like a portal for large amounts of energy. You have a very large off world intention group. Those are beings that are related to you and work with you and through you.

"I am sorry it has taken so long to say this but I am just amazed at how you are doing this and that it is quite remarkable. Essentially you are a walk-in, in the sense that your off world essence is now fully functioning and fully operational all in one swoop which is quite odd.

Mystical Puzzle

"By your definition, yes it is a walk-in. They want you to know that it was not a soul swap. They explained to me that it is very important that you know that. There is no soul swap going on here. They are showing me that you carry a most beautiful essence. That essence was always there and if you think about it, it would be like talking to a stranger in a strange land.

"They say that by the time you were three years old, you knew that you didn't belong here. You were too young to articulate but you just knew that things were kind of off and upside down in this place. If you look back, you will see that you were always different.

"Just in order to survive, you had to cut off from your real essence, which is now fludding you in a big way. It's like your higher self; your other dimensional self just walked in and showed up.

"I am still finding this totally remarkable and I have never seen it happen this way before. It is usually a process. This is pretty intense! I don't know why but they keep making a heavy point to the fact that there is not a soul swap."

T – "I completely understand why they keep assuring me that I am not a walk-in because they watched me freak out looking for the old Tanya."

M – "Your guides are asking you to honor your courage that it took to come here and be here until now. They say that if it had been a soul swap, it would have been like a human evolution person and they wouldn't have had such a difficult time. The difficulty that you faced was because you are not from here. They are stressing this point very firmly! They say that there is an honoring."

TG – "And Tanya there is a type of death here. In a sense, yes walk-in because your spirit, your full presence your full off world essence has now entered and walked in taking up residence. There has been a death of the Tanya that was. A death of the Tanya that compromised and twisted and contorted herself to fit into the box.

"We are in great celebration of this death / transformation for there is disintegration. However, it is in a much greater, higher vibrational form. What is unique here is that there is not vestige left of the old self, small self, lower personality self. This has been disintegrated very very rapidly!

"We would use the word grace. Grace. Tanya, we would recommend this word for your surroundings. Grace. Marlene, this is for you as well so we very much invite you to take note. Grace. You have been delivered. You have been delivered. This is a most, most beautiful, beautiful event."

M – "I literally see angels surrounding you and this is what is spoken of in the biblical passages where they say the angels are singing. There is literally this most beautiful, angelic presence around you.

"You are supposed to study the words grace and deliverance because they are saying that is literally, what happened to you. It was a full immediate transformation. One of the reasons you wondered if you were a walk-in because you have been wondering where is all my old stuff, angst, and pain.

"What they are showing me is grace. What has happened is amazing! This is a phenomenal happening that has occurred! It is very beautiful. When you understand or maybe you already do, the depths of this as you are operating outside the normal laws of gravity and human laws, as we know them. Grace has delivered you through something that usually takes many years and much hard work and still then, there are still residuals of energy and you have just been pulled out of that. This is quite remarkable.

"Are you aware of all the energy that is moving through your first and second chakras? What are you doing with the energy?"

T – "I went for some energy work and she removed an attachment from my second chakra. I am not sure what do with the energy because I am new to all this stuff and I am just learning about it."

MG – "We see large openings. There was a blockage removed and there was an energy attachment removed from your sacral chakra coming through the back area. A darkness attachment was removed from your energy practioner. The end result of this was a very large opening in your first and second chakras. This experience that you had during your breath work with Marlene is only the beginning. You are able to connect to this. You are able to open these channels at will."

M – "They are showing me that you are bringing up large amounts of earth energy from below through your feet and moving it up through your first and second chakra's. The experience that you had in your breath work can be accessed again and repeated anytime that you choose. You now have wide open circuits of energy that you can move up your legs and up to your first and second chakras. It is now beginning to enter your third chakra."

MG – "With this activation there is activation in your hands and your feets. There is massive amounts of energy available to you at this time. We recommend full participation in allowing this energy to move from your feet and ankles, knees and hips into your pranic tube. At this time, you are just beginning, just scratching the surface, and beginning to step into your personal power. This is a personal power that is directly aligned with spirit so it will be effortless. However, we would recommend that you begin to look very very closely at your personal relationships."

M – "First chakra is opening up to source energy and second chakra's is connected to creativity. The third one can be our emotional center where you clear out old emotional stuff but I am not getting much in that way. It is miraculous as a lot of that has moved out and it is just gone! The other function of the third chakra is when it comes into alignment when you clear out the emotional garbage and the drama and trauma, and then it becomes a power center. It's a personal power center. When you are in alignment with spirit, then it becomes true power.

"They are showing me that there is going to be market changes. You begin two things. One is becoming very discerning about whom you hang out with and number two, begin looking very carefully at your family relationships. They're not saying that anything is wrong; they are just saying that they want you to begin noticing how you begin to stand in your power.

"There are big, big shifts afoot in all of your relationships as you begin to come from a place of personal power. There is a period of time where some of your friendships are going to fall away and there is going to be a dry period where you don't have many close personal friends kind of thing. This is important that that be so.

"It is important for you to have less contact with the outer world at this time and you are not to be concerned about it or to take on anybody else's view points about whether that is ok or not ok or that something is wrong with you.

"There is very dramatic changes afoot after six months. You are doing some deep transformational work that requires aloneness and separation off from the regular world. Don't in any way be concerned about that. You're very much already prepared. You are just beginning to scratch the surface and touch into your personal power."

MG – "What is happening to you is grace, an act of God. There is an aspect of you that is chomping at the bit to move forward. It is important that you understand that this is a process of letting go and releasing which you are very much doing in some respects.

"There was this impulse to buy the tent. This was moving from inspiration and releasing all cultural expectations. We would like to impress upon you that this is very, very, very good for your soul to allow these shifts and changes!

"However, we are simply cautioning you as well only that there is another aspect of you that is very much wanting to move forward into your new life, your new work, your new being."

M – "You connect into a passion and deep knowing. It just kind of flows, it breathes and it knows what it needs to do. You are doing great but there is another aspect of you that gets impatient."

MG – "This impatience needs to be addressed. It is not Tanya, the personality self that created this process. It was the diminishing of Tanya; it was the disintegration of Tanya. And through that disintegration, it allowed the grace to flow through. It is through grace that your personality self diminished and disintegrated to allow this full integration of your soul energy.

"Keep remembering what got you here. It was letting go and allowing. It was letting go and allowing. This impatience to move forward is very admirable, but it is important to keep this in check. This process has its own time frame, its own time table."

M – "It's quite the paradox as you have transformed one hundred and eighty degrees but now you must have patience to allow the rest of the transformation to unfold at its own timetable. You must not rush the process."

MG – "There is also a level of fear here that is most natural. Whenever we transform from one vibrational state to another, especially in this process, which is such a quantum quantum leap. There is a natural fear of the unknown, a natural fear of unfamiliarity. It is important to not deny this fear for that would simply be denying a piece of yourself.

"Extend compassion to the fear. It is the part of you that wishes to know where are we going. Where will we end up? You are directly in the heart of the unknown. You are living in the great void. At this time, it is very, very sacred. You are living in the great void of the divine feminine, that great potential in which all things come.

"This is why your apartment has so dramatically shifted. Everything must go! This is your own deep knowing from inside. You are creating space for a vessel for your high self, your essence, your real true self."

It is now fifty minutes into the reading and I now have the opportunity to ask my guides questions.

T – "What star or world did I come from? Is there a name?"

M – "They are showing me Orion. There are different groups from Orion. Some of them are more benevolent than others. You are from a very, very high frequency group."

TG – "At this time, this vibrational intention group is actually working in tandem very, very closely with groups from the Pleiades. That is why Marlene is experiencing resonance with your intention group."

M – "What they are referencing is that you brought in a whole intention group with you that is different than my group but there was a blending that was very easy. There are certain off world intention groups that are working in tandem now and are working in large group energies. So even though you are from Orion, your intention group energies blends very nicely, readily and easily with mine.

"Your guides said that you are able to have direct communication with them and see them. You are to begin practicing in the dark."

T – "I thought I seen something last night in my room to be honest with you. I was lying in bed looking at it, wondering, what is that!? It was a light white cloudy type thing. It wasn't anything that I could see like. It was just like. Not in the form of a human. It had no form. It was formless. It was like I didn't see the. It was just like the. I don't know. It was weird!"

Mystical Puzzle

M – "They are telling me that is you beginning to sense them and see them. You are to validate that for yourself and there is no reason to be afraid because these are like your spiritual brothers and sisters. This is your spiritual family. They showed me that they actually had an appointment to meet with you at this time and space. This is a pre-appointed reunion."

T – "When I saw a ball of light in the daylight sky a couple of weeks ago, was that them?"

TG – "And so this was a ship. This was one of our ships."

At this point Marlene just let out a huge sigh.

M – "I don't know if you know that but some extra terrestrial energies when they come and go from this dimension, they will simply appear as balls of light. That was an actual ship. The energy last night in your room was their personal energy, their being. Those were beings. So you are being contacted through both beings and ships. You are experiencing both. They were saying earlier that it is fine to have this contact with me but you are ready and able to connect with them directly. You don't need a third party."

T – "How do I connect with them?"

TG – "This left handed writing would be recommended. It is also very important that as you are sensing us in the dark, you allow yourself to begin speaking. Simply relax and allow and we can begin direct conversations. Simply empty your mind and relax. Drop into love and ease and grace, reminding yourself that there is nothing to do, simply be. Simply open and be."

M – "They keep stressing that you need to remember that this all happened by grace. It's like an act of God, a gift. Without work, it was just given to you. You have been released. They keep pressing the point on how did that happen. You don't know how it happened, it just did, right? It was this huge gift! Keep remembering that and keep remembering that that is how everything is going to come. Not by you, but by spirit. Everything!"

T – "What was the attachment and how long was it there?"

M – "They are showing me age three. This came on quite early this lifetime. Interesting, didn't they mention age three that you were having difficulties. The first thing they are saying is number one, know that this is a divine appointment.

"So this was a negative attachment, a negative energy, but the greater purpose was, it shut you down! Ok, it shut you down! It kept you in the box! Ok, so it was a dark energy that was an attachment. There was an opening through your father. It came through your father.

"Again, this is not judgment, but there was some dark energies attached to him and at that time, moved onto you. It is important the guides are saying that you frame this. That it is properly framed. In the small picture, the 3D life, it created a lot of pain for you, a lot of discomfort and dysfunction and frustration, ok.

"But in the big picture, it served a purpose. And that purpose was to keep you shut down until the appointed time. Did you remember when the guides said that you are now swimming in water? And that the water wasn't here before. And if you had been opened up too soon, you would have not survived it. So this dark energy served a greater purpose of keeping you shut down until the appointed time and now it is safe for you to allow this full expression of your true self, ok?

"And you don't even know what that true self is. Which is so fun! You have no idea. You are just meeting yourself for the first time. You are beginning to meet who you really are. It's a very beautiful process that you are going through."

T – "Is there anything I need to know to move forward other than what was already said?"

M – "They are showing me the color green. Sort of like a lime green but more like the color of grass when it is first coming in. That is a very important color for you right now. Start bringing that color into your environment. It will help bring in your off world energies as they are in this frequency of color. There are certain plants that carry that color too."

TG – "There is much joy, much joy, much joy! We are most pleased, most pleased to make this conscious contact with you."

M – "Again, I am seeing all these angels singing! They keep saying it is what is mentioned in the bible. Your situation is a biblical re-birth. It is a total rebirth. It is like being resuscitated from the dead by no act of your own. Simply by the act of grace you have been resuscitated."

T – "No matter what was going on in my life at this time, this process would have happened regardless?"

M – "That is correct."

TG – "Our other advice would be simply place focus on the new. The death of the old does exist in that the old Tanya is now gone. She is gone! This must be acknowledged, however."

M – "They are showing me that there will be challenges with friends and family who in a sense want to interact with the old Tanya. Keep focusing on the new part of you. It is not appropriate to tell anyone about your situation and origin at this time. Later yes, but not now during the shift.

"By telling people now, that would create an obstacle and create an opening for the dark energy to come back and shut you down. Only share what is appropriate. A lot of your friends are going to fall away. Don't worry about others and what they think about you.

Mystical Puzzle

"Don't tell others not to be afraid, just stress how happy you are. The planet just got ready for you. If you came out any earlier, you would have not been accepted and your energy would not be able to flourish in this environment. But you're ready now and it is very exciting!"

Oh my god! Everything made sense! It is like my whole life made sense! The people who have crossed my path, and the reasons for it. At last, I knew why I always longed toward the sky, and would gladly offer my life for a ride into space. When I am in a plane, I spend most of the ride staring down in confusement at the earth.

Why I always felt different and felt alone even if I was in a room with fifty thousand people. Why I wondered if people see what I see and think how I think. Why I just knew things and did not know how I knew them. Why I have been walking around for the last few years thinking that I had forgotten something really important.

I was always fascinated with shows on UFO's and abductions. I used to joke around and tell my friends that the reason I was so tired in the day was that UFO's abducted me when I was supposed to be sleeping. I was always joking around when I used to say that, only deep down I used to wonder if it was really true.

Ok, I needed to look up Orion and see what it looked like. See what kind of feeling I got from it. I did a search on Orion constellation and just about loaded my pants! I could not believe it! This was so amazing!

I never knew what the Orion constellation was and what was staring back at me on my computer screen were the stars that called me to my window. The stars that I saw, as I had never saw before. The stars that were trying to tell me something that I did not understand, but could not stop staring at them.

I can not explain what this felt like. To finally know. To finally know that I really was different. I also learned that Orion's belt was in exact alignment with the three main Giza Plateau pyramids in Egypt. (*Bauval*, 1995) That was what I was seeing during the breath and sound session in Sedona, the pyramids of Egypt.

My beings said they have been communicating with me at night. They say I could communicate with them using my left hand to write. I will prepare to try next week. I had to dig out my baby book and see what kind of information I could obtain about my early years.

From reading my baby book, it was very clear that I reached development milestones much earlier than the average child did. My mom also wrote that I had a good imagination. I wondered what I use to say for her to think that.

I could not believe what I found out by reading my baby book. At the age of three, my mom wrote that I had a kidney infection so bad that I could not eat solids, and only had liquids for one month. *Oh my god!* This was when I received the dark energy attachment on my sacral chakra.

I phoned my mom and tried to pick her brain regarding the first three years of my life. Of course, she never remembered a thing. Thank god she did a great job of recording my development milestones in my baby book.

I asked if she remembered when she bought me the creepy Eskimo doll. Surprisingly, she knew the answer. She bought the doll while she was on a bowling tournament in Nevada. I was three years old. There was that age again, three. I cannot stand the presence of that doll!

When I was ten or eleven years old, I was in my bedroom cleaning up the mess. I was definitely not cleaning it by choice. The doll was on the floor approximately ten feet away from me. I glanced over at the doll and it turned its head one hundred and eighty degrees.

I screamed, ran over to the doll, and started to beat it! It did not take long for my mom to enter my bedroom from all the screaming and commotion going on. As soon as she entered, I begged her to get the doll out of my room as I threw it to the doorway.

My mom was appalled at what she just witnessed, as the doll was expensive. She picked it up and placed it in its usual spot on top of my bookcase. I cried and begged her to get the doll out of my room! She asked me why. Through my crying fit, I blurted, "Because it moved its head! I don't want that creepy doll anymore!"

Naturally, my mom thought it was my imagination and insisted that it be ok that the doll stayed in my room. There was no way in hell I was keeping that doll in my room! As soon as she left, I smashed its head some more and then threw it in her bedroom!

For many weeks and months after that incident, my mom continued to put the doll back on top of my bookcase and I continued to beat it and throw it back into her room. She kept telling me that it was a nice doll. "If the doll is so nice, it can stay in your room!" I use to tell her.

Eventually, I won the battle and she kept the doll in her room. She still has that doll. Thirty-three years after I received the doll, and I still would not go any where near it! I know what the doll did and it was not my imagination! I remember as clear as day how frightened I was when the doll moved its head. I am sorry but dolls did not move their heads like that all by themselves!

Therefore, what made the head move? I did not need to know. At that age, all I knew was that was not normal and I did not care to ever see that doll again! What significance does this doll have in all this?

Holy mother of God! I am living something that was so amazing that I could not fathom or put into words, and I could not share it with anyone! They would think I was a total nut bar!

Mystical Puzzle

Even the old Tanya would think the new Tanya was a nut bar. However, I knew that this was the sanest I had ever been and felt in my whole life. I was still at the realizing what was going on and confusing stage. I had a lot to learn and a lot of balancing to do with my new body.

My channeling with Marlene was so amazing! I wanted to tell the world that I finally knew what I had been struggling with all my life. I knew why I had most of my experiences and I understood my thoughts even as I was a child.

I originate from Orion, not Earth. I know why I met the girl at the crystal shop in uptown Sedona. She was a reiki healer and perhaps I would be as well. My healing was within the energy of my hands. Why else would I think that I could heal my friend and remove her kidney stones. Who even attempts such tasks unless deep within them they knew that they had the ability to do it?

I knew why my favorite part of Lindsay Lohan's song *Rumours* is "I just need to free my mind." That was the clue for me to the answers of my existence. Once my mind was free, the answers shall come. I had not done nearly as much meditation as I should.

There was a small part of me that was scared, as I knew the more I did it, the more my sixth sense was strengthened. The funny thing was that I wanted my gifts now in one sense but there was another part of me that was afraid of them. My family from Orion had already warned me to be patient that they would come to me when I was ready and when the time was needed.

I understood why I was always panicking that I was running out of time. It was because I was. I had to be ready for my ascension and when I was panicking, I had not started. When I was panicking, I had no idea why. I know now. It was because I had not awakened.

All the places that I planned to travel to around the world are power spots. I only recently learned of power spots when I went to Sedona. For some reason I have no desire to go to Europe what so ever! I would go to Cambodia and Israel but not Europe. Go figure.

Perhaps my ascension and awakening would have happened while I was travelling. However, the energy on the Earth at that time could not sustain me. That was why I had to have the dirt bike accident. My awakening was pre-planned. Had I gone on the trip around the world that I had originally planned, it could have triggered an earlier awakening.

Oh boy! I just thought of something. If my awakening were pre-planned, like the guides said, it would have happened no matter what was going on in my life. Had this happened and I never went to Sedona, I could have seriously lost it! I did not seek to awaken. In fact, I did not know it existed. I did not go looking for it; it found me.

Finally! I Now Know Why I am So Different.

As blissful as the state I was in, this process had not been easy. Believe me, there were days where I questioned my sanity. However, at the same time that I was questioning it, I knew without a doubt than I was perfectly sane. I did not have answers and so many, many questions. Something told me that I had quite the ride ahead of me.

CHAPTER 6

Getting Use to My New Skin

I had a few errands to run in town. I missed being able to walk around to do my errands. It seemed ridiculous to drive a half block and back. As I was driving down the main street in town, I heard *the Voice*.

It told me to stop at the health food store. I do not know why because I rarely go there. I said no, I was not going there because I did not like the energy of that store. I would only go in that shop if it were necessary. Why would I need to go there? I continued with my errands and *the Voice* would not leave me be.

I went to the health food store. I never knew why I was being called somewhere until I got there. I walked in the store and pretty much started to loiter around trying to figure out why I was there. Ah ha! I could see why they wanted me to go there. There were salt lamps for a very decent price and crystals for fifty percent off. One of the crystal clusters was a piece of citrine, which was very expensive, and I have been keeping my eye open to buy one.

Wow! Who would have thought that I could buy crystals at a health food store? There was a box of tumbled stones but none of them was labeled. As I was new to collecting stones, I did not know what they all were just by looking at them, as there were so many. I asked the sales woman if she knew what any of the stones were. She did not have any knowledge on crystals but mentioned a store in town that would.

What was the chance of that? There was a store in town that sold crystals?! This was too good to be true. Alex tried telling me about a huge crystal he saw in town for two thousand dollars. Here I thought that he was exaggerating. I really must learn to listen to the kids more as they were much brighter than we gave them credit.

Ok, so I bought a little more than what I had planned, but I could not resist because I received great deals! I also could not resist the smoky quartz crystal ball. Apparently, it had been in the store for four years with no offers to purchase it. I purchased my first crystal ball!

I was glad that I listened to my guides. I loved it when this happened. They led me to finding information as well. I cannot count how many times that I had found very pertinent information on the internet by fluke. I came across stuff that I did not know existed. It was amazing how it came right when it was needed. I saw the connections all the time.

One of my other stops was the post office to pick up my mail. Once I arrived home, I proceeded to open my mail. Holy doodles batman! I was seeing 3D letters in the color orange now! What was going on? Was anyone else seeing it like this? I guess there was only one way to find out. I asked Lorne to come over to my place so I could show him something. I showed him the piece of mail and asked him to look at it.

"What!? Why are you showing me this?"

"Look at it! What do you see? Do you see anything different?"

"I see a stupid piece of mail and don't know why I need to look at it!"

"No! Look at it! Can you not see the 3D letters? The orange colored letters! Look at them!"

"I don't see what the fuck you see!"

Ok then. I guess that answered my question. I was seeing red and orange colored letters in 3D.

As I shut off my bedroom lights to go to bed, I noticed the most amazing thing on my ceiling. Angel wings! That is right. Angel wings. I knew what was making them. It was the way my belly dance coin belt was the positioned on the table behind my bed. The only thing was, everything was arranged in my room just as it had always been, and I have never had angel wings on my ceiling.

Another thing, there was a number eleven on my wall in light where my rainbow usually was. Again, there was a simple explanation for this. The street light was shining through my blinds. However, nothing had changed. The same old street light and my same old blinds closed the same old way. That was the only time I saw the wings on my ceiling and the number eleven on my wall. Most nights I usually just have a rainbow on my wall.

Lorne had told me to stop researching and start studying my schooling because I would find the answers along the way. Why would Lorne say that? He also started talking about energy. My guides during the channeling with Marlene also warned me to be patient. I looked over at him and wondered who was speaking through him, as those were not his words, not his language. He insisted that it was him speaking, not someone else.

I felt compelled to read and learn as much as I possibly could in regards to history, paranormal and the metaphysics. It was like an addiction that I could not stop. It was as if I was looking for answers specifically made for me to find. What did I think? That I was going to come across a website that said, *Tanya*

Ebert, please enter this site. All the answers are here. I was looking for a needle in a hay stack.

Honestly, I did not know what I was looking for. I could feel something. I had forgotten something. I was so close to whatever it was that I could taste it. Only I did not know what *it* was.

As soon as Lorne painted my living room and I have my apartment set up, I am going full board with my meditation, schooling and balancing myself out. That was the key with me, balance. It was interesting how I bought an antique balance from a second hand store in town about a month ago. I was not fully sure why but knew that I had to have it. Now I knew, to remind me of balance.

~ ~ ~

I was in the bath and heard the phone ring. I listened to the message and it was Becca, my energy practioner, wondering if everything was all right. She said she did not know why she was calling; she just had an urge to phone to ensure I was all right. Yes, everything was good. I would be seeing her later in the day to buy some crystals.

After my bath, I dressed and was ready to leave. Before I went to Becca's, I needed to stop off at my place of employment. As soon as I started up the car, I smelled gas very strongly. Hmm. My nose was very sensitive to smell. Was it in my head or was the smell really that strong?

I proceeded to drive to work. It was only five kilometers from my place. I rolled the windows down and lit a smoke. I figured the smell must be in my head because it was strong and it did not smell like that yesterday. When I got to work, Amber noticed the smell right away and so did others.

As I was picking up my nephew Michael from Surrey the following day for his birthday date weekend, I thought that I had better get my car checked out right away. Dumb ass me lit a cigarette and smoked it too! I left work and I immediately went to my mechanics. When I got there, he asked me to pop the hood.

The first thing I noticed was some plastic stuffed down the side of my car just under the hood. I had no idea how it got there. It baffled me, as I knew that I or anyone else that ever went under the hood would not stuff that there. Then I noticed a cluster of shredded up paper, plastic, Styrofoam, etc.

Oh my god; the rat was now trying to build a nest in the hood of my car. It had been five days since I found his nest in a baseball cap in my garage. I bet it chewed through my gas line. My mechanic found where he chewed through and the line and gas was pouring out when the car was running. He yelled to ensure that no one lit a cigarette.

Mystical Puzzle

Then it hit me. I could have been blown up to smithereens! If not by my own cigarette, someone else could have thrown one out the window, and if I drove over a lit cigarette. Kaboom!

It was interesting that one of my errands was going to the post office and picking up books. One of them happened to be, *How to Communicate with Your Angels*, by Doreen Virtue. It looked like they saved my ass yet again. I could not count the amount of times that I should have been dead or severely injured.

Looking back, they have graciously spared such incidents throughout my life. I use to joke around saying that I was a cat with nine lives. I am thankful to have all the angels and guides that I have. I could only imagine at how hard they had worked in the first thirty-six years of my life to ensure that I was safe and alive.

It was no wonder I have so many. I have been such a handful that I had a team assigned to me. I could just hear them. I am sure that it would sound a little like this. What?! What is she doing now?! Is she crazy? Does she not realize she has a physical body? Miiiichael! We need your help! She is at it again!

My mechanic repaired my car in time so that I could pick up my nephew Michael for his birthday weekend date. I was surprised that he came over this particular weekend, as it was Halloween. He had just turned thirteen so maybe he was not so interested in trick or treating anymore.

He wanted to help me set up my gazebo in the living room and decorate my new peaceful sanctuary. Anything would be fun for him at this point since he was grounded for life! I did not think his parents had figured out that after thirteen years, continual grounding did not work. All that grounding he had would probably cause him to rebel even more.

Together we did a smudging ceremony. He was very excited to do that as he had a little bit of native background in him. He also used to belong to a pow wow club. There was something about the pow wow dance that filled my being with intense emotion. I did not know why that was. I could not explain it. I would get goose bumps all over and I found it hard not to cry.

It was the same when I witnessed the Indian Thaipusam ritual in Malaysia. It was something I would never forget for the rest of my life. It was the feeling of utmost peace and empowerment. I became extremely emotional when I heard bag pipes as well.

My nephew soon lost interest in putting up the gazebo when I could not figure out how to get the first two pieces together for about two or three hours. Not to mention I started to put the gazebo together at 1am. You have to be kidding me! It was no wonder three hours had gone by and I still did not have two pieces put together. The store I purchased the gazebo from gave me the wrong directions!

This was too comical! Lorne said there was no way I was putting up the gazebo by myself. Did I just hear a challenge? Now for sure I was putting it up without the help of anyone! I had a new challenge. I had never put anything together like this before. It was ten feet by ten feet by eight feet high and my living room was thirteen feet by eleven and a half feet by eight feet high.

I was handicapped with limited mobility and it was an outdoor gazebo. I highly doubt that there was anyone in the world that had an outdoor gazebo in their living room. My nephew was afraid that people might think I was crazy. Several times during the long hours that it took to put the gazebo up, Michael told me that I might as well give it up. That there was no way I was going to be able to accomplish putting the gazebo together.

Oh, looked like another challenge. It literally took me forever to put that thing up! Michael played games on my computer while I slowly put together the gazebo. I guess I really could not take full credit for putting it together as I did have some help. My guides and angels led the way once I asked for their assistance.

As soon as I figured out that I had the wrong directions, I threw those out the window because they were useless. Each time I was stumped, which was every five to ten minutes, I would leave the living room and go into my bedroom to smoke a joint and to contemplate what was the next step and then asked the angels to guide me.

When I left my bedroom and went back to building the gazebo, somehow I just knew what to do and started to put it together. At so many times during the night, I mean early hours of the morning, my nephew insisted that I give it up. I on the other hand was not giving it up!

After many, many, many hours, I finally had the frame together. You have to remember that most people set up the tent outdoors; where there were no walls that could get in the way of putting it together. Michael was impressed.

He soon questioned how I was going to get the canopy on when the frame could not get any closer to the ceiling. It took what seemed like forever, but I pulled that troublesome canopy millimeter by millimeter while pulling down on the center of the gazebo to try to free some space to work with. Oh yeah baby, I did *it!*

You must be wondering how a cripple could put up a canopy on such a huge tent. Michael helped me move a four foot tall dresser to the middle of the living room. I used my step stool to try to get on top of the dresser, but the stool was not tall enough. Somehow I had to leap up onto the dresser, without it tipping over, (all the contents were removed so that we could move it) and without banging or hurting my knee.

Mystical Puzzle

I had Michael stand at the back of the dresser so that when I leapt on top of it, his weight would stop it from tipping over. I planned it all out so that I would not bang my leg while getting up. Where there was a will, there was a way.

Both Michael and Lorne were amazed that I actually did it. When you ask for guidance, you shall receive it. Michael finally went to bed at 1pm. Now that the gazebo was up, it was time to start decorating and putting my sanctuary together. I had decided not to go to sleep and to just stay up until about midnight and then go to sleep.

I would have gone to bed much earlier but I had to let Amber's dogs out to go pee just before midnight. I was not sure why everyone else got breaks at work except for her. That was the reason that I had to take care of her dogs two to four times per week.

I started to do this over a year ago to help Amber out so that she would be less stressed, and not have to worry about rushing on her work break to deal with her dogs. It started out as a favor, but it did not take long before it became my job, and I had to revolve my life around it.

As I had not slept, it was a long, tiring day, but I was quite pleased with what I had accomplished. My sanctuary was really starting to come alive. I pretty much had the base of it done in the living room, kitchen, hallway, and bedroom. The only thing that was left to do was the bathroom and then to add a little bit of peaceful touch to each room.

~ ~ ~

I went to my first spiritual church. There were none in my area, but I found some in Burnaby, Cloverdale, and Vancouver. Something did not feel right to me about that particular service, yet everyone else was stating how powerful the energy was that particular night.

There was a guest at the church that travelled around the world and was supposed to be some holier than thou person. Something was not right about him! Everyone kept saying what an amazing person he was, but my instincts were telling me different. I did not care what others were saying, I know myself, and I know the warning signs that I get. That man was not to be trusted!

After the service, I decided to go up to the front of the church for a healing. A woman sat across from me and she placed her hands over top of mine. She asked me to chant, "Ra Riaz." There was a lot of heat energy transferred between our hands. I asked her if she could feel it, and she said that it was the energy from her hands. Oh was that what it was, her energy, and not our energy.

She abruptly stopped the healing and asked me to continue chanting. She walked over to the creepy visitor and started to whisper in his ear. What?! She was with him! I was trying to listen because I was getting the distinct feeling that something was just not right. All I could hear her say was that she could not do me anymore.

She came back over and asked me to go talk to the creepy man. They asked me what my plans were. Huh? They wanted me to leave with them and said that I could live in the UK with them free of charge. They explained that all I needed was airfare, and they would take care of the rest.

Who were these two? I was not going anywhere with them! I knew something was weird about that man. He also offered to heal my knee on the spot. I did not let him anywhere near my knee! That man was not from the light! Why did no one else see that?!

I also spoke to a psychic while I was there. She was sketchy too! She was literally trying to get away from me. What was with her? I asked her if anyone had any messages for me. She said that my leg would not be like this forever and that I had a grandmother type person around me all the time. The only person I could think of was nana Ebert.

I get a weird sense from intuitives and psychics. They are either so happy to have met me as if they knew something about me that I did not know, or they behaved nervous and somewhat sketchy around me.

I would like to get my aura read one of these days. Perhaps I have a spaceship in my aura and that freaks people out that have never saw that in an aura before. On more than one occasion, some of the intuitives that I seek healing from tell me that they had never had a session like that before. It was as though they were completely overwhelmed.

November 6

I had an energy session with Becca. She had told me that she had been excited for the last few days anticipating our session. I too looked forward to the sessions. I trusted her in a sense that there was nothing that I could not tell her. She was one of the people that I could talk to that did not look at me as if I was crazy.

I told her about my channeling session with Marlene and disclosed to her that my origin was Orion. She then told me, that was her origin as well. That was probably why I felt very comfortable with her. We come from the same place.

During the session, some of the things that came out were, Becca and I were brothers during a golden age. She was quite excited, as she never experienced that kind of session before. My higher self was speaking to her. At one point, she said that she was so excited that she almost forgot that she was healing me and wanted to ask my higher self more questions.

Mystical Puzzle

Most of this session was about the etheric body and not the physical body. She mentioned that I did come in with a negative attachment, but nothing like the hook that she removed in the last session. She got a glimpse of what we look like in original form. A golden glow not shaped like a human. It did not stay the same shape. It moved into other shapes.

Becca asked me what the singing bowls sounded like to me while she was playing them. She also asked how I felt. The sound they made was very different. I could see how some people would find it haunting but I felt at home while they were playing. I told Becca they sounded like something that I should not know what it sounded like. They sounded like what a space ship would sound like. She agreed with me.

She also discovered that I was a fairy at one time and one of my wings was damaged. My higher self led Becca to show her my broken wing that needed fixing. Becca healed it for me and said my wings were amazingly beautiful. That could be why I was scared to accept my gifts. Maybe I showed my fairy self to someone and they chopped my wing off.

Becca also mentioned that we did quite a bit of work in regards to past life karmic debt. She said I should hold off on past life regression because I might have cleared quite a bit in our session. She said that I have had many dark lives in the past. That would explain the deep routed pain I use to have.

My guess was I had learned most of my most painful lessons. Now I was being prepared for what was to come. Maybe that was why Gods given grace was delivered upon me. I had lived so much hurt and trauma that now was the time to remove the hurt, so that I was able to help lead, teach, and heal others.

I asked Becca why some intuitives / healers were excited to work with me and others avoided me. She explained that it was an ego thing. Either they could not read me, or they could, and they were somewhat jealous so to speak. She did not use the word jealous; those were my words. By using the word jealous, I was by no means trying to judge here. I just simply wanted to know why. Because we have incarnated as humans, we tend to act like humans; therefore, ego tends to get in the way. We are not perfect, nor shall we ever be.

I felt heart beats in my legs during the end of the session and I felt gentle brushing on my shoulders. Becca did not physically touch me during the session. It must have been my guides. I found it hard to open my eyes after an energy session. The reason for this was that my eyes felt so sensitive to the bright lights that I would always see. Only, there were no lights on. Becca explained to me that those were the angels.

My mom and niece, Sara, came over for a visit the week after Michael had left. Mom was curious and wanted to see what I had done to my living room. When she came for weekend visits, she usually brought one of the kids with her.

Mom said she had liked what I had done. I told her she did not have to lie, and that it would not upset me. She assured me that she liked it. We will see how much she liked it when I turned my place into non smoking.

They brought air mattresses to sleep on in my peaceful sanctuary. I removed my crystal singing bowl just incase something happened to it. I moved it to my bedroom beside a few miscellaneous items that I had not hung up yet, as I needed to finish painting the rest of my apartment. More like I needed to wait for Lorne to finish painting my apartment.

As I placed the singing bowl down, something told me that it would break if I had left it there. My eyes gazed to the shoe rack holding eighteen pairs of shoes hanging off the back of my door. Something told me that it would fall off. However, it had never done that before.

I listened to my instincts, and moved the crystal bowl far and clear from the shoe rack. Low and behold, the shoe rack fell the next day exactly where I would have put my crystal singing bowl. There was also a full length mirror in that area and it was knocked down, but it did not break. Thank you again to my guides and angels, they really took good care of me!

~ ~ ~

So far I have had positive responses from those that had saw my gazebo sanctuary. Most people's first reaction was, what the?! However, once they walked inside and checked it out, they actually liked it. It was different, but very relaxing! I had invited a couple of the town's big mouths over to see how quickly the rumors fly.

One of the books that I ordered and just received was *Angel Numbers 101*. I looked up the numbers during the time of my dirt bike accident and the following was what I found. I knew the exact time, minute by minute because Amber filmed my entire accident with my camcorder. The page number that 432, 433 and 434 fell on was page 111. Triple numbers again!

At 4:32pm, I asked Amber if she thought that I should do a wheelie. 432 = Trust that you are accurately hearing trustworthy divine guidance from your angels and the ascended masters. This guidance may come in the form of feelings, ideas, visions, or signs.

At 4:33pm, the accident occurred. 433 = You are completely surrounded, loved, and supported by the angels and many beloved deities.

At 4:34pm, I was still screaming and crying from the accident. 434 = Give any worries or concerns to the angels and ascended masters, who are embracing you right this minute with healing love. (*Virtue*, 2008, p. 111)

Mystical Puzzle

November 28

I went to the city for the weekend. I wanted to check out a psychic fair at one of the churches. Besides, I needed winter tires for my car and a chair bed for meditating. If I wanted to sit and meditate, I kept it folded up. If I wanted to lay and meditate, I simply unfolded it. The closest I had found to what I was looking for was at Ikea.

I did all the last minute checks before leaving my apartment and then shut my computer down. Interesting as it was 4:20. I used to see 4:20 almost everyday at work. I did not clock watch; it just happened that I glanced at the clock at 4:20. I used to think that it was a sign that it was almost doobie time. As I was off work at 4:30, ten more minutes and I would be at home smoking a joint.

I usually stayed at my sister's house when I went to the city. She had more room at her place than my mom. Besides, my mom's boyfriend drove me nuts when he was drinking and there was no place to get away from him.

November 29

I had woke up and realized that I was supposed to be at the tire shop for my appointment in five minutes. There was nothing like getting up and running out the door. I decided to go in my pajamas, as there was no time to piss around. I was fifteen minutes late. I explained to the owner that I was sorry I was late and that I did not take the time to change out of my pajamas.

I brought a book with me to read, as I did not have the patience to sit there and do absolutely nothing. Before I knew it, my tires were on and off I went. The owner gave me ten dollars off. He said that since I had started rough that morning, he would give me a discount. You have to like that! I had been going to the same tire shop since I was a teenager. Always good service and he never tries to rip me off.

On my way back to my sister's, I heard *the Voice*. Go to the furniture store, it told me. I started to think, but which one. I had just passed six in a row. Besides, I was already going to Ikea. The item I needed was not going to be in any of those stores. I continued to drive down the highway.

The voice continued to tell me to go to the furniture store. As I continued to drive away from the furniture stores, the voice continued to tell me to go back. I was almost at my sister's house and the voice was being relentless. Ok, ok! I turned around and went back to the furniture stores.

Why did I do that? I knew better to just listen and not argue. I wasted a lot of time and gas ignoring the voice instead of just listening in the first place. I stopped at the first store and asked if they sold chair beds. Of course, they did not, but off I went to the next store. I continued to do that until I went to the sixth store. The sales clerk told me to try Ikea. No kidding; I was planning to go there tomorrow.

I left the sixth store and noticed a futon furniture store next door. Why did the sales clerk not mention that store? Surely, they would know where to get what I was looking for. I walked in the store, and as I was about to ask the sales clerk if she knew where I could buy a chair bed, there it was.

I just about leapt out of my skin as I screeched, "There it is! That is exactly what I am looking for!" If I could jump up and down, I would. I asked the sales clerk if I could pull it out and lay on it. Hello, of course I could. I was in a furniture store.

It was so comfortable! I asked for one in green. The sales clerk climbed up a ladder to the location of the stock. She turned around to tell me, "You better buy a lottery ticket. I only have one in stock and it is the color you want and the size you want." "Honestly, I do not know what I am doing here. I had not planned to come here. My angels guided me here." I blurted.

She glared over at me and said, "You believe in angels?" Oh great, what did I get myself into. "Yes." I stated matter of factly. "You believe in the divine?" She said as she was examining me over. "Yes." I squeaked with squinted eyes.

She turned her head, showed me her angel earrings, and said, "Honey, could I tell you stories." I smiled and said, "Honey, I'm writing one right now." We both giggled and immediately felt comfortable with each other to exchange a few stories. She told me that she had felt like she was going to die soon. That could not be. She looked amazing! She told me that she had just turned sixty-five. Whoa! She looked more like fifty.

I reassured her that she was not going anywhere. Just as I was paying for the chair bed, some other customers had walked in. She walked me to the door and said, "There is a reason we have met. We must get together and talk. I have your phone number. I will call you."

I nodded and she opened my hand and put something in it. I did not dare look at it until I was in my car. Once I settled in the car, I opened my hand. It was a pendant made of pewter. On one side was an angel and on the other side, *Always With You*, was inscribed.

Who was that woman? I could not describe the utter bliss that I had felt. It was as though I just met a true angel. I felt like I was in la la land and I was floating on cloud nine. I so love life! I could not wait until she phoned me! I really must learn to just trust *the Voice* and listen to it right off the bat. It had never done me any harm and always brought a world of good!

I went back to my sister's to shower and get dressed. I wanted to check out a psychic fair at a spiritual church. I purchased a thirty minute reading with one of the medium's. She told me there was a beautiful cat that was by my side. At that moment, her tail wrapped around my leg. It must be

Mystical Puzzle

Molly! I burst into tears! I think that was a sign that Molly understood why I had her put down, and that I was not to feel guilty.

The medium also told me that there was an older man coming in. He was gesturing something but she said she was not sure she should show me. I asked her to show me what he was doing. Maybe I would know what it meant. She did not want to show me because she thought that I might think she was being rude.

She started to shake her finger at me while pointing her finger towards me. Oh my god, that was my papa! He always did that to me. Just before he died while he was in the hospital, he started to forget who everyone was. When I walked into his hospital room, he started to shake his finger at me. That was a sign to me that he knew exactly who I was. He had been shaking his finger at me since I was a little kid.

I left the church and was on my way to buy a waterfall. My mom had showed me one in a flyer and said that she would buy it for me for Christmas if I wanted. I arrived at the store that sold the waterfalls. The one in the flyer that mom showed me was not as nice in person as it looked in the flyer. However, there were several other waterfalls in the store. There was a four foot one on display but I could not find that same model for sale in a box. It was only ninety dollars and waterfalls of that size are usually two hundred dollars or more.

I asked the store manager if I could buy the display and she said yes. I could not wait to get it home! It was such a cool waterfall and since it was the display, I received an additional ten dollars off. Not only did I buy the display waterfall, but I also ended up buying six different types of table top waterfalls. I could not help myself. I wanted them in every room. I found the sound of trickling water most peaceful. I went back to my sister's for the evening. It had been a long day and I was pooped!

November 30

When I woke up in the morning and tried to get out of bed, I immediately knew that I had forgotten to take Effexor. My head felt like it was going to fall off! That stuff was like Paxil. If you forgot one dosage, you were screwed! During my state of bliss, I forgot to take my meds after meeting the woman at the furniture store.

I was planning to go home that day but I could hardly move without feeling dizzy, so I decided to stay another day. I sure the hell could not drive for two hours to get home. At one point during the day, I glanced over to the kitchen and noticed the time on the microwave, 4:20 again.

I pretty much spent the day in bed because every time I tried to get up, I would feel dizzy and get that sensation in my head that I could not describe. What ever it was, it made me grab my head in agony.

December 1

When I woke up, I felt so much better than the previous day. The crazy dizziness in my head had gone away. I was about to phone a friend to buy some weed but something told me to wait just a little while. I had arranged to meet him about an hour after I had that feeling.

Low and behold, on my way to his house, I came across a road block. Had I left when I originally planned to, I might not have gone through the road block on the way there but would have on the way back after I had a bunch of dope on me. That so would have not been cool.

Obviously, I took a different route back as I did not want to risk going through the road block. On my way home, I stopped off in Chilliwack to pick up a few groceries. Once I arrived at home, I turned on my computer, as I had no idea what time it was. Well, what did you know, 4:20 again.

Thank god for Lorne! My car was loaded from floor to ceiling with stuff. Heavy stuff too! That one waterfall probably weighed one hundred and fifty pounds. I did not know what I would do without him. Every time I left or came home from shopping, he loaded up my car and unloaded it. I have to admit there had been times that I was so lucky he had been home.

Coming home with a load of fridge and freezer food and not being able to get it to your apartment yourself can be nerve racking. I had family in town that helped me a lot too, but sometimes it worked out that no one was around when I needed help. It was hard enough to ask for help to begin with.

I had done things myself all my life without depending on people. Growing up it was as if I was the mom and my mom and little sister were my kids. I found it difficult knowing that I could not get by on my own two feet. What a vulnerable state to be. No matter how much I wanted to do certain things for myself, I could not and had to wait for the assistance of another. People said they did not mind helping, but after time, they started to get pissed off.

It was when you were truly in need of help, that you found out who your real friends were. When people said that you could count on them no matter what, most times they really did not mean it. However, it sounded good and made them look good. Unless you truly mean it, do not ever say those words to someone. It is far more damaging not following through with what you led someone to believe.

December 2

Ok, so I met a man whom I was totally drawn to. I can not tell you how or where I met him, as you will soon find out why. There was just something about him. Was he my mentor? I had told my mom about him and she must have seen stars in my eyes because she gave me that look. "Oh no! It is not like that at all mom! I mean, he is old. Gross!" I was so not physically attracted to him. He was just a really interesting and cool man.

December 5

I had an appointment with my surgeon. He had informed me that he had canceled my surgery again. I smiled and took it gracefully. He said there had been some improvement in bending my knee and he would like to see if it would improve some more without surgery.

Everything happened for a reason! That also meant that I did not have to start taking those yucky pain medications. That is it. I am going back to my doctor to get off Effexor. I did not need it and I have not needed it since I came home from Sedona.

My doctor had convinced me to stay on Effexor until after my surgery to see if I was able to cope with the constant pain from rehabilitation. Since my surgery had been canceled yet again, I wanted off that crap! If there came a time in my future that I absolutely could not cope, I would consider anti-depressants then and only then. I did not need them!

Any time I had an appointment that was out of town, I took advantage of being in a city and went shopping while I was there. Shopping was not my favorite thing to do, especially in a wheelchair. It was such a pain in the ass sometimes. Unless I had someone with me, I could only buy so much.

Sometimes I went through the checkout several times, as I could only get what I could fit in one basket and then off to the car I wheeled to unload. It got tiring when I had nine more basket loads to go. My good leg got tired too as I used it to drag along the floor to get more speed and momentum with the wheel chair. I only had one arm that I could use to wheel as the other arm was holding the basket.

I had a few errands to run and I usually did them in some kind of order. I wanted to go to the bank first so that I actually had money to shop. I had some money on me, but not enough to purchase everything I wanted. Something was urging me to go to Liquidation World first, instead of the bank. I should probably listen to that.

I guess if worse came to worse and I did not have enough cash, I could use my bank card to pay for my purchase. For all I knew, I may come out of there empty handed anyways. It was a huge store and I liked to go through every aisle as their merchandise changed regularly.

I spent over an hour wheeling around checking every thing out and then made my way to the check out. There was a man in line two spots ahead of me. He motioned the woman in front of me to go ahead of him. "So how much do you figure you bought today?" He questioned as he glanced into my basket. "I'm not to sure. I bought a couple of storage ottoman's and an end table that I needed to pick up at the delivery bay. They were really good deals that I could not pass up." I answered.

The cashier moved his nuts and chocolate over the scanner. "Add her stuff to my bill." He said to the cashier and motioned to my basket of merchandise. "But you don't understand I have purchased furniture as well. I have about a one hundred and fifty dollars worth of stuff here. You cannot just go and pay for all my stuff. That is a lot of money!" I tried to reason with him.

He assured the cashier to put my stuff on his bill, as I stood there speechless with my jaw on the floor. He paid for everything, turned and looked at me and said, "Merry Christmas" and walked out the door. "Wait! But…. You can't… Where did you go?"

I was confused at what just happened. In a million years, I would never expect anyone to pay even five dollars worth of my stuff. Was that a sign to show me that there were decent people on this planet? Because once upon a time, I use to really love meeting new people and engaging conversation with just about anyone.

Lately, all I saw was greed and negativity in most people. Like a bunch of robots stuck on auto pilot and the only thing on their mind was, ME, ME, ME! WANT, WANT, WANT! I drove around to the back of the store to pick up the furniture and noticed the cashier made a mistake. She charged for four ottomans instead of just two.

At least I noticed before getting all the way home. I would just have to go back into the store so that the cashier could reverse the money back to his card. Back inside the store, I wheeled. I showed the cashier the receipt and she said that she could not reverse the money back to the man's card because he used his bank card and not his credit card. She explained that she needed his actual bank card to do the transaction.

Great! He had no clue that she made the mistake in the first place, so there was no way that he would be coming back. That generous man came in, bought five dollars worth of goods, and ended up paying almost two hundred and fifty dollars. Ninety dollars should have not been on that bill. Because they were paid for, the cashier said the only thing that she could do at that point, was to give me an additional two ottomans.

I really wished the man could just get his money back but unfortunately, that could not happen. I ended up taking the additional two ottomans.

Again, I would never expect such an act from anyone, but it was nice to see that there were people out there like that. Who just wanted to give and help in any way they could. I finished the rest of my errands and made my way home. I had another car load of stuff for Lorne to bring up to my apartment.

~~~

I met Takhi, a woman that owned a store that sold jewelry, crystals, and the sort. I was excited, as that was another place that I could buy crystals. The store had been around for a long time and I did not know it. I think she was some kind of medicine woman or something. She said she did not like the term medicine woman, because she said she was more than just that. She felt that labeling herself, limited her abilities.

I had always been interested in doing a sweat. I asked her if she had known anyone in the area that did that. She said that she held sweat ceremonies and that I could come to the next one in the spring. It all depended on when the snow melted as to when they began sweats for the year.

Later in the day, Natasha had mentioned that she liked the ottomans that I had bought. Or should I say, the stranger bought me. Since I had an extra one, I decided to give it to her. I was planning to give one away anyways. I left the box at Lorne's door with a note attached. Natasha spent most of her time at Lorne's when she was not at work.

Natasha and I had not hung out or got along very well in the last year. I tried to be mature about the whole situation, but the truth of the matter was, she was twenty years old and tried to play the high school routine with me. No thanks sweets, I did that twenty years ago, right around when you were born. I did not wish her any harm; I just did not like the snotty attitude. That did not matter to me. She liked the ottoman and I just so happened to have an extra one, so I gave it to her. In hindsight, it was not long after this that our friendship had grown.

Looking around my apartment, I noticed that I sure had changed a lot in the last couple of months. Although I still have a trucker mouth, drive like a race car driver, and have a problem with authority. I cannot stand power abusers! Following are some of those changes.

* I got rid of my TV's, cable, VCR's, DVD players, Play Station 2, etc. I no longer watched the soap Days of Our Lives. Old Tanya watched it since she was thirteen years old everyday! I gave up all other shows as well without any problems what so ever. Old Tanya would be more than upset had she missed an episode of any of her shows!
* I donated my couch, rocking chair, and kitchen table.
* I do not use paper plates and plastic cutlery any more. I use real dishes and try to wash them myself.
* My apartment now has plants and sometimes I would buy flowers too.
* I have a huge attraction to crystals and spirituality.
* I completely rearranged my apartment, including painting the walls the colors of the rainbow.

* There is an outdoor tent in my living room and I use giant pillows for seats.
* My Healing Hut (use to be living room) was decorated with waterfalls, candles, scent, sound, crystals, plants, etc.
* I enrolled for a Bachelor, Master, and Doctorate Degree in Metaphysical Sciences without any fear at all.
* I am reading like its going out of style. I bought one thousand dollars worth of books within a couple of months. I never ever read before.
* I am constantly researching metaphysical, paranormal and history.
* I use to love going to parties where there were many people boozing it up and having fun. Now I want to tell them to shut the fuck up!

Since miscarrying her baby, Amber had not been doing well, understandably so. She confided to me that she felt as though she just might not be able to snap out of the depression. She said this time it was different and she did not want to feel all messed up for the rest of her life.

I had an idea. Maybe I could help her with my crystals. I had never done that before and I had never received any training. Maybe there was something that I could do using the crystals to alleviate some of her pain so that she could at least have some fight in her to continue on.

Her session lasted around ninety minutes. My intent was to balance her chakras and help soothe her broken heart. At one point during the session, she started to move her feet around and giggled. I was no where near her feet. I quickly remembered what I was doing and paid no attention to that. I continued to concentrate on the healing.

The following was what Amber said had happened during the session. She felt good and positive with a sense of hope. Some parts of her skin tingled. She felt very warm in the sacral area. A shot of energy shot from her base chakra down her leg. She felt a warm sparkly feeling that started in her leg and moved up to her heart.

She also explained to me that we were not alone. She felt my cat Molly, only Molly was no longer alive. Amber had said that Molly was cuddling up to her feet and that she was being gentle and did not attack her at all. That must have been when I saw Amber giggle and move her feet around. Amber said that when I was lifting up her legs to ground her energy, Molly was purring in her ear.

This was too cool! With that much spirit activity going on, Amber would be sure to know that there really was something different about me and that I was not crazy! I have tried to tell people about the healing effects of crystals and spirit and they thought that I was a loony tune.

Mystical Puzzle

Well, I just proved it to Amber, so I was sure that she would accept the new me and that I was not making stuff up. She had encountered events during the session that she had no explanation for. Therefore, she should be able to handle some of my crazy experiences without thinking that I was making crazy stories up!

Amber had been doing well since I used the crystals to perform a healing on her. My prescription for her anxiety attacks was rose quartz for her left hand and smoky quartz for her right hand. Amazingly, it had been working well for her.

Ok, so the man that I mentioned earlier, he was very down to earth. Someone I could totally relate to. I felt so comfortable around him that I felt like he must be a part of one of my past lives. Ok, it was time to fess up. He had me how do we say, buzzing from head to toe when he was around me.

It was not physical at all. Physically he was not my type in the least. However, ever since I met him, I was drawn to him. I could not get him out of my head. He consumed my thoughts! When I was doing my angel cards, soul mate, new love, and romance kept coming up.

He kept saying he was going to stop over and he never did. Finally, he sent me a text, and said that he was sorry for not stopping by because he was nervous, and wanted to rip all my clothes off. I never got that text right away because my cell phone was dead. Poor guy must have been sweating because an hour later he sent a text, did I scare you?

I did not get that one for awhile either. Finally, I charged my phone and got his text messages. Our messages were starting to get a little randy and I asked him if he had a wife. I knew he had a young son but he never ever mentioned having a wife.

I would not have thought that he had a wife as he was always hugging me, calling me gorgeous, and telling me he loved it when I came in the shop. He answered my text, and did not hesitate when he told me that he was married. That was why he had not come over.

He was scared of what might happen if he did and we were alone together. He said that he met many people but had never been attracted to another girl like that. How could that be? Why did soul mate, new love, and romance keep coming up? Those cards had been coming up for weeks.

Another thing was. Instead of asking for a man with a list of what I was looking for, I asked for someone that brought the best out of me as I would bring the best out of them. Suddenly, I am being drawn to that guy like flies in shit! Ok, so I need to come up with a name for this guy for obvious reasons. Let us call him something simple like Bob.

What was going on? He was clearly not available. We both knew that if we were alone together we would not be able to stop fate. We were two strangers that had been drawn to each other since day one. Oh yeah, the digits to one of his phone numbers has 444 in them.

There was no doubt in my mind that we would not be able to keep our hands off each other. At first, I was trying to ensure that this would not happen. Then I started to look at all the signs and they were pointing to Bob. I was going to let nature run its course and what ever was meant to happen, would happen. My friend Amber decided to do a little investigating of her own and then phoned to tell me that he was married. You are too late Amber, because I already knew.

December 20

I was supposed to be reading and learning about World Religion and all I could think of was Bob. The next thing I knew, I received a text. Guess who and guess what time? Bob and it was 4:44. He asked if he could come over. He did and we did if you get my drift.

It felt so natural and comfortable as if we had known each other forever. I had not been with anyone for one and a half years and if I was to make a list of what I was looking for physically, he did not fit the bill.

Because we had such a deep emotional, mental, intellectual connection, I totally found him irresistibly sexy. The guy had face hair. I hate face hair! However, there was something about him. I was so drawn to him; and felt as if I wanted to be with him in all kinds of ways.

I could not think that way because he was married. There had to be a reason why my guides and angels led me to him. However, what was it? I want to let you know that I am not proud of sleeping with a married man. There was a magnetism that I could not stop, nor could he.

I kept glancing at clocks when they were 4:20 and now I was starting to see 11:11 all of the time. It was not as if I was clock watching and most of the time, I was not paying attention to the time, it just happened. It happened so often that it must mean something.

December 21

I woke up to use the washroom one morning, but I was still tired, so I went back to bed. I had a thought running through my head that I was giving Lorne heck because he did not tell me it was snowing.

I thought it was rather weird that I had that thought unexpectedly. I did not have a TV anymore, watch the news, or listen to the radio, so I had no idea what the forecast was. Two hours later, it snowed, and he phoned to wake me up to tell me.

It had been snowing all day and night. Amber asked me to let her dogs out because she could not leave work. I did not know if I would make it out of the alley of my apartment, as it was not plowed. If I ended up stuck, I was unable to walk in the snow due to the instability of my leg.

She knew all that and she had a four wheel drive truck, yet she was still asking me. Why was it that everyone else that worked there got breaks except her? More like, why would she use *her* break to take care of *her* animals when she had her brother, sister in law and me to do it for her?

It was becoming harder to have the freedom that I seek when I had to schedule two to four days per week around her dogs piss schedule. When I first offered to do this for Amber over a year ago, I did it because she was in a fragile state of mind. I was trying to do anything I could to alleviate any stress or anxiety from her life.

At the time, she was returning to work after a lengthy leave. Since I was at home on disability, I thought that it would help if she did not have to leave work on her breaks to care for her dogs. The only problem was, a year later, it became my job. If I did not do it, it would cause all kinds of anxiety for Amber.

I did not let the dogs out as late as I usually did because the snow was not letting up and I thought I had better get over to her place before more snow came down. I gunned it out of my garage into the alley and thankfully made it onto the street. Even the main streets looked as though they were not plowed. The crew just could not keep up with the snow. They were out there and they were trying, but Mother Nature was pounding us with the fluffy white stuff.

Oh, this was just great! There was at least two feet of snow on Amber's street! I figured that I had better step on it and not stop, or I would be stuck! I let the dogs out to do their thing and quickly got back into my car to get home. There was no where to turn around. She lived in a cul-de-sac but it was covered in two feet of snow.

The only chance I had was to back out in the same tracks I came in on for about a block, and hopefully I could get out of there. Well it was a nice try but my car ended up totally stuck in snow. I spent a half hour trying to rock my car out of its stuck position. I could not get out of my car because I could not walk in that deep of snow.

The entire time I was stuck, a man watched me from his living room window and did not come out to offer any assistance. Not to mention everyone else on the street that was too busy watching TV. I was beside myself that this was happening. What has humanity come to?

Were they afraid they were going to miss a part of their show? Did the man that watched me through his window not want to put his boots and jacket on? What was wrong with people?! Interesting as the man that watched me struggle for a half hour had 666 in his address. That would explain it!

I finally got free from the snow! No, not because someone finally came out and helped me. Because I trashed the crap out of my engine trying to rock it out. I hope I did not wreck anything. I have never been that hard on my car. I did not really have a choice though. I finally got home and informed Amber that she was going to have to figure out something else because I could not keep risking being stuck like that!

December 22

I had an energy session with Becca today. I always used the washroom before a session but that day I needed to stop half way during our session to go to the washroom again. I could not believe the amount of pee that came out of me. Where did it all come from?

At the end of the session, Becca always discussed what she saw. She saw a sweet little fairy on my right shoulder and she told Becca that she would help me with my lungs. I felt her walking on my shoulder.

Becca had informed me that I was killed in my sleep in a prior life from a lover / husband. I slept with a night light. Maybe that was one of the reasons. Maybe it was also, why I was afraid to go to sleep.

The doozie from that session, I have a dragon protector named Esmerelda. She did not know love, only to fiercely protect me. Becca had told me that Esmerelda tried to chase her out of the healing room. What did that mean? Was that bad for me? Becca assured me that this was not bad for me at all, as Esmerelda was my protector. If that were the case then why would Esmerelda try to chase Becca away from me?

During the Christmas season when my Auntie Karla and I were outside for a smoke, I was trying to pick her brain to see what she remembered about me before the age of three.

"Tanya! I can't remember that long ago!"

"Come on. Think! You must remember something. Anything! What stood out the most? Looking back, what is it about me that was different?"

"I don't know! You were out of this world!"

As she said that, she pointed to the sky. I so badly wanted to tell her that I was from another world, but since she was drunk and I was not ready to come out of the closet so to speak, I just smiled.

Over the holidays, I hung out with family and friends. I stayed at my sister's house for the most part. When I headed home, I was lucky that I made it there. I had just left Surrey, and was driving about a hundred and twenty kilometers an hour on the highway, and my car felt as though it was slamming on the brakes by itself. It was stopping so abruptly that my head flung forward.

Mystical Puzzle

What was going on? It felt as though something was wrong with my transmission.

I could not drive past eighty kilometers an hour as the transmission would not shift into the next gear. I decided to take the next exit off the highway and went to a gas station. Maybe I just needed transmission fluid. I poured some transmission fluid using a funnel into the ridiculously tiny hole while crossing my fingers that that was all that was wrong.

I sat back in my car and headed back towards the highway. The car seemed to be running better. I guess I would soon find out when I tried to drive past eighty kilometers an hour. Hmm. The car seemed to be fine. I had made it past Chilliwack and the car started to act up again. I wondered if maybe there was a leak in my transmission. I only had twenty more minutes of driving before I was home. Something was obviously wrong with my transmission.

I went to my mechanic's the next morning and sure enough, my transmission was toast. It was not worth putting in a new transmission because they were so costly and the car was not that new. My guess was I wrecked it when I was trying to get unstuck on Amber's street full of snow.

Oh well. Everything happened for a reason. My car could no longer drive on the highway because the third and fourth gears were gone, but I could drive around town with the first two gears. My car was becoming quite the little adventurous beater! The back brakes were rubbing metal on metal but the fronts were new so I should be fine.

There was no point in spending money on brake pads when my transmission was kaput. I love the looks on people's faces as they were walking in front of my car as I was grinding the brakes to a stop. The funny thing was when they told me, "I think there is something wrong with your brakes. You better get those checked." Gee, thanks for telling me that because I did not hear them grind as I applied the brakes for the last sixty feet.

December 31

Amber was having a New Year's Eve party and had invited me. Honestly, for one of the first times in my life, I just did not feel like getting drunk with a bunch of drunken people and acting like a bunch of yahoo's until the wee hours of the morning. Did I just type that? I guess there was a first for everything.

She assured me that it was not going to be a big piss up and that it would be more families with kids orientated. I went and it was ok in the sense that nobody was acting like complete idiots. I brought Alex with me since there would be other kids there. He thought that it was cool that he was able to stay up and howl at midnight with everyone.

Midnight seemed to take forever. The funny thing was, I would much rather be home reading a book or something. I was so not into the party atmosphere anymore. Alex and I went back to my place at around 1am.

I could not believe it! I did not have any alcohol to drink! This was the first time in twenty-two years that I had not drunk alcohol during the Christmas and New Years season! I was not trying to not drink; I just did not have the desire. I had some beer with me, but never drank it.

It was 2009 and it was going to be an amazing year. All day long, I see double and triple numbers. 10:10, 11:11, 12:12, 1:11, 2:22, 3:33, 4:44, 5:55, or 2:11, 3:11, 4:11, etc. This goes on all day. I could not count how many times that it happened.

I did not clock watch. The only time I have in my surroundings was on my computer and on my cell phone. I did not see the numbers just in time, but as addresses, license plate numbers, totals of the purchase I just made, etc.

Some of my friends told me that I was just looking for the numbers. Only that was just it, I did not look for them. Something prompted me to glance and there they were. That must mean something. I wondered if there was anything on the internet in regards to seeing the numbers, so I did a search.

I could not believe that there was a wealth of information on that. So many others were seeing the same numbers as me. I came across some videos on YouTube, "Who are the Starseed Indigos?" and "11:11 Journey of a Starseed" and was completely taken aback by the fact that those videos were describing me! There were so many more of us! Something was definitely going on!

January 8

I had an appointment with the sleep disorder clinic today to return the breathing machine. I did not have four thousand dollars for a machine so they needed to take it back from me. They explained to me that I could die in my sleep. Since I did not have money, they explained there was nothing they could do to help. What was the matter with this world? There were people out there that could help so many but unless you gave them money, they would not lift a finger.

Tonight was a big night. I was going to bed without a night light. I have never attempted remotely to try this in over ten years. The mere thought of having to sleep in the dark usually had me in hysterics. I said a prayer to Archangel Michael to protect me at all times while I slept.

~ ~ ~

I could not believe I never clued into this sooner. The last four digits in Bob's cell phone number was the old address that Julie and Misty Casey use to live. At one point, I lived there as well. What was the connection? The Casey's had been a huge part in my life without them really even knowing that they were.

I met Misty when I was ten years old. She used to live across the street from me. One day after school, I was going up and down the street we lived on looking for caterpillars. Misty was on her bike and rode up to me to ask me what I was doing. I informed her that I was collecting caterpillars and showed her what I had so far. She had a look and then continued on her way down the street.

About five minutes went past and she rode up to me again. "I found a caterpillar for you. Do you want to be friends?" "Thank you. Do you want to collect caterpillars with me?" At the time, Misty was eight years old. We quickly became best friends and if I was not at her house, she was at mine.

Sometimes we would convince our parents to let us have sleepovers on a school night. That did not happen often, but the odd time our parents would give in to our pleas. It was not long before I introduced my mom to her parents. To this day my mom and her mom are still good friends. That was not the case with Misty and me.

Once I became about thirteen years old, her parents were not so fond of me hanging out with their daughter. I was into boys, drugs, and since Misty was two years younger than me, that was not going to fly with them. They ended up moving to Nakusp.

Due to my age, interests, and Misty moving away, we did not have much contact during our teenage years. While living in Nakusp, she met Brady. The two of them moved to Surrey from Nakusp. Once Misty moved back to Surrey, we started to hang out again. They stayed for a few years before moving back to Nakusp.

Soon after returning to Nakusp, Misty and Brady broke up. Brady ended up dating Cassie and the two of them moved to Surrey. As Cassie did not know anyone, I befriended her and introduced her to some of my friends. It did not take long before we all hit it off.

Something very strange started going on with me. I was looking at Brady in ways that I should not be. For god sakes, he used to be my best friends boyfriend, he was dating Cassie, and he had been a friend of my family for about seven years. Where were those feelings coming from? I did not like Brady in that way. I wished those feelings would just leave me alone.

I secretly pined for him for a couple of years. I did not dare tell him or anyone! One night, Brady was over at Julie's and everyone that had been there that night was either sleeping or had left. He started to give me a massage. Somehow, during the massage, our lips found each other. That was the most incredible kiss. I could not believe what was happening! He was dating Cassie and he use to go out with my best friend! I could not deny my feelings, but I did not want to hurt anyone either.

A couple of weeks after we had kissed, I took my sister Corrina on a road trip to Kelowna and Nakusp. We decided to go to Nakusp first to visit Misty. Of course, I did not dare tell her that Brady and I had kissed. Even though it had been a couple of years since they had broken up, I did not think it was appropriate. Corrina and I left Nakusp and were on our way to visit my friend Dina in Kelowna.

While we were driving through the Monashee Mountains, we were stopped for about twenty minutes due to road work. Since there was going to be quite a bit of a wait, I shut my car off. While we were stopped, I was looking in my side view mirror and noticed a car a couple of spots behind me. It had a red bumper with yellow circle patch on it.

No! It could not be! The only person I knew with a red bumper and yellow circle patch was Brady! I convinced my sister to get out of the car to go and see if it was Brady. She quickly came back to inform that yes indeed, it was him!

Wow! What was the chance of that happening? We were in the middle of the Monashee Mountains and were stopped for road work, and there he was. He came up to my car and told me that he had been looking all over Nakusp for me. He had mentioned that he had given up and was on his way back home.

For those that did not know, Nakusp is about an eight hour drive from Surrey. Brady informed me that he drove to Nakusp to drop off Cassie because they were no longer going out and that he came looking for me. We arranged to meet in Kelowna to talk.

Once we met in Kelowna, he confided in me that he has had feelings for me for the last couple of years but due to our circumstances of him being with someone and me as well, he never acted on them. We had both wanted each other for the last couple of years, but never knew that the other person was thinking the exact same thing.

We ended up together and our relationship lasted five years. During that time, my relationship fizzled with Misty. When I left Brady and moved out on my own, Misty magically came back into my life for a short period. It was her idea that I go backpacking in South East Asia for a year.

My first reaction to her suggestion was, are you freaking nuts! Travel to some weird dirty countries all by myself. What about all my stuff? Misty explained to me that stuff could be sold and replaced, or put into storage. I had a strange feeling that she knew what she was talking about so I bought an open ended airplane ticket that left in a year.

That gave me one year to save as much as I possibly could to go away for a year. Somehow, it felt so right. I did not know how I was going to do this but I guess I would figure it out along the way. That was a whole other story.

An adventure of embracing other cultures, another dirt bike accident, a heroine addiction, a boyfriend that I did not know was an undercover drug agent that saved me from a Malaysian prison. If that was not enough, I came home to the person that I gave power of attorney to while I was away, screwing me over so badly that my zero dollar debt had become two hundred thousand dollars. I was forced to claim bankruptcy on a debt that was not mine but it was in my name. Again, that was a whole other story.

Anyways, I was living at Julie's house when Brady and I got together. Julie was Misty's mom. That house was the same house address as Bob's cell phone number. I believe to this day that Brady is one of my soul mates. I also believe that Misty is one of my soul mates.

I believe that you can have soul mates of the same sex as well as animals. You did not have to have an intimate sexual relationship with someone to be their soul mate. So how did Bob fit into all of this? Perhaps he is not a soul mate but someone who would have a significant impact on my life. I had to believe that what ever it was that I was doing, I was on the right path as there were synchronicities everywhere.

It had been about a month since I had slept without a night light. I was doing really well. I was no longer afraid to be in the dark in my own apartment. This was a good first step. Now I needed to be brave and not be afraid of the dark in my garage and in the forests. One step at a time though.

It was funny that every other day I questioned my sanity. I knew without a doubt that I was not crazy. However, if I tried to explain my experience that was exactly what people would think. I went back and forth continuously. However, at the end of the day I saw signs every where.

January 31

My Auntie Cynthia came over for her first chakra balancing as she had been feeling quite depressed. She enjoyed the session and felt refreshed afterwards. Some of what she experienced is as follows.

Her left big toe felt like someone touched it approximately fifteen times. She felt extreme pressure on her third eye and higher heart chakra. I found that quite interesting, as the stones used on those chakras were as light as a feather. She placed the turquoise back on her third eye and she felt a tingle coming from both her ears and her head felt like it was being squished, but it was not painful. She had tingles on her head when I was working in that area. Her ovaries hurt a little as well. She felt a little sad but she did not feel desperate. It was more of a neutral feeling.

She had forgotten to leave a clipping of her hair so that I could do distance healing on her. She had sent my Uncle Jim over to deliver the hair. When my uncle returned home, she had asked him if he had given me her hair. He just about had a bird and told her, "What the fuck does she need your hair for? She doesn't need it!" I take it that he was a little freaked out to say the least.

February 2

My aunt informed me that she could not stop having bowel movements ever since our session the other day. No pun intended but she had a lot of crap that was stuck and needed releasing. I am not kidding! My aunt was one of those people that were lucky if she had a bowel movement once per week! Since the chakra balancing, she was releasing old crap. I assured her that once the back log had been released, her bowels would calm down. She also mentioned that she felt better emotionally.

February 5

I had my usual once per month energy session with Becca. That session seemed different to me. I knew it was different somehow but did not know how. At one point, I was wondering if Becca was ok. I could also feel a presence on the massage table with me.

When it got on the table, the actual table did not move but I could hear the sound that it made as if someone was getting on to the table. It was rubbing up against my side, almost like a rocking motion. It started to feel as though I had wings and they were about to spread. It was so hard to describe this stuff sometimes.

At the end of the session, Becca had told me that she had to stop the healing and allowed the guides to completely take over. She said she had never experienced that and that St. Germaine came in and poured his purple light into me. Becca said that something was wrong and she was scared for me.

There were dark forces and energy around me. I had been on the dark side in other lives. She noticed that I had a tail in that session as well as a problem that was described as a yellow ball of light in my mental body. A couple of blockages were also released.

Before I left, Becca said that my dragon had come after her in our last session because she had been sleeping for many, many years and Becca startled her out of her sleep. In another life, I use to be a wizard. I hoped that the dark energy that was around me was gone. I was afraid of something that I did by accident in this lifetime at age fourteen. I accidently opened an evil portal messing around with an Ouija board. I hoped that they were not coming back to haunt me again! There were reasons that I use to be petrified to go to sleep!

Mystical Puzzle

February 6

I was sitting at my computer and my body started to jerk and vibrate, especially in my left hand. Several times, throughout the day, I would get involuntary movements and jerking type energy releases, but this was very different. I did not know what was happening. Were they trying to communicate with me?

I decided to grab a piece of paper and picked up a pen with my left hand to see if anything happened. I closed my eyes and tried to relax as much as possible. It felt as though I was just scribbling. I kept my eyes closed and just let the pen do its thing. While I was doing that, I noticed that my head felt like it wanted to fall back and my neck muscles were becoming sore and tense.

After a few minutes, I opened my eyes and had a look at the paper. Amongst all the scribbling was, SOS. That was the second time that I had gotten SOS while trying to channel with my left hand. SOS stands for Save Our Souls or an international symbol for help. I did not know what to make of this.

February 11

My friend Kate came over to have her chakras balanced. Kate and Amber had been best friends since they were young kids and Kate was married to Amber's brother. I hoped we would have a profound session like Amber's. It would be so much easier for my friends to come to terms with my new self if they could see first hand that there was a whole world out there that we could not see, but it was there.

I explained to Kate some of the possibilities that may happen during the session. For someone that had never experienced energy healing, it could be quite frightening when you could feel something touching you, yet the practioner had not laid one hand on you. I could tell that she was thinking, yeah right Tanya!

At the end of the session, the first words out of her mouth were, "I don't know how to explain to you what happened without you thinking that I am crazy!" "Believe me; I know what working with crystals and spirit can do. Do your best to explain. I am not here to judge in anyway. Now do you have a tiny glimpse of what I feel?" I stated.

Kate had explained to me that she was in this desert type of place and it was windy. Big tumble weeds were blowing around. During our session, she began to cry and tremble. She said during that time, I was breathing different. She had said that my breathe was the wind blowing all her troubles and hurt out of her.

I found that quite fascinating because that was exactly what I was trying to do. Release her pain and then fill the void with love and light. She also experienced tingly type feelings and an energy blockage released in her right leg.

This was great! Two of my closest friends in town have had unexplainable experiences during their chakra balancing session.

Surely, they would just accept that I was different and support me in this amazing journey. It had been so difficult living in a world that so very little people see. It was lonely when none of my friends and family understood a damn thing I was saying.

Sometimes they looked at me as if I had three heads. The irony in all of this was the old Tanya would think exactly what they were thinking. How did I convince my friends and family that I was not crazy, when my own old self would have thought the same?

I never did hear back from Kate regarding the crystal treatment for her kidney stone. I should have known not to spend so much time and effort on something before asking someone if they were actually committed to alternate healing.

I could not say that I did not blame Kate. Why would she think that I could heal something that the doctors could not? She did mention that placing three crystals on her body for twenty minutes a day would be too much of an inconvenience.

Imagine having to do that possibly to save your life. I am not going to beg people to try alternative healing and help themselves. It was very clear to me that most people really did not want to help themselves at all. Maybe it was not so much about wanting to help them, as they did not believe that they could help themselves.

February 18

Amber came over for a chakra balancing. She ended up coming ten minutes early for her appointment and let herself in with her keys. I had the do not disturb sign on my door but I guess she thought that did not include her. I was in the middle of grounding and centering my energy and doing any last minute preparations that I do before a client comes for a session.

When she disrupted me, I told her that she was early and I had already discussed with her the importance of why she needed to come on time, not early, not late, on time. I asked her to come back in ten minutes.

She looked at me dumbfounded and said, "Where the fuck am I supposed to go?" "It is not rocket science. Wait in the hallway or your truck." Amber was right pissed when I said that. It was obvious to me that she had no respect for me, or the space that I was creating for the healing that she came to receive.

I almost had to cancel the session all together but I managed to free my mind of what just happened. After the session, Amber said that she felt dizzy and was seeing double. I assured her that she had nothing to worry about and it would work itself out.

~ ~ ~

Lorne came over for a visit and told me that Flood Falls had a major landslide and that I should go check it out with him. The ground would be totally uneven and unstable. I was not sure this was a good idea. Lorne assured me that he would head the trail. If I followed his footsteps, that should stop me from hurting myself by falling through unstable ground. If it was too painful, he said we could just head back to the car.

It bothered me when I could not perform certain tasks and I stopped others from doing so because they were with me. Lorne assured me that it was no big deal if I could not make it to the falls and back, and that he did not mind if we had to turn around. On that note, I was ready to check out the landslide. Before we left my apartment, I did a silent prayer asking for a sign while I was on my walk that my guides were with me.

Then I started to wonder, what kind of sign were they going to give me? A bird? Of course, I was going to see a bird as I was going for a walk in nature. So I said, give me a really big sign that I could not miss. Hit me on the head with it.

The falls were located a short drive away, probably no more than five minutes. As we were driving along the main road on the way to the falls, my right leg started to shake so bad that the car was shaking due to my foot hitting the gas. I did not know why my leg was doing that.

I started to laugh because I could not stop it and the car ride was less than smooth. I continued to drive down the road like that, laughing and jerking about while Lorne just shook his head. I tried to explain to Lorne that the only time my leg did that was right after the living daylights had just been scared out of me. Only nothing had happened.

The drive was uneventful, so why was my leg shaking out of control like that. Oh well. We made our way to the trail head. Lorne took the lead and I followed. It was not long before his leg had gone down through the ground a foot deep. "See. My leg can't do that!" I yelled. "That is why I am leading; so that this doesn't happen to you. You are all right. Come on, let's keep going."

The trail was not long, but it was my way of still being able to get to a little piece of nature. I use to hike a lot before my accident. The walk to the falls was twelve minutes from the car, to the falls, and back to the car when I had legs that worked. I could not believe the trail! More like we had to make our own trail because the original had disappeared.

So many trees had vanished and there was so much open space. It just goes to show you how powerful Mother Nature could be in the split of a second. There use to be a bench to sit on at the base of the falls, but who knew where that ended up.

Once we arrived at the falls, we would always sit back, chill, and smoke a joint and a cigarette before heading back to the car. As there was no bench and the ground was wet and muddy, we just stood while smoking. We were only there a few minutes when Lorne said, "Oh my god! Did you hear that? I just heard rock on rock."

"Bullshit Lorne! Nice try though. You are such a bullshitter! Stop trying to scare me dumbass! Hey. What the? I just heard something too."

I looked at the top of the falls. "Oh my god! Ruuuun!" I screamed. "Get over here! Get to this tree!" Lorne screamed as he motioned for me to get to where he was. "I'm trying! My leg doesn't run even if I really need it to!" I whimpered back. I tried with all my might just to make my leg run and leap without pain, but I could not do it.

The fucking mountain might be coming down, and I still could not make my leg run for dear life! I made it to where Lorne was and he pushed me into the tree. He wrapped himself around the tree and me. "You hold on for dear life! You latch onto this tree like you're making love to it!" He screamed.

There was no where to go. There were no other trees because the last slide took them all out. It was all open. Was that it? Was there more? I will never forget that sound and sight of massive amounts of huge ice chunks, flying off the top of the waterfalls. The sound was so thunderous! As I was trying to get to cover, I did not know if there was more right on my heels.

"I don't like this anymore. I want to go home." I said as tears started to roll from my eyes. Lorne climbed down a steep hill, looked at me and said, "Let's go!" "I can't go that way. It is too steep for my leg!" I cried. Great! This meant I had to walk closer to where all the ice just fell, and walk around to where Lorne was. I hobbled my way over to where he was and we decided to get the heck out of there and not look back. That was way too much adrenaline! That was just way too much!

Hey, my little angel friends. When I said give me a sign, a big sign; hit me on the head with it. I did not literally mean, hit me on the head with it! Did you all figure I had not had a good adrenaline rush in awhile and needed one? Good grief! Ok, so now that I was safe, it was quite the experience. One I would never forget! Oh Mother Earth, you are one powerful source!

March 4

I borrowed my aunt's car today as I had two appointments out of town. One was in Chilliwack with my surgeon and the other was in Abbotsford with my lung specialist. I left town and had been driving on the highway for about ten minutes.

The car started to behave strangely. I did not know what it was doing and if I should pull over or not. I continued to drive and just paid attention to

Mystical Puzzle

see if smoke would come out from under the hood. There was no smoke but the car was sputtering as if it wanted to stall.

This could not be happening! I had two very important appointments. "Michael, can you please fix the car?" The second I finished saying that, the car stopped sputtering and drove as though nothing had been wrong with it. "Thanks Michael!"

Well, my surgeon was now giving up on me. In the last year, he had booked two surgeries, canceled both surgeries, never looked at my leg, and then told me there was nothing he could do for me. It had taken him that long to figure out that, I did not respond well to surgery the first time. He suspected that I would end up with a permanent disability.

Ok, I could take this. Everything happened for a reason. Maybe I really was going to have to heal my leg myself. Well, not by myself. I would definitely need the help of spirit. I did not care what the doctors had said; I knew that my leg would heal with or without their help.

The lung specialist said that I had lung disease. He told me to take two puffs of an inhaler in the morning and in the evening and that was it. Huh? That was it. I have lung disease and all you could do was tell me to take puffs off a puffer. Were you sure that I really had lung disease? All he did was listen to my breathing, and tested me for allergies.

I made my way back home from my appointments. I explained to my aunt what her car had done but it drove fine on the way home.

The following day my uncle drove my aunt's car to work. On the other hand, I should say tried to drive. The car broke down about twenty minutes from home. The alternator had gone on it. Thanks to Michael, I made it to my appointments, and back safe and soundly.

I had come down with a nasty little cold. I had it for a few days before the light bulb went on. Hello, I could heal myself. I was always eager to try to heal everyone else and ended up forgetting about healing my own self.

I used my pendulum to pick out the most appropriate crystals to bathe with to heal my cold. I placed the chosen crystals on the table at my bedroom entrance. I cranked up the heat in the bathroom to warm it up because I felt so icky and cranky that I could not imagine having to get out of a hot tub of water and then having to step into the cold air.

I ended up falling asleep waiting for the bathroom to heat up. I had the heat cranked all night wasting electricity. That was not the first time I had cranked the bathroom heat and fallen asleep before having my bath.

March 6

I had procrastinated having my bath most of the day. I was given the message that it was time for the bath if I wanted to be rid of the cold! That message came in the form of the picture of myself and my cousin Lori falling over on the table that I had placed the crystals on. Ok, ok, I got the message.

I proceeded to crank up the heat in the bathroom, only this time I did not fall asleep. I placed a tumbled clear quartz and ametrine in the tub with me. For thirty minutes, I concentrated on that every *in* breath I took, was full of healing energy, and with every *out* breath, any negativity, and illness from the cold, would leave me and be transferred back to Mother Earth, so that she could transmute the energy back to love and light.

I got out of the bath and wrapped myself in my robe. You have to be kidding me! The sniffles, headache, aches, stuffiness, and whiny voice, had disappeared. To think I could have done that four days ago and the suffering would have been gone. Thank you so much to my crystals, Mother Nature and Spirit for this healing!

March 12

I still did not know why my angels and guides were guiding me to be non angelic with Bob. The soul mate card came up all the time when I thought of him while doing a reading. I could only trust that everything was happening just as it was suppose to. What was the link though? There were so many coincidences.

I did not normally know what day it was because I try to live in the now as much as possible. I happened to glance over at the calendar and noticed the date. It was Brady's birthday today and Bob and I were intimate tonight. The last four digits in Bob's cell phone is the address where Brady and I were first intimate.

March 13

I went to all the places in town that sold crystals in hopes of finding brown jasper. I had almost every jasper there was, except for brown jasper. I had not had very good luck in finding one. I stopped at the crystal shop in town and he as well had several types of jasper, but not the brown.

A friend of the owner just happened to stop in the shop to show him a couple of pieces of crystal he had found. His friend had heard our conversation and reached in his pocket, "Is this what you are looking for?" The look on the owner's face said it all.

Yes! Brown jasper! I offered to buy it from him, but he just gave it to me. This was too cool! What was the chance that a complete stranger to me just happened to have found the stone that I was looking for, and then gave it to me? I love it when this happened!

Mystical Puzzle

March 14

Amber invited me over for lunch. While I was there, I mentioned that crystals could be used on dogs for healing. Amber told me to stay the fuck away from her dogs with my crystals because she did not have enough money to fix her dogs if I made them go blind. Ok then, on that note, I thought it was time to go home.

March 16

My mom and Michael were visiting for spring break. Mom and I were in my bedroom when Michael called out, and said he was having difficulties getting the lid off the ketchup. How could he be having difficulties when it was a flip top lid? I walked into the kitchen and my mouth hit the floor.

"You have got to be kidding me! What are you doing using my display condiments? You know damn well that those came from New York and Arizona, and that they are for display only! You know that the condiments we use are in the fridge, not on top of the stove! Have fun finding replacements as I bought them in New York and Arizona!"

I was so pissed that I went back to my bedroom to calm down. I came out of my bedroom to get some water and noticed my mom trying to tape the label back on so that it looked like he had not opened it.

March 21

I stopped at Bob's place of work. It was quiet without any customers, so it gave us an opportunity to talk freely without interruption. He told me that he had been with his wife for over twenty years and it had been hell because she was so money hungry, bossy and demanding while he was so laid back, gentle, and easy going.

He wanted to make a break but was afraid of losing everything he had worked so hard to build. Well I was not going to count on that. It was not as if we were having an affair or that we saw each other all the time. Each time we saw each other, I learned something amazing about him, and I was becoming more and more smitten with him.

I left his place of work and went to check on my nephew at the skateboard park. I was approaching the train tracks when the train warning flashing lights came on. I usually gunned it over the tracks before the arms came down, but since the transmission in my car was hooped, with my luck, it would get stuck in neutral when I was over the tracks.

I decided to play it safe and stopped. I was day dreaming about Bob and the train car number on the first train was the last four digits to his work phone number. This happened all the time and I really did not know what to make of it. He was married and I had no plans of messing that up. Somehow we must be deeply connected.

~~~

Kate and Toby invited me over for dinner. Toby and I were outside having a cigarette, and I asked him if Amber had a boyfriend because I had not heard from her since the bear rug incident.

"Oh, the bear rug." Toby said as he rolled his eyes back. I also told Toby that I mentioned to Amber that she should use that experience to finally realize that her dogs needed some training. "You said what!? You know you two are not friends anymore. You do know that, right? Nobody but nobody says anything about Amber's dogs!" Toby said wide eyed. I was sure Toby had to be joking. I mean he should know Amber well as she was his sister, but I highly doubt she was not going to be my friend over that.

March 26

I was excited as I received a free fifteen minute reading with Brianna. Brianna lived in the same province as I. The following was what came from the reading.

"First thing that came in is a brown and white horse that is travelling very fast. The meaning of this is things are happening really quickly.

"I have chills running up my arms because you have such a strong connection to spirit.

"Are you doing any writing?"

I had mentioned this book and that I was afraid to publish it because of the content.

"You must find the courage to keep going with the book. It will transform lives. You are here to help so many people and to inspire others. You must not give up on the book.

"You need to meditate and silence yourself more. You need to play more."

We started to talk about relationships. I had told her that I was smitten with Bob but he was married. She had asked if he was happily married, and I told her, no. When I said no, the time into the reading was 4:44.

"There is an opening coming up for a relationship in September. This does not mean that it is Bob.

"Are you doing any healing with others?"

I had mentioned that since coming home from Sedona, I have bought over four hundred crystals and it was my intention to use them for healing.

"You are a healer, especially in your hands. Your attraction to crystals comes from your lifetimes in Atlantis and Lemuria. Keep amethyst around you. (Bob bought me an amethyst. It was the first crystal he bought me.)

Mystical Puzzle

"You need to be true to yourself. Your path before the dirt bike accident was destructive and if you had kept on that path, it could have killed you. You will heal your leg. You need to forgive someone as it is connected to your leg. Focus this year on healing your leg and writing your book.

"I see a white dove around you. You are surrounded by magic, high energy and angels.

"You will be very successful.

"You should be giving readings.

"Your leg is what transforms you.

"It is a joy to connect with you.

"Are you doing any automatic writing as your guides are trying to connect with you? 11am and 11pm are the times that they would like to work with you. (Funny she should mention that because it was one of the questions I was going to ask her.)

"You need to connect with your past lives in Egypt as it will help you with what you are writing about. You are very gifted and you don't even know what all those gifts are yet."

We ended our call with Brianna telling me, that she could not wait to read my book and that I was such an inspiration, and to never forget that.

The first thing I did when I hung up the phone was cry my little eyes out. They were tears of joy, not sadness. Things had been happening so rapidly that I sometimes questioned my sanity. I knew I was not crazy, but I was afraid that the world would think that I was.

I was also afraid that people would think that I was evil because of my gifts. I must have been killed several times in past lives because of my gifts. The short time that Brianna spent on the phone with me had done so much. She told me exactly what I needed to hear and confirmed my knowing.

After talking with Brianna, I felt like I was so ready for this world, and I was learning to embrace who I was, and not to be ashamed. I did have quite a bit of fear regarding who I was during our reading, but I was learning how to let go of that fear, and be proud and accepting.

I had decided to confide pretty much everything to my Aunt Cynthia. I let her listen to the entire channeling session that took place last fall. I was so scared that she would think that I had really lost it, but something told me that said it was safe to tell her. Before she left my house she told me that she loved me know matter what or who I was. I know it was a lot to hear and take, but I believed that she would let me be whom I was.

CHAPTER 7

Mental Health Comes For a Visit
My Friends Think I am Crazy

March 30

As I had an energy session with Becca and my car could not drive on the highway, I borrowed Amber's truck. Becca said that she was concerned as my energy field was so small. She said that it use to radiate out of the room and now there was next to nothing.

She said that she had brought my energy level up by the end of our session, but that I was very fragile right now. She had asked how I was doing and I told her good except that my friends thought that I was crazy. She told me to stop worrying about people thinking that I was crazy when I knew that I was not. She said that I was being over dramatic and that they did not think that I was crazy, and that we lived in a different era. I was not going to be burned to the stake.

After the session, I proceeded to Amber's to drop her truck off. I decided that I was going to tell Amber that I was a starseed and share the channeling with my guides with her. My instincts told me that she thought that I was a crack pot, but Becca had just told me that I was being dramatic and exaggerating. I was just going to go for it.

When I arrived at Amber's, I went inside the house to give Amber her keys. She was not there. She knew that I would be there and my car was still there, so how did she get to where ever she was? Was this a sign that I was not supposed to say anything to her? Something did not feel right. I was not going to tell her just yet.

March 31

Kate phoned me just after 11pm, which was unusual for her to be phoning that late at night. She started the conversation with, "I have to tell you something, and we might not be friends after I tell you."

"What?! I am confused. What did I do?"

"You didn't do anything. I did something, but I did it because I care about you."

Mystical Puzzle

"Kate, what is going on? Just tell me whatever it is."

"I called mental health on you because I am afraid that you are depressed and suicidal."

"You're kidding me! Right?" (I started to laugh my head off.)

"No Tanya, I am not kidding. I am really concerned for you."

"Kate, I have not the foggiest idea why you would think that I am depressed and suicidal. I have been so happy most of the time that it is almost sickening. Everything is falling apart all around me and I am totally ok with it. Why would you think that I am suicidal?"

"Amber told me that you told her that you are going to kill yourself by the end of this year."

"What!? Why would she say something so stupid? I never said anything of the sort!"

"What do you mean? You never said that to Amber?"

"No Kate. I never said anything like that to Amber. I mentioned to her that if it were not for Sedona, I would have killed myself last year. I do not want to die. I love life! Each day I awake, I am excited to see what the day will bring."

"Tanya, I am really sorry. I honestly thought that you were suicidal and that I was doing something to help you."

"Kate, don't be sorry. If I thought a friend was in trouble, I would do the exact same thing."

"I'm so sorry Tanya! Whatever happens between you and Amber, can we please treat our relationship separately from that?"

"I know what this is about. It has nothing to do with Amber thinking that I am suicidal and everything to do with her thinking that I am crazy!"

"I just did what I thought was right Tanya."

"I know Kate. I am not angry at that. I am sure they are going to call my doctor so I will call her tomorrow to give her a heads up."

As I hung up the phone I started to think, last year when I really was suicidal, nobody phoned mental health then. In fact, I phoned mental health myself and they put me on the wait list. Something did not add up. I was right. They really did think that I was crazy. My worst nightmare was starting to come true! I knew this would happen. I knew this would happen as soon as I realized that something very profound had happened to me.

It was a good thing that I never told Amber that I was a starseed because we all know where I would be right now; locked up in a padded room! It really made me wonder how many people were in mental institutions that did not belong there. There are people on this planet that are gifted and ahead of our time, not psychotic wacko's.

April 1

I phoned my doctor's office and spoke to the secretary. I let her know that mental health would be contacting them and the reason why. I just had a doctor's appointment about a week ago. I am sure my doctor was going to laugh at them.

She had been wondering herself what happened to me in Sedona. I use to spend my appointments bawling my eyes out and telling my doctor that I could not do this anymore. I could not live! Now when I go to the doctor's, I glow from the inside out. Maybe once mental health talks to my doctor they would not bother me. I was sure that they would not come today, as it was April Fools day.

April 2

The phone rang in the morning and guess who? Uh huh, that is right, mental health! I tried to assure them that this whole thing was one big mistake and that they should just go talk to my doctor. The woman on the phone told me that they did speak to my doctor, but they would like to see with their own eyes that I was indeed ok.

I started to think that this could be rather entertaining. Therefore, I asked them when they would like to come over. She suggested ten minutes. Wow. What did I do to deserve this prompt attention? I told her to come on over. As I just finished smoking a joint, I thought I should at least try to spray the place down and air out the smell of pot.

A woman and man came together from mental health for the visit. I could see as soon as they entered that they were quite curious of my environment. "Why don't we just nip your curiosity right now, and I take you for a tour of my home." I took them in what I call the Healing Hut.

We all had a seat in the kitchen while they asked me all kinds of questions. None of them had to do with me being suicidal. They all had to do with my frame of mind. By the end of their visit, they were apologizing profusely for bothering me and told me that it was clear to them that I was not psychotic or schizophrenic. Bingo! As I had thought, they were not there to see if I was suicidal at all!

I asked why they bothered coming over if they had seen my doctor. Surely, she could verify all of this without them having to come over. Their response was my doctor gave me a clean bill of mental health and they had thought that I was so good, that I had fooled my own doctor.

Wow! I could not even imagine what Kate and Amber told them. Thank god I never told them everything that had been really going on. Before they left, this is what I said to them.

Mystical Puzzle

"I'm going to tell you a little something. Last year I was a complete mess! Due to my accident and losing the mobility of my left leg, I no longer had any desire to live. I know myself pretty well. I was on my way down a deep dark hole and the only way out was suicide.

"You see, I have been down that hole many of times. There is only one other time that I was this deep in the hole. I was twenty-two years old. I did try to commit suicide. I did die. I was kept alive with machines. As I could feel this happening again, I did not want to have to struggle with the constant thought if I should do it or not. You know, kill myself. I did not want to do it. I did not want to die! However, I could not go on feeling that pain any longer!

"I tried to get help. In fact, I phoned your very office. And do you want to know what happened. You put me on the waiting list. That is right! You put me on the waiting list!"

"Oh no. We don't do that."

"Oh yes! You do, do that because you did it to me. That was not the first time that I have cried out for help during my lifetime. Each time I have been put on a wait list. Now suddenly you are at my door because I talk to angels. So that is how it works?

"I am going to tell all my friends. If you are suicidal just tell them you talk to angels and they will come right away to help you.

"My name is Tanya Ebert. Keep an eye on that name. I am writing a book and this little bit that just happened here, just made it in the book!"

I said as I shook my finger back and forth in front of my face. They again apologized profusely and out the door, they went.

Once mental health left, it all hit me. This was for real! Amber really thought that I had lost my mind! She never called mental health last year when I really was suicidal. It was happening. This was how Amber leaves my life.

No soul mate that has had a profound part in my life experience stayed in my life. About six months ago, I told her she was not going to be apart of my life soon, and she told me that she was not going anywhere. She sure the hell was going somewhere. I could not have this in my life. I was going through something amazing, and I could not share the tiniest bit, with someone that I thought I would be growing old with, without them thinking that I had totally lost it.

This meant that I never knew Amber and she never knew me. I did not get this! Why could she not see what other people saw? They saw strength and love, she saw whack job! As I was quite upset, I wanted to get together with Amber and talk.

She told me that she was not feeling well because she just had a medical procedure done. Not feeling well?! Well I was not feeling well either, and I wanted to talk about it! Apparently, when a cyst bursts, your ears and mouth stop working as well. I found out that she was over at the neighbor's house and drinking alcohol, but could not talk to me about why she lied to me, and why she called mental health. I had forewarned her that if she lied to me, I would know.

I pretty much spent the day devastated that I was losing what I had thought was a good friend. What seemed worse was I was losing her because she seriously thought I was crazy. There was a chance that I lost more than Amber's friendship. There was her mom, her brother Toby, her sister in law Kate, her three dogs, cat, and bird as well.

I stood to lose a lot. Was this what it was going to be like with everyone? Were they all going to think that I was crazy? I did not want to walk down the street and have everyone start to point at me saying, she is that crazy woman! I cried to the point that my eyes were swollen shut. This was the first time that I had felt this hurt since I had been back from Sedona.

Later in the evening, I saw Lorne and Natasha and broke down crying. "Do you guys think I am crazy? Just tell me the truth!" Surely, they would know. They see me every single day. Amber saw me once a month if that. I spent more time with Amber's dogs, than I did with Amber these days.

"Tanya, you're not crazy and you know that! Tell them to phone us. We are the ones that see you everyday. They do not. You are different and that is ok. Amber is just an idiot! Do not worry about her. I told you that you would find out who your real friends were." Piped Lorne.

Natasha explained, "You know Tanya. I am going to be completely honest with you. When I first saw the tent in your living room, I went home thinking, she has lost her mind. She is crazy. She really is crazy! Then each day that I see you, you are not crazy at all. You are always happy. Yes, you are very different than you use to be, but you are definitely not crazy! Besides, we love the tent!"

Here was a strange coincidence. It is Misty's birthday today. I believe Misty has played a major part in my journey. Just as I believe that Amber has played a major part and this was the day that marked the start of the end of our relationship.

I headed into bed as I have had an emotional day to say the least. I felt so wrecked inside. So hurt and lost. It had been six months of heart ache free. I did not want to feel like this. I had not come this far too just feel like a waste of space. Screw that! I said a prayer at night and asked my guides to help me leave today where it was, and start tomorrow fresh, energized, and ready to take on the world.

April 3

As I went to bed early for my standards last night, I was up early in the morning. The hurt that filled me yesterday was gone, and was replaced with strength, and the will to keep moving forward on my journey. Ok, who was next? I thanked my angels for clearing all of yesterday's ick.

It was interesting that my friend Janice, unexpectedly, popped over and told me about a man in town who did tarot readings. She thought that I would probably be interested in meeting him. He just happened to live across the street. She gave me his name and phone number.

I emailed Becca my energy worker to let her know that mental health was at my place yesterday. I tried telling her at our last session that my friends thought that I was crazy, and she tried to tell me that I was being dramatic. It did not look like I was being so dramatic after all.

April 5

Janice came over for a visit and brought me over a smudge stick. What?! Were you reading my mind? I was just thinking that I needed to smudge my apartment after all the emotions that I just went through. Good call Janice!

I phoned XYZ Radio to speak with the intuitive named Darla. I asked her, "How many times have I incarnated on Earth?" This was the feedback she gave me.

"You are among the soul group of the Christed spirit. In this lifetime, living your truth is paramount."

Darla mentioned that she did not come from Christian based before mentioning, "The guides are showing me the sacred heart of Jesus with the knife in it and that you have known betrayal in this lifetime that only the Christ spirit could contain it, and actually live through it. You have observed others that are not living their truth and betraying themselves.

"Your mission is to heal your heart as a way of modeling the movement of light and the aspect of hope for those who have lost it. Step into your power of truth and you're at the aspect of your own confidence of your own knowing.

"I rarely use these words but a pre-determined time capsule within you, set off when you went to Sedona.

"Read Byron Katie. Read how she woke into her power.

"You have your own system to develop. As you are writing your book, you will receive information on a new system of understanding for humanity. This is a very important time for you; document everything you hear, see and feel. You have a lot of wonderful work ahead of you. You are in total alignment and willing to receive information."

Darla had asked if she had answered my question. I told her no, my question was not answered, but she gave me some valuable information. Darla explained to me that my question was too light weight and the guides will share what was most appropriate at the time. I thanked her before ending the call.

April 6

Apparently, Amber was now feeling well enough to send me an email, but never did have the balls to talk to me in person. The first time I read the letter, I thought to myself, it was terrible that this was happening to two good friends. Then as usual, my sixth sense kicked in and I started to smell a big pile of crap! I had warned her several times not to lie.

You see, Amber was not aware of a lit bit of information that I had received. She should know better that this was a small town and things have a way of spreading like wild fire. Before she had even sent me the letter, she was already trying to convince others not to hang around with me. It was a sick, sick feeling to think that I thought she was a good friend, and that we would be growing old together, and over time found out something opposite.

It made me feel as though I never knew her at all, yet I called her my best friend. It was truly amazing how dirty some people could become. I wanted this to be a case of a person that changed so much that there just was no common ground anymore. Therefore, you part ways thanking each other for the good times that were had, and wished each other well.

This was ridiculous! It was as if I was in the twilight zone. I was in total disbelief on how Amber was handling this. I did not quite know how to respond to her yet, so I was going to give it some thought, and a little bit of time.

April 8

I sent the following email.

Amber,

I have put a lot of thought into the recent events and I am clear where we need to go with our relationship, as I am sure you know as well.

When I came home from Sedona, I had forewarned you that there will be many changes happening, and I will be spending the next year pretty much hanging out with myself. I asked you not to take it personally. You are not the only one I had said this to. I said it to everyone whom I normally spend a lot of time with. Just because you can not go without human contact on a daily basis, does not automatically mean that I am the same way.

I still do not know how you misinterpreted the following, "If it was not for Sedona, I would not be here today," as I was planning to give it the rest of the year, (2008) to make my decision whether I would kill myself or not. I am not depressed or suicidal in the least.

In fact, I am so happy it is almost sickening. Now last year, no doubt about it, I was suicidal. I do not believe that you really think I was suicidal; I believe you thought I was / am psychotic. You are close though, but its called psychic, not psychotic.

The anxiety you sensed from me was me worried that you and the rest of the world would think I am crazy, which turned out to be correct. The part about you anyways, I do not know about the rest of the world yet.

As for you telling me on the phone that I cannot leave my apartment because I do not want to hang out with all the losers. Who are these losers you are talking about? The reason I do not go out often is that I am so extra sensitive; I pick up all of everyone's negative energies. I do not know how to control that yet.

It is not easy sitting at a table with people and not only hearing the conversations that they are saying, but also the thoughts that they were not. I am still dumbfounded that you actually thought I was depressed and suicidal.

The kind of feedback I have been getting from people is, wow, you look really good, you look happy; you are such an inspiration, that is the most powerful thing anyone has ever said to me, etc.

When my cousin went from being a junkie on the street to "Father God Christopher," it scared the shit out of me! I swore to god he was being brainwashed and I often had thoughts of kidnapping him and saving him. I kept my distance because we were not speaking the same language.

Although, there were times that he had asked me to go to church. For the most part, I cannot stand church, even today. I went to church for some of the ceremonies as they were important to him, and he was important to me. I sucked it up and I did it. I did not go every Sunday, but I went to his christening as that meant everything to him.

As time went on, I noticed that he was not brainwashed, he was still Christopher, just different. He is doing amazing things and helping so many people. I admire him for the courage it took to go from a drug dealing junkie on the street, to helping the people on the street.

Do I believe what he believes? No. Do I understand him? Not fully, but I am starting to. Will he and I ever see eye to eye on our beliefs? Not a chance in hell. His beliefs and my beliefs do not make us who we are, but I can put those aside because I care for him and love him.

I do not expect anyone to believe what I believe. I do not expect anyone to understand what I am going through. That would be impossible. It is one of those things that you just have to live to understand. I do not believe that I am holier than thou, and that I am any better than the next guy, because I am not. I am not perfect. I am content with not being perfect.

Mental Health Comes For a Visit – My Friends Think I am Crazy

You say that I said that I am going to ditch those that do not understand me or support me. I did not say that. I said that I would ditch those who thought I was crazy. How can I stay friends with someone who looks at me as if I am crazy?

I predicted about six months ago that this would happen, and you assured me that you were not going anywhere. I guess deep down, I knew otherwise. You see, you only lose one relationship; I have the potential to lose five people and five pets.

Remember when your anxiety attacks were bad, and it used to comfort you to lie on the bare kitchen floor? Where was I? Right beside you on the floor? Or looking from the sidelines thinking you were crazy?

God for bid if Kate or I show any signs of weakness and cry. Yet, it is ok for you to fall apart, and for us to stop what we are doing to help you. Yet when it is one of us falling apart, quite often you will tell us to suck it up.

Amber, me not being who I previously was, is an understatement. I have changed so much that I do not even know who I am anymore. I, like everyone else is meeting the new me too.

I know what you mean about not being able to converse with me, because I am having a hard time conversing with others as well. You hit it on the nose when you say we are in two completely different worlds.

I have changed so much that I do not fit in society too well. I have no intention of conforming and contorting to the way society or anyone wants me to be. Funny you should say that everything I speak about is metaphysical. Remember I am studying to be a doctor of Metaphysical Sciences, not just any doctor. One who is knowledgeable, and actually cares for her patients and their well being.

Overall, I still believe that you are one of my soul mates, but our time has come to part. I will always hold a place in my heart for you regardless of what happens. I thank you from the bottom of my heart for saying those words "Can you pop a wheelie Tanya?" For those words have led me to where I am today.

I can only hope that one day you will see your part in making whom I am and what I am going to accomplish in this life. Who knows, maybe our paths will cross again. I hope you do not turn into one of those petty women we use to speak of, tell all my deepest secrets, and try to encourage people to ostracize me. I will have that challenge all my life without your help.

I have been getting visions of you in Sue's garage, and during future family get togethers saying some not so nice things. I do not look at this as two people whom did rotten things to each other and can no longer be friends. I look at this as one person changing so much that the two people just do not fit anymore. It does not mean that any one of us is wrong or right. It simply means that I am going on a new path, one that you do not care to join.

Lorne does not believe or understand what I am going through. But he see's the changes in me for the good. He even has a cup here that has "666" on it and I could care less. He does not believe in my crystals, yet he will go to the creek for me and get me water, so I can cleanse them with creek water instead of tap water.

Does it matter to him whether its tap or creek? Nope! But he knows it matters to me and I cannot get to the creek so easily. Honestly, he could care less whether I cleansed them or not. He even told me that it makes no difference that I talk to rocks.

Out of everyone, I would have to say that Lorne has seen everything from before the accident, after the accident and after Sedona. I had expected him to make fun of me and not be my friend. It turns out he has been the most supportive through my entire last two years of my life.

Had he not lived across the hall, his and my relationship would not be what it was today. Had he not lived across the hall, I would have not made it to Sedona. Had he not lived across the hall, I would not be alive. He has been encouraging me in ways I didn't think he had in him.

Natasha even admitted to me a few weeks back that at first she seriously thought I had gone crazy. But each day she also noticed that I was always happy and content. After observing, she came to the conclusion that no, I am not crazy. Am I different? Oh yeah! Does she believe everything I say or understand it; no.

I am glad that phone call was made to mental health as it brought all of this into the open. It devastated and killed me inside at first to think my worse nightmare was coming true, my friends think I am a whack job!

I cried to the point of swelling my eyes shut and thought oh my god, what if this is how I am going to be now, depressed! I woke up the next day, feeling amazing! This whole situation gave me strength and courage to go on and share my story, instead of shutting me down and conforming.

If I can get through losing my best friend because of who I am, everyone else will be a walk in the park. Get your Oprah speech ready, because I am still bringing you. It will be interesting when Oprah asks you, so…. What do you think of your ex best friend now? I am even going to give you an autographed copy of my book.

I would like to visit you for closure and I guess we should exchange our keys back. I would really like to take a few minutes with each of the animals if you do not mind, because they are the innocent ones in all this and I will miss them terribly.

Mental Health Comes For a Visit – My Friends Think I am Crazy

I am shedding tears right now, thinking about how they are going to wonder why I am not visiting them anymore. It seems rather weird not to be your friend, as I had always thought we would grow old together. But like I had said earlier, who knows what the future will bring. Anything is possible.

And for gods sakes, I hope you know me well enough to know that I am not going to do anything, (hence – your old neighbor Karla who had your keys and it bothered you) and maybe on Friday we can get together as I am going out of town Wednesday, and not sure when I will be back on Thursday.

I wish you all the best! Love and light,

Tanya aka the crazy temporary cripple

xoxoxoxo

April 9

Amber sent me an email and insisted that we exchange our keys using a third party and she would not let me say goodbye to the pets. Oh how classic. She knew I really wanted to say goodbye to them and now she was withholding that from me, real nice Amber. Well, there you have it. Amber and I were no longer friends, just as I predicted about six months ago.

CHAPTER 8

Still Trying to Put the Puzzle Together

April 12

I phoned XYZ Radio to speak with the intuitive named Darla. I asked her, "Who is trying to connect with me when I try automatic writing and all I get is scribbles and SOS. What is blocking me?" This was the feedback she gave me.

"Ask who is trying to connect with you when you get scribbles and SOS and notice how your body feels. Do you feel good? Anxious? Be aware of who you are connecting with and how you are feeling at the time.

"Part of this block that you think you have has again to do with stepping in to what you believe to be your greatness. Another part of it is guides can play games. Ask them not to play games and that you need to get work done. Ask who are they? What are their intentions? Why do they want to work with you at 11am / 11pm?

"When we work with guides, they are serving us, we are not serving them. They assist us on moving forward to whatever plans we set up prior to coming in. It is very important to ensure that you are working with your guide and not a lower vibrational energy. You can identify with lower vibrational energies when you don't feel good or you feel anxious, your throat gets tight. Be sure to set the intention of only working with divine love. Work with what ever is light, white and the highest.

"You have a connection with Mother Mary. Your connection is to do with your connection to the earth and her nurturing of the earth. More from a nurturing point of view with healing issues with your mom. Move into forgiveness and compassion of being willing to be open with yourself and not listening to the essence of the relationship with your mother. Releasing old beliefs that block you based on fear and lack of stepping into your power based on your relationship with your mom. She doesn't need to understand you. You just need to forgive her and love her for who she is. People will not understand the path of a lightworker because they are not there. They do not need to understand. You need to accept the child within that your mom did not.

"Lack of acknowledgment within you and a fear of being wrong. You are blocking yourself due to a fear of being wrong. You need to self nurture to move into a space of light. You need to trust yourself and the process and allow yourself to not know. Be willing not to know why you are saying what you are saying."

I thanked Darla before ending the call. I had decided that for now, I was going to stop automatic writing. I am very much aware of the benevolent energies that surround me, but I am also aware of the dark energies. I did not want to take the chance of channeling them. I did not want to mess with something that I did not know a whole lot about.

April 13

I briefly saw Bob today. It was so hard to be in the same room as him. How did a person whose physical appearance happened to be the opposite of what I was attracted to, have me so smitten? If someone had shown me a picture of him a couple of years ago and told me that I would be smitten with him, I would have thought they were on glue! Yet I found him irresistibly sexy.

April 14

I awoke in the middle of the night with my left leg in the air and it was moving around. When I say in the air, I mean in the air. I was confused as I had just woken, and I was watching my leg move around in different positions. Rather than wonder by it, I just let it do its thing. It was obvious to me that this was some sort of spiritual healing.

April 16

Lorne and Natasha popped over and Lorne noticed that the smudge stick that Janice brought me had not been used yet. He pulled it out and put it on top of my desk in front of my monitor and said, "This better not be here tomorrow." It was so strange to hear Lorne talk like that.

Lorne had been trying to tell me that he was my mentor. I had tried to tell him that my mentor was someone older that I had not met yet. Lorne insisted that it was he. I swear to god that my guides and angels speak through him. He encourages me in so many different ways that was just not him. Sometimes I would stop him mid sentence and ask him, who was speaking through him because it was not Lorne.

It was interesting that I was upset that he had to do the midnight move, as he had not paid rent for four months. He had been there through thick and thin with me, and I really could not imagine that we would one day not be living across the hall from each other. Natasha moved in to the apartment next door to me and Lorne started to bunk with her. I guess that meant that I was able to keep my buddy around for a little bit longer.

It was going to take time getting use to having a neighbor again. I had forgotten how thin the walls were. If we were both using our bathrooms at the same time, no privacy if you know what I mean.

Lorne and I had conversations through the bedroom wall. I could hear when Natasha's alarm clock went off and every time they move around in bed. No one has lived beside me for six months and the previous tenant never slept in his bedroom. He slept in the living room.

April 17

My Aunt Cynthia phoned me and said that she has not had a bowel movement in a couple of days. She said she was doing well in that department after a couple of healing sessions with me earlier in the year.

I told her that this would give us the perfect opportunity for us to try a distance healing. I used my crystal singing bowl with the intention of my aunt's bowels releasing. I figured she should have a bowel movement by 9pm.

April 18

I phoned my aunt to see if she had a bowel movement last night and she said that she had not, but the cramping had gone away. I asked her what time the cramping was gone by and she said around 9pm. I told her that I would do another distance healing from home today, and hopefully that would be enough to bring upon a bowel movement.

April 19

I talked to my aunt and she finally had a bowel movement this morning. We would never know or have any solid proof that those distance healings worked. It made no difference as she was back to having bowel movements.

I finally decided to share my channeling with Lorne. He kept bugging me to tell him what had been really going on, but I would usually break down in tears and told him not to bring it up. I would tell him when I was ready, when I was ready to lose him as a friend.

We listened to the channeling together and he told me that he was not going anywhere. He was still my friend. Did he believe that I was a starseed? I did not think so. However, he allowed me to be me, whatever that may be.

Then the dumb ass said that he wanted to play himself in the movie. What?! What movie are you talking about? According to Lorne, this book would turn into a movie and the only way I was to allow it to happen was if Lorne could play himself.

We started to laugh and joke around about it. With my Aunt Cynthia's help, we came up with the perfect actress to play me. Drew Barrymore. We have a lot more in common than you would think, and the fact that she was in the movie, "ET" made perfect sense. Ok, back to reality.

April 21

It was a gorgeous spring day so Lorne and I decided to go for a walk through Othello Tunnels. Normally he pushed me while I sat in the wheelchair but I wanted to try something different today. I wanted to see if I could walk all the way to the last tunnel and back.

Actually, I would be pushing my own wheelchair but I would not be in it. I did not want to take the risk that I could not walk that far. If worse came to worse, I could just sit in my wheelchair and continue on that way.

We were walking through one of the tunnels and I could feel a spirit behind me. If it were any closer to me, it would be right on my back! I decided to try to communicate with him. Telepathically I said, I know you are there. Why don't you materialize in front of me instead of walking behind me?

I waited to see if anything would happen. Nothing had changed and he was still riding my tail. Again, I said, why don't you materialize in front of me instead of walking behind me? You don't scare me!

Just as that thought finished in my head, I was tapped on the shoulder repeatedly about eight times. I screamed and jumped over to the opposite side! Those were not light taps. They were very distinct!

"What are you screaming at? What is the matter?"

"Never mind! Just keep moving."

"Tanya, it is ok. Just tell me what happened."

"It doesn't matter what happened. Let's just keep moving!"

Lorne blocked my wheelchair and demanded to know what just happened. Then he sat in my chair and said that we were not going anywhere until I told him what happened. Usually I won those battles but since we were not in my home or my car, and he was sitting in my wheelchair in the middle of nowhere, I did not have much of a choice but to give in and tell him.

Once I explained what happened, he laughed and asked me why I screamed and jumped if I was not scared? "I will tell you why! I asked him to show himself to me, not tap me a whole bunch of times on my shoulder! I know it is a male. He is not evil or mean, just a mischievous little bastard!"

Lorne hopped out of my wheelchair and we laughed as we continued. I could not believe it. I went just past the last tunnel and back to the parking lot without using my wheelchair. It was not easy and I had to push my limits. I could feel the pain getting stronger, but that was the farthest I had gone since my accident.

Actually, I did use my wheelchair once. It was for fun though. There was a little bit of a hill leading back to the parking lot. It was amazing at what little of an incline could do for a wheelchair.

I sat in the chair at the top of the hill and used my good leg to give myself a big push down the hill. I had no control of the chair and I just hoped and prayed that I did not end up off the trail and into the bush.

I laughed and screamed for everyone to watch out so that I did not run into them! I did that every time we went to Othello Tunnels. Sometimes you would never know that I was thirty-seven years old. I tried to get Lorne to try, but he would not try it.

Later in the day, I phoned XYZ Radio to speak with the intuitive named Victoria. As soon as I told her my name, she asked me if I was working with my angels because I have strong angels around me. I asked her, "What was happening with my sight as I have been seeing red and orange colored letters in 3D and I am starting to see through the air?" This was the feedback she gave me.

"You are beginning to breakdown in your knowing what the frequencies all are, that make up reality. It is a weird thing. I often see weird things too. What is happening Tanya is you are having a waking up of your perceptions. If you can bear it, I mean I have done this work for a long time and all my waking up was very strange and sometimes it can be very scary because you don't know if you are losing it or what and you can't really talk to most people about it.

"You are beginning to awaken to perceiving other dimensions. You are just awakening your senses to be able to handle that. For you it is just going to keep unfolding. Bear with the weirdness now and it will get a little weirder but a little more explainable. You are just on route honey. You have tremendous support.

"Honey I will tell you something, the life you are going to live is so magical. I'm excited because you are going to be perceiving beyond your wildest dreams.

"I suggest that you watch the movie the *Peaceful Warrior*. Sometimes we need to be broken (your dirt bike accident) to be activated."

I thanked Victoria before ending the call. I believe I may have the *Peaceful Warrior* book but I will watch the movie as Victoria suggested.

April 22

I met Justin the tarot reader at one of the local coffee shops in town. Nice guy and knows his stuff, but I have decided that I would not do tarot readings as I much preferred channeled readings.

Justin emailed me after the reading to let me know that the interesting thing about the reading was there were no Major Arcana cards at all. He mentioned that it almost never happened that way.

I responded back and shared some of my awakening and that many of the intuitives and practioners that I had worked with have tripped out after a session with me. I was afraid that he might take my email the wrong way and that I should not have to explain to him that, I have my ego in check. I did not think I needed to explain to him that I knew that I was not Jesus reincarnated, nor his sister.

He responded with, I think you sort of got the wrong idea about the unusual nature of your cards. Turned it around in a sense, by making it into something "special."

I decided not to respond, as I did not want to have to explain that my ego was in check and that I was very well aware that I was no more "special" than the next person was. God, I feel like I could not even share bits of my story with awakened people without them misunderstanding me for having a remarkable experience.

Perhaps Justin had been awake for so long that the excitement I shared from my experience was a bore to him. You know like a been there, done that, I am way beyond that stage kind of attitude. One good piece of advice he gave me was that I needed to ground myself more and come out of la la land so to speak.

After the reading at the coffee shop, I came home and I set up my computer monitor in the Healing Hut so that I could comfortably watch the movie the *Peaceful Warrior*. As soon as I started to watch it, emotion started to well up inside of me and I began bawling my eyes out. I did not know why I was crying like that as the movie had hardly begun. I was an emotional mess!

I had no clue what the movie was about so I should not be crying already. It turned out that I cried during the entire movie. There were parts that I giggled through the tears. I felt his pain. I *know* his pain. How ironic that he had a motorcycle accident as well.

Unless you have actually lived through it, you have no idea how the words feel, when someone tells you that you were never going to walk and be the same again. There was no describing how the deep cut and despair felt, while hearing those words.

I thought I was ok with my disability. That it did not matter. That I was going to get through it. That I was going to take on the good, the bad, and the ugly with grace. Why was I bawling my eyes out and in such an emotional mess?! Did this mean that I had not made peace with my leg and my disability?

I was so confused! Where was my strength, courage, and oomph? I did not feel it. What if I did not make peace with it? I could not let it get me down. I had to keep moving forward. The only one I could count on to fix my leg was spirit and me. The doctors had clearly been useless in my healing.

Maybe that was part of the plan. That the doctors would not figure it out and I would fix it myself. That I would inspire people by showing them that you could get better and beat the odds just as Dan Millman did. He was quite the inspiration, and I could only hope that I continued to find strength and courage to beat the odds. His story had hit home so hard for me.

April 24

I phoned XYZ Radio to speak with the intuitive named June. I asked her, "Could you please shed some light as to why I sweat profusely while I am sleeping?" This was the feedback she gave me.

"Try rubbing a mixture of the following essential oils in a lotion and rub it on your ankles before going to sleep. Clary Sage, French Lavender, Tangerine, Bergamot. Your body is changing and transitioning.

"Are you aware of how much you travel when you are sleeping? You do a lot of work on the other side. You need to start recording a dream journal. Record even little things such as rainbow or saw a horse. This will help you to become aware that you are doing work on the other side.

"Your physical body is reacting to the work that you are doing in spirit, which is very vigorous. You are not transitioning slowly and easily back into your body. You need to become aware of the work that you do while you are sleeping because this is part of your path. You need to get a handle on what is going on, on a conscious level during your sub conscious dream time."

I thanked June before ending the call. I definitely believe that I did a lot of work on the other side. That was probably why I was always so tired when I woke up in the morning.

April 26

I phoned XYZ Radio to speak with the intuitive named Darla. I asked her, "How is writing my book connected with my past life in Egypt?" This was the feedback she gave me.

"You lived a variety of different lifetimes in Egypt. In one, you were a queen who dictated to a scribe. In another, you were a scribe who took information from a king. You felt that there was more information that the king could have shared, to be beneficial to his subjects. In another, you were a priest and you were prevented from sharing the secrets that you wanted to share with others. Do you have any other questions?"

Tanya – "Why was it so important to have this activation no matter what?"

"The guides responded with, why is it important to get up on time for work? Your job is to allow yourself to be an open vessel for information to flow freely. If writing, continue, if not, get going on it. Even if it doesn't make sense, it will prime you for the flow.

"Don't put the cart before the horse. Get in the cart and enjoy the ride, as the horse knows where it is going. Relax, the awakening has happened, there is a plan, but you do not need to know the end result as it will hamper the now. All will be shown when it is meant to be shown.

"You're in flux, do not worry. Get clear what you want to create and it will happen. Don't try and figure it out, just be open and willing to receive the financial abundance and everything more that you have contracted in this life time."

Before ending the call, I thanked Darla. Now I understand where the connection in Egypt lies. I was stopped from sharing the truth. I will not be stopped in this lifetime. I really did hope that the horse knew where it was going.

April 30

I phoned XYZ Radio to speak with the intuitive named Jessica. I asked her, "What is my spirit guides name and what are my most profound gifts unfolding this year?" This was the feedback she gave me.

"You have many spirit guides, about a group of ten. You can refer to the group as Michael.

"You are on the right path. Your heart is opening and expanding wider everyday. Your guides are happy with your progress. You have so many gifts expanding this year that it would be easier to say what gifts you will not have. You are in for a wild ride and do not forget that you asked for this. The more you relax and be, the more you will be guided.

"You are expanding in many, many huge ways. You need to ground yourself more. You need to clear your energies daily because you are so sensitive now that you are collecting a lot of other people's energy. Because your light is becoming brighter and brighter, there are psychic vampires that don't want the light shining that brightly, they feel that it needs to be dimmed so they will try to suck it from you.

"Drink water with a little sea salt with the intention of clearing any energy that is not yours and is not for your highest good. You can also bath in sea salt to clear negative energies. It is very important to ground and clear your energies because you are getting very bright with your light.

"If they are turning up the power a little too fast, tell them to filter it. You are in control of how much you are getting and as fast as you are getting. Don't say turn it up, turn it up, and then when it is turned up, get overwhelmed by it. You need time to adjust and align to the energies. It is advisable to smudge your home every week."

I thanked Jessica before ending the call. That was interesting because it was not that long ago when I did tell them to turn it up, and when they did, I was completely overwhelmed by the energy.

May 1

Something had been bothering me lately. Remember when my nephew Michael opened up my mini ketchup bottle that was for display only. I was a little pissed and told him he had to find me another one. Then I told him good luck because I had only seen them when I was in New York and Arizona. What was the matter with me?

I allowed something so ridiculous to get to me. With every thing that was happening in the world and I got upset over a stupid mini bottle of ketchup being opened. I had an attachment to those cute mini condiment bottles. I did not want to be attached to them. I had an idea. I phoned my nephew Michael.

"Hey buddy. How's it going?"

"Hey Auntie, I'm just watching a movie."

"Remember that mini ketchup bottle that you opened and I told you that you owe me a new one?"

"Yeah, I think I know where I can get those."

"No, no, no. Buddy. That is why I am calling. I have an idea. When you come up during the summer, we are going to the river, we will build a fire to cook hot dogs and roast marshmallows and we are going to use all the mini bottles; the mayo, ketchup and mustard."

"Auntie no, I know how much you love those bottles!"

"Exactly; there is no point in loving such a material item. Regardless if I have those mini bottles or not, it is not going to make or break me. This is my way of saying sorry for getting upset with you over something so ridiculously stupid!"

"Auntie, you don't have to do this."

"I want to do it! Not only are we going to use all three of the condiments, who cares if we get ketchup in the mayo or mayo in the mustard. We will mix them all up!"

"Auntie, are you feeling ok?"

"I'm feeling awesome! Woo hoo! We are using the mini bottles!"

"Oh my god Auntie!"

"Ok buddy, I will let you get back to your movie. I just wanted to let you know that you don't need to buy me a new mini ketchup bottle and that we are going to use them when you come up for the summer. Have a good day and I love you!"

"I love you too Auntie! Bye."

"See you later buddy."

I hung up the phone and felt so much better. I could look back now and laugh about how ridiculous it was to be attached to material objects.

May 6

Bob came over tonight. It seemed the more I talked to him and saw him, the more I was smitten by him. I could sit and talk to him forever about everything and anything. What was it about that man that made me so that I could not think straight? He was married for god sake! I could tell it was hard on him when we were intimate with each other. He had a young son and he just worshiped the ground that he walked on.

After Bob left, I went next door to visit Lorne and Natasha. Natasha answered the door, and could not look me in the eyes. She gazed down to the floor with a big smile and said, "I can't believe you! I am mortified!"

"Huh? What are you talking about?"

"I was in my bedroom trying to sleep! There is no way I could sleep through that and I had to come in the living room!"

"Oops! I thought I had turned up the music loud enough."

"My poor little head! Just for that you better smoke a doobie with us!"

"Ok, ok, let's go to my place and smoke a joint."

My first thought was did they really want to smoke a joint with me right now? When Lorne and Natasha read this part, they are going to kill me! I really do not think I need to explain it.

Poor Natasha. She was young and thought sex was somewhat disgusting. That girl had a lot to learn. I explained to her that one day she would be in her thirties and she would not know what hit her. I was sure that other women in their thirties could attest to this. Sometimes I actually felt like I was in heat! It was most painful to be in my prime and single. Prior to Bob I had only been intimate with a partner three times in four years.

May 7

I went to Becca's for my monthly energy session. She informed me that my heart and solar plexus chakra were not connected. She also suggested that I did not talk to any channelers as they were confusing me and to stop writing my book. She said I needed to start trusting and may need to move to an area to be with like minded people.

I left Becca's in utter confusement. I felt like I was living in two different worlds. One that I was living in all by myself and one that everyone else lived in. I dropped off my aunt's car as I had borrowed it to go to the session.

She noticed that I was a wreck and asked me what was wrong. "I live in two worlds. Everyone else lives in one world and I don't know how to live like this!" I blurted through the tears. She hugged me and told me to talk to Lorne.

She was right about talking to Lorne. I had been fortunate to see a side of him that I was sure most did not get the chance to see. He was such an ass sometimes but when it really counted, he was always by my side. Somehow, he was able to put his shittiness aside and had all the right words to convey to me.

I had no idea where those words came from. He did not believe in just about everything I said, yet he always encouraged me to keep focusing on why I was here. Whenever I was in a whirl, he always said the right thing to ground me.

He had truly been my rock for the entire last two years of my journey. I really believed that I would not be here writing this right now had he not been in my life. He had been a crucial part in keeping me going. I wonder if he really knew the big part he had played in all of this. The part he had played in my life, my journey.

I had decided not to go to sessions with Becca anymore. I felt like we just did not resonate with each other. The last three or four sessions had been somewhat frightening for her. Every session we have had, she told me that she had never experienced such happenings.

The first sign I received was when my dragon tried to chase her out of her own healing room. My first reaction was if the dragon was my protector, why was it chasing her away from me? My initial instincts at that time told me that I should not have any more sessions with Becca. Then I started to think, we have had many helpful sessions as well and I had continued to see her.

She told me that she could not continue one of our sessions and she let the guides completely take over. Next, she was worried for me and my energy was doing things that she had no clue about. I am not saying Becca was a bad practioner. She was a wonderful woman and practioner.

I think the straw that broke the camels back was when she told me to stop writing my book. I would continue to purchase crystals from Becca, but I believed it was in both our best interests that she not perform any healing sessions on me.

I had the weirdest dream the night after the session. The toilet would not flush because it was stuffed with too much toilet paper and clothes. Why would I be flushing clothes? I did not know what to make of it. I did a little research on the internet on dream interpretation and this was what I found.

Eliminating, cleansing, releasing, purifying. A blocked toilet may represent repressed emotions or an inability to express yourself. (*Dreams, Toilet, Blocked*, n.d.)

May 10

My aunt and uncle paid me the money for the car they bought from me a couple of years ago. I now had money to get myself a vehicle. I only had one thousand dollars and my uncle knew a guy that he worked with that was selling his van. I did not care about anything other than I needed something reliable.

It looked like it was in immaculate shape. I told the guy that I was handicapped and that it was of utmost importance that I had a reliable vehicle, and one that was not going to suck me dry with continuous repairs. He was originally asking fifteen hundred dollars but said he would give it to me for eight hundred dollars.

I took my new van to my mechanic and as soon as I pulled in his driveway, he told me that he hoped that I did not buy it because it sounded like there was a cylinder missing. He tested the van and sure enough, one of the six cylinders was completely dead. The only way around it was getting another motor.

I could not believe the nerve of some people. I told the guy that I was handicapped but all he cared about was the money for him. It made sense why he sold me the van for eight hundred dollars because he knew something was wrong with it but failed to tell me when I flat out asked him. He lied right to my face.

Another thing I had wondered was why my uncle did not look at it or test drove it. Perhaps he just assumed it was ok because the guy from work was selling it and he trusted him. My uncle was no dummy when it came to vehicles so I did not know how he did not realize that I should have never bought the van in the first place.

May 13

I had my first chiropractor appointment this morning. My doctor suggested that I try the new chiropractor in town as he specialized in helping patients with mobility. I had his phone number for about one month before I made the phone call for today's appointment. Had I known that his phone number consisted of 555, I would have phoned him long ago.

During my appointment, he pulled out a stainless steel looking instrument and said that he was going to use it to remove scar tissue from my knee and surrounding area. I asked him if he was using the graston technique on me. He informed me that he was.

Had I known that he used that particular technique, I would have been there long ago. My angel guide Marlene from Sedona had mentioned the graston technique to me. What I would like to know was why had no doctor recommended that kind of treatment?

If scar tissue could be removed without surgery, why were the surgeons not informing patients of that? Although the graston technique would not reach the scar tissue inside of my knee joint, it would break up the scar tissue surrounding my knee and area.

As the chiropractor was using graston on me, I kindly informed him that I had one good leg and it was about to kick him in the head! It was unbelievably painful! He warned me that it would not feel good, and that I would be in pain afterwards as well.

Somehow, I needed to get myself in a frame of mind that would help me get through the pain. I could not find that place. It was hard to find that place when your entire head and being was consumed with unspeakable pain. I had to find a way to get through it. If some of the scar tissue was removed, I may just get some more mobility.

May 14

I woke up completely soaked! That was one of my worse sleeps for wetness! I was really getting tired of not being able to sleep because I was soaked and my bed was soaked! I decided to take pictures of what my bed looked like because I did not think my doctor understood it when I told her that my bed was soaked!

On a good note, I just took my last Effexor pill. It took me forever to wean off! I think it had been a good four or five months since I started to wean off it. That was how bad the side effects were to come off it. I could have stopped taking it sooner, but it was actually painful and very hard to do. I know people that are reading this and have been on Effexor or Paxil, knew exactly what I was talking about. I was so glad that I did not have to take that crap anymore!

May 21

I phoned XYZ Radio to speak with the intuitive named Jessica. I asked her, "Do my guides think I should continue seeing the energy practioner that I have been seeing for the last six months?" This was the feedback she gave me.

Before she gave me the answer that she was getting, she wanted to know what I thought. I was not sure why, but I did not think I should continue with her.

"No. You have outgrown the sessions. Meaning your energy has grown so much and you have moved out of that modality of healing. The practioner is doing good work, but you have outgrown it. It is time to empower yourself more.

"You are becoming a very, very powerful young lady.

"I suggest you write a journal that is not for publication to help release changes and see growth and progress. Your book will be very successful. It will be out by the beginning of next year to the public. It will be done this fall and will take a couple of months for editing.

Mystical Puzzle

"Don't lose touch with human beings. Try the local coffee shop to do some writing and interact with people and observe."

I thanked Jessica before ending the call. I guess in order for my book to be on the shelves by the beginning of next year, I should have finished writing it by then. Unfortunately, that never happened.

May 26

I phoned XYZ Radio to speak with the intuitive named Victoria. I asked her, "Can my guides offer any advice as to why I am sweating profusely during my sleep? I literally soak my bedding at night." This was the feedback she gave me.

"You know what is interesting, you are boiling something out. I can feel it in me. They are showing me in your second chakra, have you had a check up lately because you have some old subconscious stuff boiling out of your body like mad."

Tanya – "I had a hook removed from my second chakra a few months back."

"But honey you know this, in the second chakra we have a lot of subconscious programming. The first thing they are showing is that you have a process going on that is literally boiling out of your second chakra, some tremendous like old old soulier collection of energies, ancient stuff girl. Old abuses, old beliefs and old stuff; you are evolving like mad.

"You need to have daily baths with Epsom salt or apple cider vinegar. Not both at the same time or you will foam over.

"Bless this transformation because it is changing your brain and the way your mind works. All your systems are adjusting.

"Are you seeing a chiropractor?"

Tanya – "I am currently seeing a chiropractor for my leg."

"You have subluxations in the sacrum area. Your spinal vertebrae are out of whack. Partly because of your removal of the attachment, and partly because of your leg. Where you are having the transformational sweats emanating from, there are blocks in the vertebrae.

"It is all coming together, keep going as you are doing fine. You're going to be quite an amazing woman. You're going through a tremendous healing phase in your life and you are going to be awakened majorly in the next while.

"A lot of the stuff that is boiling out of you is resistance, reaction, and defensive, fears boiling out and boiling out."

I thanked Victoria before ending the call. She was not kidding when she said this transformation was changing my brain and the way my mind worked. I could not look at anything like I used to. Just watching people go about there day was different. Looking out my window, I did not see what I used to see. The word change almost seemed an understatement.

June 2

I saw Bob today. He had not worked in town for the last couple of months or so. His wife and son were in town as well. No, we were not intimate. I would never attempt that knowing that his wife and son were across the street. It was bad enough that he was a married man.

I never knew it that day, but that was the last day we saw or spoke to each other. I sent him a couple of texts and wished him a happy birthday and he never did respond to them. I was not going to chase someone who was unavailable. I would have never gotten involved with him had he not made the first move.

Oh well, it was not as if I expected him to just leave his wife and son and we would live happily ever after. Life did not work like that. I did not understand why so many people stayed in relationships that they were clearly unhappy in. I wish him and his family all the best.

June 6

There was a spider crawling on my bed. It reminded me of something weird that happened when I woke up in the middle of the night. It is so hard to explain this stuff sometimes. When I open my eyes, I see strings of energy coming from above. They were all over the place like a web. I was not dreaming that as something usually awoke me and when I opened my eyes, I could not really make out what was going on.

It was as though stuff was being downloaded into me. I did not understand the language, but I could feel it entering within me. I was guessing that when the time was right, I would know all I needed to know. I did not understand what was going on when that happened, so I would just go back to sleep.

June 8

I had a reading with Brianna today. This was the feedback that she gave me.

"The first thing that I am getting is with your left leg. What is happening with your left leg?"

Tanya – "I had a dirt bike accident two years ago."

"Have you ever placed lemurian seed crystals on your leg?"

Tanya – "I can't believe this, but I have a lemurian seed crystal in my hand right now as we are talking."

"I'm seeing seven to eight different crystals on your leg. I'm seeing them placed with four wands pointed towards your knee, starting from your ankle and three wands coming from your thigh pointing downwards towards your knee. I see a round black stone placed on your knee, maybe tourmaline, or obsidian.

"When the stones are in place, put out the intention and ask what is blocking the energy from flowing? It is ready to flow, it wants to flow, but it is blocked. Place the intention and ask if anything needs to be released first. Pay attention to what comes up. You might feel an emotion or a memory or a feeling, etc.

"Merlin's energy just came through to help heal your knee with his huge full on laser wand. He will guide you for this process. He wants to bring me to a past life in Avalon and Glastonbury, England."

At that point, I explained to Brianna that I had planned a backpacking trip around the world before my accident. At the time that I had planned my trip, I unknowingly picked places all around the world that were known as energy power spots. However, for some reason I had no desire to go to Europe. I would go to Israel and Cambodia but keep me away from Europe! I had also explained that since I had gone through that huge awakening last September, I had been scared shitless of someone trying to hurt me because of it.

Brianna explained the following.

"You are stepping into your power. You are embracing your power. You are really connecting with your truth. There is definitely something there. This may come forward through this reading. If you feel comfortable with it, we can proceed.

"Yes, definitely England. You have a lot of past lives in England and a lot of old witchy stuff as well. I'm actually seeing the top of Glastonbury Tor, Saint Michael's mound. That is a very powerful spot. There is something linked with you.

"I am getting an image of you being initiated into power into some sort of sisterhood and you were the leader. You were there all day at sunrise, sunset, and moon ceremony. It was a transition period.

"The number three comes up. The sunrise, sunset, moon, your knee, and the process I am going through are all linked. My body has chills and I am so excited for your journey. The sunrise is the awakening. The sunset is the acceptance. The moon is embrace your power.

"As the moon sets, you are completely in your power and have your arms up towards the sky. As soon as you accepted your power, someone shot a sharp object into your knee. Someone came and put an arrow or sword or something through your knee. This is pretty potent!"

Brianna brought me back to that past life. It was emotional. Emotions were coming up from places I did not know.

"The retreat is going to be transforming. I have chills. You are going to be at the right place with the right people to help you through the next huge shift. An Asian guide has come in like an old age prophet and will connect with you at the retreat.

"You have many stories to tell Tanya, and I am sure that you will be writing more than one book.

"There is another door opening for you in September. Be aware of doors opening for you.

"Intuitive training in Vancouver will be extremely good for you. You will be able to meet like minded people. This will bring you great freedom.

"There is a soul mate coming in that is like minded. This may be linked with the retreat or meeting in nature. Or perhaps in your relationship you will spend a lot of time in nature. There is a number three linked to this person. This could be linked to three weeks, three months, the month of March; the number three in some way is linked. There is definitely romance coming and an awakening of some kind in a relationship. Your body is going to come to life in many ways. Snake energy is coming through. This is linked to sexuality and healing powers.

"Bob is from a past life in the Mediterranean, Italy, or Spain. That is why you feel such a connection to him."

Tanya – "Can you offer any insight into my severe night sweats?"

"The first thing that comes to me is your body is detoxing. I don't feel concerned. I actually think it is apart of your ascension process. A huge awakening is happening, not only spiritual, but mental and physical as well. Your body is really waking up. You will be experiencing sexuality in a big way and I see your body glowing golden right through.

"You will inspire so many people.

"You were a catholic nun in another life. You are here to become totally enlightened in this life time. You have lived so many difficult past lives because of whom you were and you are always going to voice your opinion. You are that type of person except for your life as a nun.

"You have come into this life with a huge purpose and along with huge purposes come huge challenges and that's why you have gone through what you have gone through, but you are coming out to the other side now.

"You are going to connect with a lot of totally like minded people. You have got some great new friends coming into your life."

Tanya – "Thank you Brianna for all that you shared with me."

Mystical Puzzle

Good grief! A nun? I have no idea why I would pick such an experience. Maybe to witness how corrupt the church really was. Fuel for the fire so to speak.

June 13

I went to my first native sweat in the evening. Considering I have sleep apnea and lung disease, I found it easy to breathe. One thing I found quite odd was during the sweat, we would each take turns sharing what we were grateful for. One of the men said that he was grateful for all the people he fucked up.

What?! That did not sound right to me and the person heading the ceremony did not say anything. I found that to be quite negative, and why was he grateful for the people whom he had hurt in the past? I really did not get much from the sweat. I have had some profound experiences lately but nothing really happened during the sweat. I did not feel cleansed or received any visions, insight, or anything.

Once I got home from the sweat, I went over to Lorne and Natasha's place. They were camping, so I was taking care of their cats. It did not take long before I ended up falling asleep. I woke up with my arms and legs thrashing about in the air. Something kept trying to bug me when I was sleeping and I was fighting it.

I was not feeling comfortable there anymore so I left. Spirits were bugging me. I went next door back to my place to discover that I was next door for three and a half hours, not one hour as I had thought. I went to bed right away and no spirits were bugging me there.

I was having extreme difficulties seeing my light body when I closed my eyes. In addition, I was not seeing through the air as I use to. Did something take part at the sweat or next door? What was going on? I had a dream during the night that someone was chopping off my hair. I looked up the dream meaning on the internet and one of the meanings was loss of power. (*Dream Moods – Haircut*, n.d.)

June 23

I phoned XYZ Radio to speak with the intuitive named Victoria. I asked her, "Can my guides offer any advice as to whether I should go to sweat lodges or just not the one I went to a week and a half ago?" This was the feedback she gave me.

"You picked something up, didn't you? What I feel is you just took on a lot of darker frequencies there because everyone is clearing their energies, right? Your energies need to be cleared. Try bathing with Epsom salt.

"You need to better protect yourself and not go to sweats for awhile. I'm getting a belly ache from someone that was at the sweat. That is just evidence for me that there was something really dark. It is not nasty, nasty; it is just that someone had a deep pain and depression. And you sucked it in. It is right in your navel area.

"Don't panic but you need to find a better way to clear yourself up and protect yourself. As you clear this you will pop open further into your intuitive knowing."

I thanked Victoria before ending the call. I knew something happened at the sweat!

June 30

I had been waiting for this day for over six months. The angel woman from the furniture store phoned me. Her name is Carol. She just got my message today. She had mentioned to me that when she had woken up yesterday, she had a feeling that she needed to go to Hope for some reason.

She did not know that I lived in Hope and then proceeded to ask me where I lived. I love it when those things happened. We were planning to meet during the week. She was going to drive here from White Rock. I was so looking forward to meeting her again!

July 2

Carol, the angel woman from the furniture store came to Hope to visit me. She explained to me that the accident she had was in the furniture store that she worked at. She tripped and fell. When she went to the hospital, the injuries she sustained were so severe that they had thought a truck hit her. They could not figure out how she sustained such injuries in a fall. When she tried to explain it to me, she said it was as if she was picked up high in the air, and then dropped.

I took Carol to a local restaurant for a bite to eat. She tried to pay for the bill but I insisted as she came all that way to visit me. Next time we got together, I would go out her way. Did I mention her home phone number had 888 in it.

We had a nice visit and I was so glad to connect with her again. We shared a lot of our woo hoo stories. There were not too many people that I could share such information with. Most people did not understand and or thought that I was a bit cuckoo. It really was hard to believe that she was sixty-five. She did not look it at all, and did not act like an old fuddy duddy. She was such a joy to hang around.

A couple of hours after Carol left it came to me. I knew why she thought she was going to die, because that was exactly how I felt before I had the soul death and rebirth. I bet she was going to have a dramatic awakening too! Because I had already gone through one, I would be able to assist her. It had to be something. I did not hear *the Voice* that often, so there must be an important reason why we had crossed paths.

July 3

I had been feeling quite tired and had next to nothing for drive and energy since the sweat lodge. I drove over to Takhi's shop and asked to talk to her about the sweat I attended that she facilitated. I explained to her that I had extreme difficulties seeing my light body and over time noticed that I was no longer seeing through the air. Not to mention I had been extremely tired and had no drive.

I asked her to please help me understand what had happened and asked for advise on what to do to reverse what had happened. Immediately she stated that what ever it was that was wrong with me, did not happen during her care because she always made sure that everyone was grounded. What ever it was, she said was my fault.

I was clearly upset with what she was saying, as she would not even discuss the possibility that something negative happened to me during the sweat. I was in near tears and she was smiling while telling me that perhaps I did not need to see my light body anymore and that maybe I needed to eat some wheat. What?!

Something did not feel right. I could tell you one thing; I would never do a sweat with Takhi again. Nor would I purchase anything from her. I always wondered about her. I wondered what side she was on and if she could be trusted.

A lesson I learned was do not trust someone because they stated that they were from the light and were healers. Some people out there pose as healers only to steal the energies of their patients. I went in blinded, ungrounded, and trusting Takhi to the fullest.

July 4

I phoned XYZ Radio to speak with the intuitive named Candace and healer named Sharon. The first time I called in, somehow I was disconnected. It was 2:22 when I was disconnected. I phoned back and I asked them, "I went to my first sweat lodge about three weeks ago and I am wondering if my guides have any feedback on that?" This was the feedback Candace gave me.

"Before we ask Sharon to comment on that, let me ask you something. When you went through that experience, how did you feel afterwards?"

Tanya – "Not good."

"That's the point that I am trying to make."

I explained everything that happened since the sweat.

"Tanya you really know what happened, don't you? You are developed enough to really know what happened. You are a developed individual spiritually and I would say metaphysically. Because of the nature of who you are, you need to be careful of the places you go to, especially when you place yourself in someone else's direction. You are a master in the making and before you go and commit yourself to anybody else's influences, you need to connect with your higher self and make sure that it is in your best interest."

Sharon – "You were not grounded. There were some dark energies attached to you at the sweat lodge and I have released them. A portal was created so that they can never come back. Your guard was down. Always ask your higher self for guidance."

I thanked the two of them before ending the call. That was two confirmations that I have had. I knew something had happened. It just felt better to have it confirmed from extremely skilled intuitives. I guess I needed to learn to trust my instincts more no matter how ridiculous they seemed sometimes.

CHAPTER 9

Spiritual Retreat? Yeah Right! More like a Cult!

July 5

I had just been informed that I was the last participant accepted for a nine day retreat in Heffey Creek, coming up in less than two weeks. I had my eye on that retreat center since last fall. I tried to attend a four day retreat in May, but all the spots were taken. I was actually on the waiting list for the nine day retreat, and because a few people had canceled, I made it to the last participant accepted. The maximum number of participants was eighteen.

I was really looking forward to a peaceful spiritual retreat. What really intrigued me to that retreat was the facilitator was an awakened teacher. I had been feeling so out of sorts and lost lately, that I really needed somewhere to ground myself, and learn to relax and not be in fear.

I hoped that I would meet other people like myself. I really yearn to have contact with others like me. To be able to talk to someone who really knew and understood what I was going through. I just wanted that connection that I was not all alone with this phenomenon.

July 7

On the way back home from Chilliwack, my friend David and I noticed a hitch hiker. David proceeded to pull over. The hitch hiker approached the van and he had piercings and tattoos all over his face.

The sad thing was, because of the way he looked, most people would be frightened to give him a ride. I learned during the thirty minute drive what a cool person he was. Many people were missing out by not connecting with him.

David introduced me to a documentary called *Home Project*. After watching it, I could not imagine why everyone just kept doing what they had been doing. Do people not know that we are abusing the natural resources so much that we will run out in this life time? It was not going to matter how much money you had if the resources have been used up. Before my awakening, I was not an aware person. David was not awake but he was definitely aware.

Mystical Puzzle

Well I was all packed and ready for Heffey Creek. I hoped that the van would make it without any problems. I was sure it would be fine if I just took it easy. I was really looking forward to some peace and quiet and balancing myself out. I felt like I had been holding on for dear life waiting for the retreat. I really needed the time to balance myself.

I was also using that time at the retreat to quit smoking. I figured that if I could go nine days without smoking, it would be pointless to start up again when I got back home. That would also give me an opportunity to cut down on smoking pot. I smoked much more than I cared to.

I said a prayer to keep me safe during my trip and then walked around my van with my lemurian seed crystal to place a ring of protection around it. I would not have to worry about getting a speeding ticket, as I probably could not do the speed limit. With one of the cylinders blown, it made the van gutless. The entire drive was through hilly mountains, so I was sure that I would be in the slow lane the whole way. I left town at 4pm.

Ok, I did not know what was wrong with my van or should I say right? I was passing new cars going up the hills doing at least one hundred and fifty kilometers. Sometimes I caught myself doing one hundred and seventy kilometers! I was fricken flying! It only took me one hour and forty-five minutes to get to Heffey Creek. I smoked my last joint for nine days and my last smoke before arriving at the retreat.

Upon arriving, I discovered that the tenting area was a switch back of a climb to the top of the property. I guess the only time I would be going to my tent was when it was time to sleep. It was a hard enough to walk on regular ground and that was all up hill. Volunteers at the retreat carried all of my stuff to the tent area.

I did not have long to set up my tent as the retreat would be commencing at 7:30pm. That evening was a welcome kind of night and we ended it with a meditation. I could not get comfortable and my knee was killing me. It was hard to concentrate on the meditation when all I felt was pain.

The evening was uneventful. I found out that I was the only participant that had never been to one of these retreats. I headed up to my tent at 10:30pm. There was one other man tenting there. He had come all the way from England to attend the retreat.

Between the noise from the highway, my tent neighbor snoring, the dog that would not seem to shut up, and the trains bumping into each other at the train yard, I could not sleep! What a great way to start my relaxing retreat.

Spiritual Retreat? Yeah Right! More like a Cult!

July 18

It was nice to be woken up with tingshaws instead of an alarm clock. Wake up time was 6:30am. It was hard to have a shower when there were only two bathrooms and eighteen of us.

First meditation was at 7:30am. I was laying there with the group of eighteen and all of a sudden, I felt sadness come over me and my eyes were welling up with tears. I did not know what was going on because those were not my emotions. I did not have anything to cry about and nothing just happened. I opened my eyes and noticed one of the participants near me was crying. Oh great, I was picking up other people's emotions.

After the meditation, everyone got up and started to move around. Not just regular kind of moving around, it was something that I had never seen before. One part of it was somewhat interesting as some people were very free in expression. They were all milling about wrapping their bodies around each other but not physically touching.

It started to get a little out of hand, as people were flailing about. My leg was not that stable to be in an environment where people were moving about all over the place. I was almost knocked down a couple of times. I ended up walking out of the room and sat on the stairs outside of the meditation room.

I was a little upset because I was not able to participate and I really did not know what they were doing. I was open minded, but it felt somewhat weird what ever was going on. It also struck me that I was not feeling good about my disability. I thought that I had put it behind me, but I realized that I had not when I was put in situations that I could not participate. I had been tricking myself by only putting myself in situations that I knew I could participate. I did not feel solid. I did not feel ready to take on the world.

I did not know if it was my leg or that I was picking up other peoples emotions, but I was feeling quite messed. Something was not right. I had not been there twenty-four hours and I have wanted to leave a few times. I would try to stick it out, as I believed everything happened for a reason. There was a reason that I was there.

Our next session was at 10:30. There seemed to be a lot of crying and emotional stuff going on. I did not quite understand why. I thought that this was supposed to be a peaceful retreat.

After lunch, I kicked back on one of the benches. The property was peaceful, but the people were not. What I meant was they were not at peace. They were all hurting very deeply. I thought I would be at a retreat with people who were awake, but I did not see that happening at all. I did talk with one man named Ruben for a bit. I shared quite a bit of what had been going on with me. He told me that I needed to be careful of whom I told, and that I could not just trust people there.

After dinner, we did some meditations and some exercises with partners. Honestly, I was not getting this place. I did not know what was going on and it did not feel right. This was not what I signed up for. I felt like I wanted to go home again.

The participants were nice and it was not as if I was not enjoying their company. It was just, I did not know. I did not think anyone other than the facilitator was awake and that was what I was really looking for. Connecting with people that had gone through what I was going through, learn, and grow from our exchange of information.

I was hoping to gain some strength, courage and answers; answers that I was not alone, that there were others like me. I knew there had to be, but where were they? It was disappointing because I had been looking forward to going there for almost a year. Now that I was there, I just did not get what that place was and what the purpose was.

I headed to my tent just after 10pm. I hoped that I would get some sleep. It was extremely windy. It felt like my whole tent was going to blow off the mountain. I hoped that with all my belongings, and me, it would keep put.

July 19

As usual, I did not sleep last night. I was lucky if I got any actually. My tent was thrashing around in the wind. All my tent pegs were lifted. My tent neighbor was yapping all night with someone and then once his guest left, he snored his face off. At 8:30am, the group left to go on a blind folded hike. I was going to take advantage of the peaceful property and hung out by the pool.

I found myself questioning what this place was again. I was just not getting it and I was not getting anything out of being there. With all the meditating we did, you would think that I felt something. I did not feel like I had been guided to any kind of altered awareness. More like, what the fuck was this place awareness! I felt like I wanted to leave. I would try to stick it out, just not sure how long.

I asked Sara the coordinator, if she could ask Liz the facilitator to put aside some time to talk to me. Liz never did talk to me.

July 20

Again, I did not sleep. Again, I was questioning what this place was. I was really starting to feel resentment to having to spend nine days there. I could not sleep, I did not feel good, and there was nothing spiritual about that place. I had not seen any crystals around the home and there had been no talk of the higher self or angels. What there had been was a whole lot of was staring into each other's eyes while sitting across from each other.

I did not understand why I was having such a hard time there when I had always felt that I was supposed to be there for some reason. I guess I would just keep plugging away and just go with what ever reason that I was supposed to be there. Without a doubt, I was supposed to be there, but why? I had wanted to leave since I got there. I was just not getting anything there. There was nothing balancing and peaceful about this place other than the yard.

I guess what I was looking for was some kind of routine and balance; and to find others like me. Were they awake? Did they know what it felt like? I just wanted to find someone like me! I was not finding that there.

During the evening exercise, we were asked to find a partner. I usually hum and haw whom to partner up with, but for some strange reason, I got up and went straight to Mitch. We had to sit across from each other and stare left eye to left eye without blinking.

After about ten minutes of that, something weird started to happen. Mitch's face was shape shifting. What ever it was shifting into, it was not good, and it was not from the light. I stopped it from developing. I did not want to see what it was.

Every time his face would start to shape shift, I would stop it. Did he realize that he was doing that? What did that mean? After each exercise, we always discussed what happened. I was sure the hell not sharing that with the group!

Once the group was done sharing their experiences, we all laid down to do a meditation. When I lay down and closed my eyes, I felt like getting up and bolting. I did not know where that was coming from. I knew I was not having a great time there, but my body literally felt like getting up and getting the heck out of there! I really did not understand where that strong urge was coming from. I was struggling to lay there.

After the meditation, we were asked to share our experience. Good god! I was not expecting what was about to happen. Before I knew it, Liz the facilitator was in an argument with Mitch one of the participants. He got up, said fuck this shit, and out the door, he went. Mitch was the man that shape shifted on me and he was lying beside me during the meditation, when all I could feel was to bolt and that was exactly what he just did, bolted!

Everybody else seemed to already know, but I did not until then that Liz and Mitch was a couple. Then Liz said to Belinda, "Perhaps Belinda you shouldn't have been massaging Mitch the other day. I'm not jealous or anything and he can do what he wants, but perhaps it was in appropriate."

Then Liz said, "Mitch likes all the pretty young girls, doesn't he Ruby. Mitch knows he is free to do what he wants." Ok Liz, I thought you said you were not jealous. You had jealousy written all up and down you.

We then spent the next two hours discussing how to get Mitch back into the group. Liz said that she just needed to give him space and he would hopefully return. Some of the other participants, whom were also volunteers that worked on the property, were quite upset and felt that they did not want their relationship to change with him, therefore they concluded to walk on egg shells around him, so as not to upset him or their relationship with him. That place was just too much drama! I did not come to live in my own live soap opera for nine days! Had I wanted that, I could have just arranged a family reunion.

I found out that dinner was our last meal for twenty-four hours as we were told we were starting a fast, silence and a vision quest. Most of the participants hiked up the mountain during their vision quest. Some of them even did it at night. Due to my leg, I would be unable to do that.

As Liz did not really give much guidance on the vision quest and everyone else had done them several times, I was not sure what to do. I heard they could be very powerful but I also heard that there was lots of preparation involved beforehand. As there really wasn't much of any preparation or discussion on what to do, I had to assume that it was just some kind of mini vision quest and not like the one I was going to do for four days in a cave.

We were also informed that after the twenty-four hours of silence, we would be doing a sweat at 3:30am. Oh my god! There was no way I wanted to participate in the sweat. The facilitator was an emotional mess after her big fight with her boyfriend. I did not want to have any part of the sweat.

I had seen what happened to me after my sweat with Takhi and I did not want to mess around with that. You can not facilitate a sweat if you are an emotional mess. Clearly, she must know that! This place just got weirder by the minute.

You know what? I just thought of something. Ruby looked disturbed during the day. Almost trance like. I could not put my finger on it, but she was not herself. She seemed so robotic with nothing behind her eyes. Liz referenced her and Mitch during all the drama. Mitch shape shifted on me. What the hell was going on?!

I was so glad to be back in my tent! This place was ridiculous! I could not believe the facilitator was a part of so much drama. By the way, the non smoking had been going good and I have not had one since I had arrived there.

July 21

Of course, I did not get any sleep! It was impossible with all the snoring that came from the tent next to me and the noisy train yard. I did not know what they did down there, but it was loud! It sounded like the train cars were smashing into each other.

I was supposed to be doing a vision quest and had been given no guidance other than do not talk, do not eat and listen for the messages. I read one of the books that Liz had written. From reading the book, I believed that at one time, good things use to happen there, but I really question that now.

While I was sitting out by the pool, I noticed a humming bird across from the pool. I tried telepathically to talk to it and asked it to come over and visit me. Low and behold, the little guy came over and buzzed right above my head. That happened three different times.

I always went to the bathroom before going to bed. I did not know how or why but something told me that we were not having the sweat at 3:30 in the morning. I went to my tent around 9:30pm. I was hoping to get some sleep. Although I did finally get some sleep during the day.

I was tossing and turning for a good portion of the night. At one point, I heard a dirt bike or quad up the mountain just above where I was tenting. It was dark and I did not want that person to go through the fence and land on my head. I got out of my tent and started to flash my flash light so that who ever was out there, knew that I was there.

He was saying something to me, but I could not hear what it was. I knew that I was supposed to be in silence but I yelled up the mountain that I could not hear him. Out of curiosity, I turned on my cell phone to see what time it was. It was 11:11.

July 22

We were woken up with the tingshaws at 3am to end our silence and start the sweat. Liz informed us that the fire department would not renew her license to burn so we were unable to do the sweat with hot rocks. I knew it! Thank you my angels!

I was worried about having to do a sweat with the condition that Liz was in. We still did the sweat; we just did not have the fire and all the heat. At the end of the *pretend sweat,* we were asked to go for a dip in the pool. Huh? I was not told about this. I did not have my bathing suit with me. Oh, what the hell, I dropped my sarong and went in naked like everyone else. No one else seemed to have a problem with being naked, so why should I?

That was one thing that I would like to work on. I did not want to be ashamed of my naked body around others. If my leg were not screwed up, I would start hanging out at Wreck Beach. For those that did not know, Wreck Beach was a nudist beach in Vancouver. The only problem was it was a long steep hill to get to the beach. My leg was not stable enough to do that. Besides, once I got on the sand, it would be difficult to walk on because the ground was not completely level.

We sat for four hours to listen to the experiences of all the vision quests. My leg was just killing me! I did not share anything, as I did not feel like I really had a vision quest. You know what? I have had it with this place! I was tired of all the drama and picking up everyone else's emotions.

I could imagine they were going to give me all kinds of grief about wanting to leave, so I was not going to be able to ask for help to carry all my belongings down the mountain to my van. I had no choice but to slowly do it bit by bit throughout the day.

Now here was the challenge. There were eighteen people milling about. I needed to carry all of my crap from my tent to my van without anyone seeing me. Well, I guess it would be a good time to practice being invisible.

I put the thought intention in my head that I was invisible to all on the property. It was a little difficult being invisible with a cane in one hand and all kinds of luggage and crap in the other. I did not know how I pulled it off, but I did it. I just focused on being invisible and getting all my stuff to my van without being noticed and it worked.

I talked to Sara and told her I was leaving. She told me to tough it out. I buckled and said that I was not guaranteeing that I would stay, but I would take it hour by hour. I did not think it was doing me any good picking up everyone else's emotions and negativity. They seemed to think that it was, and that I should stick it out.

I was ready to bust! I could not handle it there anymore! Since Liz ignored my request to talk to her a few nights ago when Sara asked for me, I was going to ask her myself. When I asked if she had a few minutes to spare for me, her response was, "Well I am kind of tired and want to get some rest. But, ah, ok, if you really need to."

Wow, does that not warm your heart. Gee, I hope I was not putting her out too much for a few of her minutes. I explained to Liz that I was picking up on other people's emotions and it was fludding me to the point that I could not function there, and that I wanted to leave. I also told her that I had a strong urge to bolt during the meditation when I was lying beside Mitch, and he ended up bolting that night.

Liz immediately pointed the finger at me. She stated that maybe it was my fault that Mitch had bolted and perhaps he was picking up stuff from me. Then she told me that everything that I was feeling was mine and no one else's. I just love it when people tell me what I was feeling, and what I was not feeling. I could see this was going no where and left Liz's room.

Mitch had returned to the group for the last evening session and Sara mouthed to me that she was glad that I was staying. I looked at her and shook my head no. Once we were finished discussing the exercise we just did, Sara mentioned that perhaps I should share with the group what I had been feeling.

I proceeded to tell everyone that I was an empath and I was picking up other people's emotions and was having a difficult time with it, as I did not know how to turn it off. I also shared that I had a spontaneous kundalini awakening and had been looking for others like me and that I wanted to learn how to deal with all the changes.

Before I knew it, every single person there was guilting me, and trying to put the fear into me if I left. Some of the things that were said to me were:

"You can't leave now. You are only half way through it will be dangerous for you to leave in this state."

"I heard you say that you wanted to dedicate yourself to humanity and planet Earth. If you leave, you are not dedicating yourself now are you?"

"You need us. You are not going to find what you are looking for outside of here. You are a part of us now; a part of the community."

"Each and every one of us here tried to leave on our first time, but we were convinced to stay and now we keep coming back."

"It is your ego that is trying to get you to leave. Do not listen to it. You have to stay."

"A lot of strings were pulled so that you could be here. You made a commitment. You are wasting a good opportunity here. There are people that would die to be in your position. If you leave now, how is it fair to them?" (Sara, the coordinator said this.)

"I thought you said that you just knew that you had to be here. Now you are saying that you just need to leave. Well, what is it? It doesn't sound like your intuition is very good." (Liz, the facilitator said this.)

"You can't leave. We have shared sacred space and personal information with you. You had better not tell anyone what goes on here. This is sacred! How do we know we can trust you? You told us you were committing to the nine day retreat and now you are leaving." (Liz, the facilitator said this.)

Well I had just about enough! They were worse than religion! Did they hear the words coming out of their mouths? I thanked everyone for their feedback and told them that my mind was made.

Mitch smirked and said, "Did you notice how we parked the cars? Unless you have chitty chitty bang bang, you are not going anywhere. There are two vehicles in front of yours." He seemed quite pleased with himself at that point. I was about to wipe that fucking little smirk right off of his face.

My energy just did a *huge* shift. It went from nice to warrior in less than a split second. I glared over at him and said, "Are you keeping me here against my will? I suggest you get those cars moved because I am leaving!"

I proceeded to walk to my van and three different people tried to stop me. I figured enough time had passed for the two cars to be moved, so I walked over to my van. I noticed that they had not been moved, so I started to walk back to the house and all the lights were turning off.

I found Mitch and asked him to move the cars. He puffed out his chest at me and gave me the dirtiest glare while saying, "I am not disrupting this retreat for you. You can wait until after our walk in the morning! You are not going anywhere. You are staying here!"

I was thinking, ah, I do not think so! Was that all you had, Mitch? Nice try with the intimidation. "No actually, I am leaving tonight!" I said as I walked back to my van. Did they actually think that after all that had happened that I would actually stay? No way!

I went inside my van and locked the doors. That place was really screwed up! What was I supposed to do now? I knew their plan. Keep me over night and then try to convince me to stay in the morning. Screw that noise!

Ok, what were my options? I could keep my hand on the horn until someone moved the two cars. On the other hand, I could just smash into the cars and push them out of my way. Shit! That might get me into trouble and cost a lot of money. Scratch that one.

I could not call 911 because my life was not being threatened. They were not physically hurting me; they just would not let me leave. I did not have the Heffey Creek Police phone number nor did I know where I was.

Think Tanya think! Where was the piece of paper with the address on it?! My van was in such a mess! I did not pack anything up nicely as I just wanted to get my belongings in the van, so that I could get out of there. There was stuff piled from the floor to the ceiling.

It was just after midnight, so it was making it hard to see. I figured I had better find someone to phone the Heffey Creek Police to let them know that I was going to need their help. I tried Lorne but I received his voice mail. I tried Natasha and received her voice mail as well. Great, now whom could I call?

I guess I could try my sister. I phoned her to let her know what was going on and that she had to phone the police for me. I was sure by the time the police phoned me back, I would have found the address.

I found the address just in time for when the police phoned me. I explained to them what was going on and gave them the address. They arrived in about twenty minutes. I flashed my van headlights so that they could see where I was. I was not unlocking my doors or getting out of the van!

They had the cars moved so that I could finally leave! Sara was standing at the bottom of the driveway with her arms folded and looked all pissed off. All I could think was what did you expect? That place was crazy! They were holding me against my will. What else was I suppose to do? They did not give a rat's ass about my well being. There was something very weird going on there!

It was 1am and dark out, and I did not know how to get out of there. I saw a gas station so I filled up with gas, got directions, and bought smokes. I knew that I was using this experience as an excuse to start smoking again. I went for five whole days. I had never quit for that long in twenty-three years.

I did not even roll a joint for the ride home. You would think that was the first thing that I would do given the circumstance and the fact that I had not had any for five days. I remembered that I had a half of one, so I just smoked that.

I finally figured out how to get on the highway and I was on my way back home! My focus was straight ahead and I was not looking back! There was something about that place that was not right. I felt it from day one, and had wanted to leave since I arrived.

I was not sure how I toughed it out for five days. It did not feel right there. There was something very, very weird going on. Very weird! There was definitely something up with that Mitch guy. No one has ever shape shifted on me, and it was not as if he shape shifted into a pretty, white wolf!

I think I just figured it out! I think I just spend my last five days at some sort of cult. It all made sense now. The way they referred to themselves as the community. However, the participants were not bad people; they were just very weak and hurting people. They thought that the retreat was the only place where they could receive unconditional love that they so desired.

God I wished that I had their email addresses so that I could let them know. At least tell them what I thought and let them make up their own minds. I wondered if they donated money to the retreat. What exactly were they so worried about me telling?

Right on their website, it stated that a cult had secrets. There were no secrets in this work. If there were no secrets, what were they worried about me saying? I just got the feeling that something very, very strange was going on there. I could not sleep almost the entire time that I was there. There was something not right about that place!

Four or five participants were also volunteers. They did everything from cooking, dusting, housework, work in the yard and garden, administrative work, preparing for activities and exercises.

Not to mention, for each meal, additional volunteers came to prepare the meals. Sara, who had been a full time volunteer and had been working with Liz for many, many, many years, still could not look at herself in the mirror and love what she saw.

What kind of master was Liz if Sara after all those years being side by side with Liz, still could not love herself? I did not believe that place was healthy and I was glad to be on my way home. I could not believe that I drove all the way home without music, without using my glasses or using my high beams. I just got in the van and went! I never go anywhere without music.

It was so good to be in the safety and comfort of my own home. My knee was killing me, as I had to go up and down the mountain all day loading up my van. I left everything in my van and went straight to bed. What a day!

July 23

I just remembered something about one of the participants at the retreat. He knew Takhi, the woman that facilitated the sweat that I went to. What a small world. I had a negative experience at the sweat and I had a negative experience at that retreat. Was there some sort of link there?

I started to think, why I would believe so strongly that I needed to be at that retreat, and then had such a negative experience while I was there. So negative that I had to phone the police and leave half way through.

I started to think about the participants. They were so weak and hurting. Maybe I was there to show them that if something did not feel right, it was ok to leave. Do not let other's try and guilt you or put fear into you, to do as they say.

They admitted to me that they wanted to leave prior retreats as well. I showed them what it looked like to stand your ground. To have eighteen people staring at you and trying everything under the sun to put fear and guilt into you, but to still get up and walk away in the middle of the night.

I also believed that was a lesson for me. A lesson to teach me not to allow others to bully me or make me do things that did not feel right. Another lesson was to trust my instincts! Perhaps a test that helped me step into my personal power. That was another message to show me that all people that claimed to be from the light and had your best interests at heart, was not.

I could just imagine circle time in Heffey Creek this morning. To only be a fly on the wall. I still could not wrap my head around what that place was. I was just glad to have gotten out of there!

I went over to David's for dinner. While I was in his front yard folding up my tent and sleeping bags properly, a van was slowly driving down the street. As the van drove by, I locked eyes with the passenger. The van stopped and backed up to where I was.

I thought that they were probably lost and were in need of directions. The couple in the van was in their late seventies to early eighties. The woman's name was Delores. They were not lost. At first, she just started to make small talk and then she started to tell me that she helped people. They just seemed to find her, she told me. She shared some of her stories. Her husband was looking a little uncomfortable at that point. He looked like he wanted to crawl under his seat. He said to me, "I'm sorry. She is a little crazy sometimes."

"Oh no dear, she is not crazy. I know what she is. She is a lightworker. A human angel if you will."

"If you know that about me, then you must be one too!"

"I know why you are here. I am ok. There is no need to worry."

With that, she hugged me and gave me a kiss on the cheek and off they went. Wow! What just happened there? She was checking up on me. Probably to make sure I was ok after the whole Heffey Creek fiasco. I know that in my heart of hearts.

David scrubbed all the algae off the rocks in the river on his property. He knew that I used the river to cleanse my crystals and offered me to do it at his place. When I tried, I noticed all the green algae, so he scrubbed all the rocks while I was in Heffey Creek. That was so sweet of him. I usually went to Sucker's Creek to do it because there was no algae there. Now I could do it at David's as well.

CHAPTER 10

The Puzzle Continues

July 24

I was listening to music on my computer and selected random rather than picking what songs I wanted to listen to. It was hard to pick songs when I had almost two thousand. I found myself daydreaming about my experience with Delores yesterday. As I played it through my head, the song *Battle of Evermore* by Led Zeppelin came on.

There was something about that song that pulled at my soul. The feeling I get when I listen to it, was struggle. Like there was a struggle going on between good and evil. That struggle was going on behind the scenes of humanity. I could feel that struggle. I could feel the pain within humanity. The struggle was soon ending where it shall be known who wins.

I have stopped using a wheelchair while I grocery shop in town. It was mostly because I was embarrassed around David to use the chair. It was not easy going up and down the aisles and then standing in line. Sometimes we were going up and down the same aisles because he could not find what he was looking for. He obviously did not know how painful it was for me to walk, or he would not have me go up and down so many aisles. When I did big grocery shops and went to the mall, I still used a wheelchair.

July 31

Today was an exciting day. Many of my friends were meeting in Hope for a get together for the August long weekend. We did that last year as well. Only this year, there were more people. My nephew Michael was already at my place. My mom was on her way from Surrey. She was staying the weekend and then taking Michael back home with her. Ten other people from Surrey were coming, one person from Grand Forks and seven people from Saskatchewan. I have known most of them since I was thirteen years old.

When the group from Saskatchewan and Grand Forks arrived at my place, they said there were eight hawks circling the roof of my apartment. Wow! What were the hawks doing right in the middle of town? Why were they circling the roof of my apartment? I did not know if this was any kind of connection, but on August 4th, there were eight of us plus one new born baby travelling back to Saskatchewan together. We were all in the apartment that the hawks were circling.

Mystical Puzzle

August 4

I could not believe this, but my friends were here at 7am ready to pick me up for our road trip to Saskatchewan. We stopped in Cranbrook for a couple of nights before continuing. We arrived at Michelle and Clay's on August 6 around 8pm.

I felt as though my connection with the kids was stronger than with their parents. They seemed so much more open minded and curious and willing to accept. Did I mention that Dustin drove us in his truck? Now that was weird considering once upon a time I use to change Dustin's diaper, and now he was driving me in his truck. They grow up so quick!

It was probably a good thing that I only had three days to spend there, as Michelle and I did not connect as we usually did. I wanted so badly to share with her the channeling that explained that I was a starseed. From the conversations that we had, I could clearly see that she was not ready to hear such a thing.

Michelle was having a hard time finding the old Tanya and very much wanted to hang out with her. I tried to explain to her that the old Tanya was gone and she was looking at me as if I had three heads. She asked me if I was just looking for some drama and making shit up. She also mentioned that maybe I did one too many drugs in the day.

I started to laugh at her and reminded her of all the times I had fallen hard on my head as well. The funny thing was, pretty much everything she said to me, I had already predicted that my friends would say such things about my change.

I felt more alone now, and sure, that no one was going to understand me, and what I was going through. My own family and friends did not get it, how was anyone else? I was really hoping that since Michelle had known me since I was thirteen that she would just instinctively know that I was in a good place. Instead, she asked me why I was throwing my life away. I never looked at dedicating my life to humanity and planet Earth as throwing my life away.

I could only hope that in time, we would make some sort of a connection again. Right now, that was not happening. We have been through so much with each other that I was sure that our friendship would hold out. She was not just a friend; she was family to me.

August 8

We went to a Native Pow Wow in the evening. There was something about pow wow's that felt so powerful to me. It always brought up so much emotion and brought me to tears. I have never understood why that was. The drumming, the music, chanting, dancing, and costumes, awaken my soul.

During the ceremony, some elders were making there way out of the ring and walking the outskirts where we were sitting. One of them stopped dead in front of me, turned to look at me and put out his hand. I took his hand and shook it. No words were spoken.

I assumed that he was going to shake everyone's hand. However, he did not. He just continued on his way. That was strange. Why did he stop to shake my hand and no one else's? Did he see something in me? Did he know something about me?

August 10

I was up at 4am and Michelle had me at the airport for 6am. I fought tears the whole way to the airport. I so badly wanted that trip to turn out differently. She did not get a chance to meet the me that was ready to take on the world, the confident and blissfully happy me. The me that she did get to meet was the one who was fearful of no one understanding her. The one that did not have the words to explain what had happened and what was happening.

My flight arrived in Vancouver at 10:30am. I love plane rides. I particularly like the window seat. Looking down at the Earth below totally tripped me out. When you were on the ground, the world seemed so big. However, once you are up in the air, it seemed so small.

Corrina, my sister met me at the airport with my van. From the airport, I drove her home. You would think she had never driven with me before as she actually covered her eyes. She was the one the backed into cars, not me. Sometimes, she did it twice in one day! Ok, so maybe I have had a few oopsies too. After dropping off my sister, I was back on the road again and on my way home.

August 21

I had been having weird visions. There was a man that was on the loose that was suspected of killing his wife. The investigative team believed that he was in British Columbia somewhere as they found his boat on this side of the border.

I envisioned that I would come face to face with him and that somehow I needed to send a text to notify the authorities. Why was I thinking such nonsense?! BC was a big place. I had no idea why my imagination was running so wild.

I was at David's in the evening and he made some sort of a comment about how some people were whack jobs for saying they had been abducted by aliens. I could not remember exactly what he said, but it was something to that effect.

It was so hard for me to not to break down in tears when he said that. I went to the bathroom to try to compose myself. I had to keep it together or else he would wonder what was wrong with me.

Mystical Puzzle

I went home that night and tried to sleep, but found myself bawling my eyes to the point that they were almost swollen shut, and my eyelids were dark purple. Why did it have to be like that!? No one was ever going to understand me! I did not want to lose everyone because they thought that I was a freak!

How was I supposed to tell David that I did not originate from Earth and that I was a starseed? He used to think I was a soul mate and that he was glad that I was in his life. What would he think of me when I told him that? I cocooned myself in bed and sobbed for hours.

I was going to have to tell him the truth about me and just go from there. I could not risk that he would make comments that destroyed me. If he could not handle the real me, than I would rather know now and not six months down the road when we were closer friends.

August 23

Lorne, Natasha, and I picked up Alex and his friend Mitchell to take them to Flood Falls. They were good kids and they enjoyed hanging out with us. Alex had come with us several times, but Mitchell had never been. The boys particularly liked Lorne as he ran around with them and played with them.

As we were driving down the road towards the falls, the boys pointed out to me that we drove past a bunch of police. I quickly glanced at my speedometer, only twenty kilometers over. Perhaps they were busy and did not notice.

I did not know how I did not see or sense them. I have internal radar for police. They must be busy as no flashing blue and red lights came after me. That was probably why I did not sense that they were in the area. They were too busy with something else.

The falls were almost dried up; there was a little bit of a trickle but nothing like after the spring run off. There were not many places in nature that I could enjoy and get to by foot. I was thankful that my leg could make it to the falls and back. I had to be extra careful because the ground was uneven. One wrong move and I was going to be in a lot of trouble and in a lot of pain!

I found out why the police were on Flood Hope Road. They found the murder suspect who murdered his wife. Only he was dead. He hung himself at the motel. That was creepy! Somehow, I sensed his presence or his energy. That was why I was having visions of me seeing him in town. It was because he was in town! Oh my god, I think I may be more sensitive than I thought!

August 25

David came over and I shared my channeling with him. I have only shared that with two other people, my aunt and Lorne. It scared me to death to think of what he might think of me after hearing the channeling. Think about it. How many friends do you have that have told you, "Hey man, so it is like this. Like, I am not from Earth and I have all kinds of unexplainable things that

206

happen to me. Like telepathic conversation with ET's and spirits that are always trying to get my attention, etc."

You get the drift. This was fucked up shit! I was very well aware of that. Why do you think that I was so damn scared of telling my friends and family? If they already thought that I was losing it, imagine what they would think when they read this book.

To my surprise, David accepted the information that I shared with him. He shed a couple of tears while listening to the channeling. A big weight had been lifted off my shoulders. Before he left, he hugged me and told me that he was glad that I shared that with him.

September 4

I noticed some marks on my skin by my ankle. If I were to connect the dots on my skin, it would be a triangle. I was not sure what that was all about if anything. It was not the first time that I have found unexplainable markings on my body after I woke up from sleeping.

September 9

It had been awhile since I had tried the breath and sound meditation. I figured today would be a great day to try it. Maybe something cool would happen, as it was the 9th day of the 9th month of the 9th year.

I was having difficulties in getting to the state I was in while I was in Sedona. Perhaps it was because there was a small part of me that feared where it could take me. To this day, I could not put into words what happened when I did that meditation in Sedona. I did not feel as though the meditation was successful. Near the end, I think I fell asleep. I would have to try it another day.

I started to think about that crazy place in Heffey Creek and remembered that right before I went to Sedona, I came across the link on the internet to the so called retreat in Heffey Creek. Here is a scary thought. Had I gone to Heffey Creek instead of Sedona, my awakening would have still happened, as it was pre-planned before I incarnated. Had that happened, I could have very well thought that it was the people at Heffey Creek, that brought on the transformation. They could have had my mind right twisted by now. I was so glad that I never went there first!

My friend Brittany came over, as she wanted me to show her how to download a movie from the internet. I went to the appropriate website and showed her where to type the movie name. I began typing the name of a movie when something made me delete what I had typed, and then unexpectedly I began to type *Marley and Me*. I did not know why I did that, as it made no difference what movie I typed. I just needed to show her an example of how it was done.

Mystical Puzzle

Brittany's eyes went wide. "Oh my god, you just typed in the movie that I want to download!" That would explain why I stopped typing what I was originally going to type and then typed *Marley and Me*. Somehow, I must have sensed that in Brittany.

Maybe I pick up other people's thoughts without realizing it. Had she not told me that that was the movie she wanted to download, I would have just chalked it up as nothing. Brittany and I high fived each other and I said, "Brittany, don't bother asking because I do not know how or why these things happen." She smiled and accepted it as that.

It had been awhile since I had phoned XYZ Radio. I phoned and spoke to the intuitive named June. I explained to her, "Since my dramatic awakening last fall, I began to see double and triple numbers. For the last few months, I have been seeing 911 everywhere. I was wondering if you could enlighten me on that." This was the feedback she gave me.

"A little bit of that is because of the seasoning and the time that we are in. Definitely being the power number that we are running in with today. I am definitely seeing that. I am seeing that there is an awakening that has come to many people to understand what is happening within the world. Yeah, they are showing me within the world.

"With the awakening that is happening within the world, that sometimes events like the 911 event that transpired, that happened, there is a new awareness and a new awakening within our, within our processing, within our connecting of understanding are strengths, of who we are, where we are at in the big game that we are going to call life so to speak. For some reason that is what they are showing me. There is significance to with it there.

"I don't do a whole lot of numerology. I just know that when there is a power number. If it is the 8th month, 8th year, 8th hour, that type of thing. I know that those are really strong alignments and I know that the 911 alignment has become very strong because of some of the different things that have happened. That even though there were mass destruction and mass losses and that type of thing, there is an awareness that has come with that.

"And it is kind of like I am feeling that there is an awareness that is coming to you that is huge. It is not just something you go, oh now I'm going to start doing this. No. This is a huge awareness. This is a 911 type of awareness type of thing that is coming into your time and space to be. I'm not saying that there is destruction coming, I'm not saying that you need to be afraid of anything. I'm saying that you have something that is going to be huge coming into your life.

"It feels very exciting. It feels very anticipatory. It feels like it is a change and a switch that you have been working on manifesting and drawing to yourself over the years. You are going through within yourself that there is something that you have been building on for many years.

"So you have been working on the different things in your life. It almost feels like somebody who has been building a house and doing this massive re-model and this re-construction. I'm hearing re re re re re. All of that going on is now finally going to get handed the keys.

"One of the strengths that would be wonderful for you is drawing in that higher vibration. Setting that higher awareness within yourself is really going to help itself open up and show itself to you.

"I'm hearing the saying, and I don't like the saying but I'm going to say it. I'm hearing the saying, you didn't choose us, but we chose you. But you had chosen them before you came. The feeling that they are expressing it to me that it is your time. That is the wording. I feel better with that one. It is now time that you come into the power of who it is and where it is you're going with your life.

"There is an older woman that you are doing some kind of work with right now. She has bits and pieces of wisdom that they are helping you to fill in a puzzle. A bigger puzzle than you even have an imagination to create. I have a feeling that this older woman is an excellent resource for you right now but I also have the feeling that you are going to expand beyond that.

"I'm also seeing a white fluffy cat. She is coming in to say hi. She is fine. She moves very calmly and gracefully.

"I'm also getting that as you start to develop some of the things that you are going to be doing, that you are going to want to stand back and say what the? I don't? Where did the? How? Why? Let it flow, don't push the river. Let if flow. Let the information come to you that is going to help fill in the blanks for you. They are showing me that even though this can be the farthest thing almost like you are sitting there watching a Sci-Fi movie. Allow the information to come and remember when you are doing this and you are adjusting only accepting and working with that which is of the highest vibration. That which is only for the highest good and always state that if you're working and something comes in and you're sitting there and wait a minute? Is this for the highest good? I only accept the highest Good. The rest of you guys got to take a hike.

"But they are showing me that it is almost going to feel like a Sci-Fi movie that you are watching and some of the information and some of the things that they are going to bring into you for you to begin doing some of the work that you are going to be doing. Like I said, don't push the river. They have used that statement a couple of times with me to share with you. Don't push the river, let things flow. (It is 33:33 into the radio program right now.) Let things happen, don't try to make them happen. Don't try to stop them. Allow the natural flow to happen."

Mystical Puzzle

Tanya – "I know exactly what they are trying to tell me."

"Good, because they are trying to tell me without telling me.

"Did some one around you just recently lose employment? You are going to need to bring words of encouragement to someone who has just recently lost employment. So if you haven't met them yet, there is someone that you are going to come across that is going to share with you that they lost employment and you are going to need to share with them words of encouragement, of hope, of love and light. That is going to be a message that you are going to be able to carry forward to them. It is going to be one of those things that when the incident happens, when the person comes to you, you are going to just know exactly, intuitively, instinctively, you are just going to know immediately, exactly what to say, how to say it. You are going to be a huge blessing to this person. They are aligning you with that.

"I don't see you doing readings sitting across the table from somebody but is that something that you are starting to practice with? Healing with crystals is high frequency work and is definitely in your line.

"Working with crystals you are definitely going to see that higher vibration, that higher frequency. One of the things that I am hearing that I need to share with you and recommend to you is if you go on-line you can find out information on Google about some of these crystal formations that are being discovered.

"There are some that are in the earth that it is so hot that man you can't be there for about a few minutes and doing exploration and that type of thing. There is something about that vibration and finding out the information about the crystals that is something that will really be beneficial to you as you are working on this path that you are working on and going towards. Finding out about crystal formations within the earth because that is not only going to help heal the people like we use with crystals and healing and doing lay and understanding where to place the crystals on the body. When you realize the crystal formations within the earth in the different locations that can then send a higher vibrational frequency of healing within locations within the planet. That is what they are sharing with me to share with you.

"You need to start going to the power spots around the world. You don't need to physically go there, you can go ethereally. That is what they are telling me. You can go through the internet too they are telling me; that you can actually make some connections through the internet. I'm definitely seeing that as a plus as a place for you to do a little bit of that connecting.

"They're showing me, they are not showing me working like, one of the things that I do intently, is I do a lot of physical healing work with people. That is not the type of healing work that they are showing me that you will do.

"There is a specific healing that you are going to do with alignment through this. That is definitely something you will want to spend a little more time on.

Do a little bit more research as you start to develop; you are starting to get some of the information that is coming. There is that, there is that word again. That Sci-Fi stuff is going on.

"Your reading about a crystal cave in Mexico that is filled with these huge massive crystals and it is so hot that people can't even spend any time in there. There is something about that information and there is something about that vibration that frequency that is really, really important for you.

"There is also for example up here in Alaska, they have discovered a crystal bed in one of our ocean places and they are not publicizing it and they are not talking about it. It was discovered by some fisherman. Because of the destruction of what it would do to the ocean floor if they messed with this crystal bed. There is something significant for you to learn about the crystal beds under the water that are under the ocean. Something about the new waters and the new life that is coming forward also with this crystal type energy that is under the water. So you are going to want to do some research on that topic as well.

"I'm also hearing that, you say you live in a little town but I am seeing a body of water. There is a body of water where there is crystal energy flowing from. I don't know why they have spun us into the crystal part of this conversation and talking about it as much as they have. I think there is a really strong connection for you with this crystal energy, with this high frequency, with this higher vibration for stuff that you are going to be doing in some changes.

"This is the big stuff they are talking about. This massive information. You are going to carry an incredible message forward. It is amazing stuff once it starts opening up and you start hearing about it and you start experiencing it.

"But there is something about this river about this body of water the crystal energy there, the crystals in the oceans, the crystal caves and they are also showing me mountains where you can go and you can actually gather your own crystals. They are showing me mountain ranges. I believe there is one called Mount Antero in Colorado that you might want to do some research on as well and find out information.

"They are not saying that you need to visit, but to find the information that can give you more insight into this vibration, into the frequency into that sound. That I think is going to bring you some healing of your own, within your own body. As you work more with the crystals, it is going to help you, it is going to help you adjust your own frequency."

June shared a story how she healed herself with herbs and crystals instead of having a pin put in her elbow. She made it happen in two and a half weeks. She insisted on another x-ray before the surgeon put the pin in her elbow and by miracle, she was completely healed. The surgeon said that this was not humanly possible.

June continued with, "They want you to know the power that you can bring in your own space with the crystals. I am sharing this with you because they want you to move into a place of being able to do this type of healing on yourself.

"First you need to work counter clockwise to remove the trauma and the injury. Once you have done that for a while, you want to take that energy and spin it in a clockwise direction over that knee as well to bring in the healing, to bring in the light. When you do that type of work you are really going to see where you will bring in that strength and bring in that new healing.

"Is there something with the muscles going up into your thigh? I can actually feel them turning like pretzels. That is exactly what I am feeling while we are talking. And what I am hearing is to get some dried arnica and go ahead and put it in some oil base like virgin olive oil and allow it to heat infuse. As you are doing that, put in the prayer and meditation, this is bringing me for my ultimate highest good and for the highest frequency, the highest vibration of healing. Go ahead and throw in a clear crystal with it and allow that to warm up and separate it out. Use that oil as massage oil and rubbing it into the top of the muscle area where you got that going on. There is something about arnica and that crystal energy that will help bring in that healing a little quicker to those muscles. Is what I am hearing to share with you on that.

"They are saying that sometimes we get put in the place of limitations so that we will sit back and evaluate how we can help it and make it better so we can help others. I am having a feeling that something is kind of going on within your space. You are developing and starting to know how to help others and how to bring this message forward. Very strongly they are saying. You know grab a hold of some of the stuff that is going to give you education. Grab a hold of some of the information that is going to help you.

"I am also hearing that you need to connect with someone who has some really strong herbal knowledge of the herbals in your local area."

I thanked June before ending the call. I was completely blown away with all the information that June provided. It was amazing how one question could bring forth so much information when I was open and willing to receive.

September 10

I woke up in the morning and felt that my energy and mood had shifted. I felt like I did when I arrived home from Sedona. So alive, and so full of oomph! Maybe something did happen during the breath and sound meditation yesterday; a type of healing of some sort.

I had a chiropractor appointment in the morning. During my appointment, I caught myself saying, "Humanity is the hardest species I have ever had to work with." What?! Where did those words come from? I covered by saying, "Like I know other species." And laughed it off.

One thing I have to say about my chiropractor. My insurance would no longer pay for visits and he did not want to see our progress go to waste, so he offered to continue treating me for half the price he normally charged. Most doctors would just say, see you later. He was the first doctor in my life that had offered a reduced cost for his service. That was something that I would always remember and appreciate.

It was such a beautiful day that I went to the river to meditate after my appointment. I had the sun on one side of me and the moon was visible on the other. What a glorious day.

I finally went to the police about Gus. The guy had a screw loose. I have not had contact with him for ten months. In fact, I asked him to never contact me again. Somehow he did not register in his head that after ten months of him texting me repeatedly and me not responding, that I was not interested.

One week he would send me a text that stated, "When you die, God is going to smack you out. Please die now!" The next week he would send, "I miss you, do you miss me?" Then it would follow with a bunch of sexual remarks. This had been going on for ten months, and I had not responded to any of his phone calls or texts.

The straw that broke the camels back was when he texted me asking me if I would like to get a room at the Thunderbird Motel. His text was sent to me after the media released that a man that was wanted for killing his wife, was found hung at the Thunderbird Motel, which happened to be in the town that I lived in.

I did not trust him! His ego was hurt and he wanted to teach me a lesson. He had been a bully all of his life. I knew this as I use to go to high school with him. He used heavy chemical drugs, and drank hard liquor all the time. In fact, it would not surprise me if he used gin for mouthwash!

I did not want to go to the police but I have had enough! I did not want to charge him with harassment; I simply wanted him to stop all contact with me. I hoped that now that the police had contacted him, he would get the hint.

Before I went to bed I was about to close my bedroom blinds and I was guided not to. I had no idea why I was to leave them open, but I did.

September 11

May peace be with those who lost their lives and to all their loved ones.

I woke up at 4am to go to the bathroom. As I was walking back towards my bed and the window, a sparkle caught my eye from the sky. You are back! My star group, Orion! It was right outside my bedroom window! It had been at least six months since I had seen it. Wow! Maybe that was why I was feeling different; my star group was back! I was going to get up every morning at 4am, just so I could look at the stars of Orion.

It was another beautiful fall day. The sun was shining and the sky was a magnificent blue without a cloud in sight. I went to the river to meditate and pray for the souls and families of 911. That was something that I had done every year since that horrid year. Even though I was not spiritual before, I carried around a deep pain for the souls that were lost and traumatized. I just so badly want to take the hurt away from others.

One year ago today, I arrived in Sedona, Arizona. It was hard to believe that an entire year had gone by since my change. I felt like I was running out of time. I had so much to do and so little time.

September 20

I woke up at 9:30am and thank god, my headache finally went away. Now here was the problem. Somehow, I had to make it from Vancouver to White Rock. Oh, I could make it all right but it might take me ten years because I did not have a sense of direction.

Carol my angel woman friend gave me directions of what highways to take but I always get confused when there were signs and exits going off all over the place. I needed exact directions or I felt like I was lost for the rest of my life!

I thought I was doing well and I was all proud of myself and then all of a sudden I swerved to take an exit. Ugh! What was I doing?! Was I supposed to do that? Oh no! Do I take the right lane or the left lane? I hate this! Where was I going? Where the hell was I?

Oh, this was just great! I was in the middle of I did not even know where I was. Now how was I going to get to White Rock?! Ok, so the worse case scenario was I ended up being late because I took the longest possible route to White Rock. I needed to chill out.

I was about to take an exit that I was familiar with and take a ridiculously long route to White Rock when something made me continue. Yahoo! I was exactly where I was supposed to be the whole time! I just fretted all that for nothing.

They really needed to learn how to label the highways so that people like me did not think they were lost. I really had to thank my angels because honestly, do not ask how I got to where I did. They swerved me into the right lanes and exits. I guess I just needed to learn to trust their guidance. They showed me that today because I had no clue of how I just went from Vancouver to White Rock in less than thirty minutes.

I had a nice visit with Carol. The last time we saw each other was when she visit me in Hope. She had told me about a younger man that she had felt a close connection. Well, that younger man was now moving in with her. They believed that they were soul mates as they had connected so quickly and so well. I was so happy for her. She had felt more love in the last few months than she had ever felt in her thirty year marriage. She was sixty-five years old and had now just met her soul mate, her true love.

Carol was so amazingly genuine. She was sixty-five going on twenty. I truly believed that she was some sort of an earth angel. Who knew? Maybe she was a starseed too. She gave me a couple of angel pendants. One to keep on me, and one to keep on the visor of my van. She figured that I needed the one specifically for my visor. One of the things we have in common was we were both speed demons. I could so see us racing each other.

She treated me to lunch and then we checked out an angel store that she frequent before we parted ways. I bought a couple of the angel pewter pendants. I had yet to figure out how Carol fit in my journey. I did not necessarily need to know. However, I did know that she was someone very important to me. As I was thinking that driving down the highway, I glanced and saw a license plate with 000.

September 21

Since my accident, the amount of doors that had slammed in my face had shown me huge lessons regarding humanity and greed. Between the doctors, the government, disability insurance companies, friends, family and sometimes even complete strangers, I could not believe that I was apart of this world. You really do find out who your true friends were in times of need.

In a way though, all those doors that kept slamming in my face was putting more fuel in the fire. I always said what does not kill you, only made you stronger. Even though I had been feeling rather weak and confused in the last while, I always bounced back. Soon I would be bouncing back with my warrior spirit intact. When that happened, look out world! I have not had the experiences that I have had to just fall apart and crumble now.

September 30

Lorne and Natasha came over and we ended up going to the tunnels for a walk. Every single time we went there, Lorne would tell the spirits in the tunnel to throw a big rock on his head if they were there. That pissed me off as I was usually walking right beside him and one of these days he was going to say it and it was going to happen!

While he rants and raves trying to get spirits to prove themselves, I telepathically told the spirits that they did not need to prove themselves to me because I knew they were there. But if they did show themselves to Lorne, please do not hurt him, as he did not mean those silly things he said.

We were finished walking through the tunnels and we were on our way back to the parking lot. Lorne jumped a little to the side and had a weird look on his face. I asked him what the matter was even though I knew damn well, what the matter was. He turned away and said nothing as he kept on walking.

"Why are you lying to me? Tell me what happened, Lorne." I started to laugh my head off because I knew something just touched him only there was nothing there. He proceeded to tell Natasha and me that he thought that something had touched him but it must have been his inside shirt rubbing on him. One of these days, he was going to be so sorry if a mischievous spirit wanted to have some fun with him.

October 5

I started the master cleanse. I was surprised that it actually did not taste that bad. I would not say that it was good, but it certainly did not taste bad. In order for the cleanse to be effective, I needed to drink at least six of the drinks per day. There was no limit of how many drinks to drink. The key was to drink enough so that I did not feel hungry.

I had hoped that I could stop smoking cigarettes and pot during the cleanse. Unfortunately, I was unable to stop. It seemed silly that while I was cleansing my body of toxins, I was filling it up with smoke and more toxins. I decided not to beat myself up. I had never done a cleanse before and if it turned out that I smoked during the entire ten days of the cleanse but stuck to it in every other way, then so be it.

I came across something interesting on the internet called soul braiding.

In soul braiding, an advanced soul joins their energy to a body formed by another soul by becoming the dominant energy of that karmic matrix (body-mind) for the greater development of both Souls.

Causes: When an individual gets to a certain level of spiritual advancement, they naturally become inclined to take on greater spiritual challenges for their continued growth. There are few tasks harder in the universe then taking on the challenges of "soul braiding." To understand why this is, compare a soul braid to the more common and less challenging form of a walk-in which is a "soul exchange."

Classic walk-in situations – "soul exchanges" are very simple: one walks out and leaves forever and one walks in and stays for the rest of that body's natural life. In "soul braiding," the walk-out is never totally out of the body and so the walk-in is never totally free to be themselves. It is like "me and my shadow" where me is the walk-in (the main energy that the body obeys and experiences) and where the shadow is the walk-out. (But unlike a shadow is not silently dragged along.)

Which is why it is a "soul braid." For, like a braid of hair, the soul energies are intertwined and lay side by side in the same field. Since they are part of the same whole, each strand of the braid, the part that is the "walk-in" and the part that is the "walk-out" is independent and each one pulling on it can unravel the braid.

When the walk-out "pulls too hard" on the energy field, it causes sensations of extreme disorientation for the walk-in which disrupts their control of the body. This disorientation can last for hours, days, or weeks at a time and it impairs the individual's functioning and usually results in illness.

When the walk-in "pulls too hard" on the energy field, they will end up leaving it altogether for hours, days, or weeks at a time. The usual result of this is the manifestation of a serious illness in body-mind that forces the walk-in to come back and "fix."

Symptoms: "soul braids" seldom have easy lives. They live for long periods of time feeling totally disoriented in their daily existence. They often will experience a string of illnesses which are a direct result of two streams of energy inhabiting their one body at the same time. Usually the challenges of the "braided" life are such that the "braided" individual knows that a walk-in has happened and is inevitably drawn to the resources which are needed to meet the challenges of the "braided" life.

After Effects: Soul braiding is a life sentence. If you are a "braid" and there have been long periods in your life when you have repeatedly experienced bouts of disorientation, then you can be sure that your "braiding" is not going well. The best way to deal with the "after effects" of soul braiding is to expand the capabilities of body, mind, and spirit with energy clearings such as Geometric Repatterning or Remote Releasement. A life long program of Chakra and Inner Body Cleansing should be followed to keep the "braid" in a continuous state of energetic harmony.

Advice: "Soul braiding" is more intimate than a marriage because the "walk-in" and the "walk-out" are together seven days a week, twenty-four hours a day. The more that the two energies can "get along" and find a way to live together "in peace," the easier it will be for "both" of them. Although souls can be braided to resolve lives long karmic conflicts, it is more likely that they have been drawn together because they share a problem that neither has been successful at resolving on their own. In working on the problem together, they have a unique opportunity to resolve their karma and speed up their growth. The best advice is for the "soul braid" is to become as clear as possible energetically by pursuing both Chakra and Inner Body Cleansing.

Case History: Soul braiding is a very rare phenomena. Given the challenges that are involved, most souls are uninterested in doing it. For, until they can master their own energy, soul braids invariably end up with cancer or another life threatening illness that takes time, patience, resources, and effort to overcome. However, as in any other karmic endeavor, the greater the challenge, the greater the reward. Soul braids who survive their challenges usually end up becoming masters of energy (because they have mastered their own) and are able to conduct it more powerfully and cleanly to others than anyone else on Earth. (*Walk-Ins – Soul Braiding*, 2000)

A lot of the above resonated with me. Another thing I came across on the internet is termed, "Early Retirement."

Although the subject of walk-ins has received considerable attention in recent years, a more recent phenomenon involving soul transfers has, as yet, received virtually no attention. Thus, I feel it is important to address this situation in considerable detail. This new phenomenon could perhaps be termed, "walk-outs;" however, I prefer the term "early retirement." Let's begin with a background perspective.

Before we came into incarnation for this final lifetime, we were thoroughly briefed on the overall transformation plan for Earth, and each of us clearly understood our individual assignments within the context of this overall mission. Although the details of the mission plan were not directly available to our human consciousness, we retained this knowledge within our oversoul. This included an awareness that group ascensions were planned to begin in the mid-1980's, and for most of us, the major part of our mission was to be completed after we were able to function within the human realm in our ascension body. So when ascension did not take place in this time-frame, there was a growing restlessness within many of the Light Workers. Aside from ascension, there were numerous other setbacks and delays in the mission. Although most of the Light Workers did not consciously understand the exact reasons for their restlessness, there was a general sense that there was much more important work that we had committed to do in the lifetime, yet the circumstances did not seem to enable clarity, or provide support for this work.

When we, as Light Workers, agreed to come to Earth so very long ago, we agreed to remain here, come hell or high water, (and we have been through both!) until the end of the cycle. It was anticipated that Earth would be firmly back on it evolutionary track by that time. But free will of the people of Earth cannot be overridden, and despite our best efforts, progress has been less than we anticipated.

The Spiritual Beings who guide the evolutionary course of this planet are compassionate beings. Most have experienced first-hand lifetime after lifetime in human embodiment here on Earth. So in March, 1994, a decision was made to make a new option available to the Light Workers. This option is limited to only those Light Workers who have been here for the longest time, those who came here as part of the original group of 144,000 or the subsequent group of 60,000. Essentially the option goes like this:

For any of these Light Workers who would like to be released from their original commitment, and to return now to their home star system, such a request will be honored. Rather than accomplishing this through physical death, or through a lift-off of the physical body, a "soul transfer" will be arranged, and a new volunteer soul will come into the embodiment to finish out the normal human lifetime.

The incoming soul will also be a Light Worker, but in virtually all cases, one of lesser evolutionary development. Thus, it will still be possible to fulfill at least part of the mission of the original soul. An aspect of the agreement related to the soul transfer is that conscious knowledge of the transfer will be "sealed," and not made available to the incoming soul. The intent of this is to minimize disruption to the human life. (*Hornecker*, 1996)

Oh my god, I just realized something. 1994 was the year that I tried to commit suicide. Did I try to end my life so that I could go back home? I guess while I was in coma, they convinced me to stay because I am still here.

I watched the documentary on Naica, Secrets of the Crystal Cave published by Discovery Channel. The giant crystal caves were found by fluke in Mexico. Something I found interesting was they were here when Lemuria was known to exist. Imagine how many more crystal caves there are deep within the earth. Perhaps it had something to do with our power vortex spots around the world. Perhaps they are ancient crystal structures from the times of Lemuria or Atlantis.

October 8

I had a horrible sleep last night. It was the first time since I stopped using my night light that I was actually petrified to be in my own room and close my eyes to go to sleep. There was something in my room and it was not benevolent.

Well you know what? Fuck you darkie! I was not going to be subjected to fear and sleep with the light on. As petrified as I was, I did not give in by turning on the light. I called for Archangel Michael to protect me, my bed, my bedroom, my apartment and the entire building that I lived in. Oh, I get it. They purposely scare me so that they can feed off my fear. Well I was not feeding them any more!

Later in the day, I was sitting at my computer when someone started to frantically bang on my door. I opened it and Lorne came rushing in by me.

"Ok, ok. I believe you now! The beads started to move on their own! There are ghosts in this building! I'm telling you the beads moved all by themselves!"

"Lorne, Lorne, slow down! It was probably the wind or something. Are any of the windows open?"

"I know what it looks like when they are moving from the wind! No windows are open! I am freaked out and I am not going back over there until Natasha gets home from work! There are ghosts in there and it is freaking me out! I also saw my cat's feet being ripped from right under him as if something was grabbing his legs. Oh my god, oh my god! I am so not going back over there right now!"

Mystical Puzzle

I started to laugh because he was the biggest skeptic and I had been trying to tell him for the last few years that there were ghosts / spirits in our building and he would never believe me that they existed. Lorne always wanted to try Ouija board and I had begged him not to go near one.

I told him if he started messing around with things like that, he was going to come to my door crying like a baby begging for it to stop. Oh and just so you know, it was not even 1pm in the afternoon. Good thing it was not night time or Lorne would be really crapping his pants!

I phoned XYZ Radio and spoke to the intuitive named Victoria. I explained to her, "I use to have night terrors in my twenties that I had no recollection of and my boyfriend would tell me about them the next morning but I would never remember. I used a night light until the beginning of this year. Last night was the first time in a long time that I was actually afraid to go to sleep. I was hoping that you could enlighten me on any of that." This was the feedback she gave me.

"Well it is interesting, did you have lots of abuse when you were three or four years old."

Tanya – "I don't remember that time period."

"So do you think you had any abuse at all? Here is what it looks like to me. It looks like you had some big shocks and some very violent things happen when you were very young and it shows that there were like programs that come up.

"Now we talked about, I don't like saying this, this tends to be kind of nice, and you know what I mean. You tended for awhile to attract, it is not demonic, its just beings who liked to trigger this hidden terror dynamic that came from being a little girl, and I think that is what you went through in your twenties.

"Were you drinking a lot during that time because you have a lot of blood sugar stuff going on at that time? Your brain pattern had a lot of trauma in it and a lot of it got triggered then.

"But then I see these beings around you. You have very strong guidance. You also have beings of a lesser form around you as well. Now that stuff I don't normally talk about."

Tanya – "Is there anything on me or in my space at the present time that I need to get rid of?"

"No but what I will say about you is you've got some frequencies, now remember this ladies and gentleman, we are all frequencies. We are entire frequencies and you are in motion inside and the frequencies on the planet are moving up. You have had three or four not shocking but really rapid changes in the last short period of time and it is jerking some deep frequencies of trauma up through your body mind. They are kind of moving up on through. So you may find yourself a little wobbly and a little precarious feeling over maybe only the next two or three days and it will bring out some funny fears. Did you have a night sweat last night?"

Tanya – "I have those just about every night. Really, really, really bad ones! Like I soak the bed!"

"Are you in menopause?"

Tanya – "No. I am not in menopause."

"To me, you have trauma that is moving out of your body; a cleansing, purification thing. There are things going on in your brain as if you are moving frequencies out and I think that you are in a cleansing. Can you get to a sauna or a steam bath?"

Tanya – "Yes."

"Can you do an Epsom salts bath? I look at you and I want to dip you into all these different things. Honor the fact that you are actually dumping a lot more stuff. You are very much an intuitive. You are very much a healer. You are being pushed to release a ton of things that came with you in this life and came from early childhood and then came from your defense of approaches when you were younger you know. Does that make sense? I'm not too worried about it. Probably in a week or so you are going to feel free and lighter than you have felt in a long time."

Tanya – "Well that's nice to know."

"Tanya, all this clearing is good for you because you will begin to step into your healing work in a big way."

Tanya – "Yes, I can feel it too. Something is shifting. Something big is shifting."

"We will send light to you. Remember; don't be afraid as you are well protected."

Tanya – "Thank you so much Victoria."

After I hung up, Victoria continued on the air and this was what she said. "Well that is a pretty good subject on how we go from having something trigger a memory because she could go into fear but she's not going to. She's got a lot of consciousness, that girl. But she could go into fear and hang into that a little longer than she wants. You know, familiar pain. The best thing to do is go in there and take a look at your identities again….. Like in Tanya's case, she's been through and a lot of you have been through life and death. Deep in the subconscious we have all kinds of memories of ways that we have died, ways that we have been brutalized, and ways that we have brutalized others. We have all kinds of awareness of what it is like on the planet. We are actually feeling what other people are feeling."

October 9

I picked up my walker from the pharmacy and went for a walk to Othello tunnels with Lorne. People stare less when I was pushing a walker than when I was pushing an empty wheelchair. It was less painful to walk with the walker as it was designed to adjust to the body.

There was a slight hill leading to the parking lot from the tunnels that I usually go for what I call, the roller coaster ride in my wheelchair. Yes, I was thirty-seven years old and riding down hills on wheelchairs without knowing the outcome of the ride was exciting for me.

I tried to ride down the hill sitting on my walker and it spun around and started to roll backwards. No way, Jose! I put the brakes to that noise right away! That was most definitely an accident waiting to happen. My leg was just starting to get better and I did not want to risk injuring it more. The thought of me falling or moving my leg a millimeter in the wrong direction was almost enough to make me pass out!

Now that I had the walker, I had more confidence to walk farther. If my legs were tired or seized with pain, I could have a seat right where I was. I never knew in any given day what my leg would do as it seemed to have a mind of its own.

October 10

I woke up a mess in the morning. I could not stop crying. I did not understand why I felt so hurt and abandoned. I felt like curling up into a little ball. I just wanted someone to hold me and tell me that it was going to be ok. That I was going to make it and know what to do. That I was not going to be all alone. Only I did not have anyone to do that. There were billions of people out there so why did I feel so all alone, weak and small! I felt like the little girl Tanya when she was five years old.

I had to pull myself together! I had planned a three hour crystal healing session with my leg today. I needed to fill my head with positive thoughts not ones of hurt and abandonment. How did I get like that? One day I was on top of the world and the next I felt like I was under it. The yo-yo of emotions was killing me! It was day six of my cleanse and maybe I was releasing emotional toxins. I guess it did not help that I was on my period as well.

It could also very well be that I was messed up because I had been writing about my early childhood. However, why was it affecting me like that? I thought I was done with that shit! I was starting to feel like I did right before I went to Sedona. This was not good! I would never survive feeling the way I did at that very moment. I was dying inside again! This could not be happening!

I decided not to use the crystals on my leg that day. I was not in the right frame of mind and could possibly bring more pain and trauma to my knee if I had tried to work with the crystals.

I pretty much spent the following four days a complete unfunctional mess. When I was that messed up, I would not leave my apartment for anything. Not even to get smokes. Lorne was usually the only person that I would allow to see me when I was in that kind of a state. Besides, someone had to go out and get me smokes. It almost felt like the energy that took over me when I came home from Sedona had been slowly leaving me.

Lorne tried to get me out of the apartment by enticing me with nature and suggested that we go for a walk in Othello tunnels. I was in no state to see people so I declined. He suggested that I wear my sunglasses so that no one would see my eyes. He knew how I thought and knew how to work me. I gave in and we went to the tunnels with my sunglasses in tow. I always figured that if no one could see my eyes, they would not see the emotional pain I was in.

By the time we arrived at the last tunnel, I did not have any more life in me to make it back to the parking lot. This was a time I really wished that I had my wheelchair. All I wanted to do was collapse, and not move another muscle. I just wanted to give up, lay on the ground and go to sleep. I hoped that I would wake up and realize it was all a bad dream.

Unfortunately, it was not a dream. I had a long walk back to the van and my body and mind said no way. I made a deal with Lorne. I would walk through the tunnels but he would have to push me while I sat in the walker through the paths in between the tunnels. It was the only way we were going to get out of there. I could not make it all the way by myself. I was giving up. I was losing the battle.

October 15

I awoke in the early hours of the day to go to the bathroom. That was a regular occurrence and usually happened between three and four in the morning. I did not wander around in the dark in case I tripped and fell on something. My leg was not stable enough to be walking blindly. I turned my bedroom light back off and slowly made my way back to my bed.

A few minutes had gone by when I heard a loud bang coming from the kitchen. I turned my head to look out my bedroom door towards the kitchen and noticed that there was a glow coming from the kitchen. I had just walked through there a few minutes ago and it was pitch black. What the heck was going on?

I got out of bed and proceeded to the kitchen with caution and curiosity. Oh my god, the light above the kitchen sink turned itself on! I sat in the chair at my desk and just stared at the light. I was not frightened but very curious. I did not bother to turn any of the main lights on because there was no need. I was not afraid in the least. Whoever turned the light on was benevolent.

I did not know if this meant anything but there was a quartz crystal and a plant on the shelf above the sink. Any time Lorne should be getting up for his middle of the night bathroom break. I had to tell him what just happened but I did not want to wake him up.

I was right. It did not take long before he was in the bathroom. I banged on the wall and told him to come over when he was done. The little bugger went back to bed and did not come over. Damn it! I needed to talk to someone! What did this mean?

I know. My guides and angels were telling me to hold on; the darkness was over, and here comes the light. They could have turned on anything or any light. They chose the light that I never use and it was above a plant and quartz crystal. That must have some meaning. However, what did it mean? I went back to bed, as I needed to get up early for my dentist appointment.

After my dentist appointment I eagerly went back home to tell Lorne and Natasha about the light turning on by itself in the middle of the night. Lorne always had the right words to say. It truly amazed me how he was able to put aside his own belief or shall I say non beliefs to steer me in the right direction.

"See. I told you your guides never left you. They will not leave you. You are just having lessons right now. Everything is going to be all right. You are going to be all right Stubs. If you would just listen to me sometimes and take my advice….."

I am no longer on the cleanse as I completed the ten days. I did not have any food of the sort and only the master cleanse drink for the entire ten days. I was so ready to eat food. The master cleanse drink was not disgusting but after ten days of drinking the same thing repeatedly, your body craves something else.

CHAPTER 11

Milestones

October 22

I had my chiropractor appointment in the morning. He was really working my leg hard. It was getting to the point that I was going to involuntarily kick him in the head. The pain was so deep that it made me light headed afterwards.

After that appointment, I had to rush down the street for my dentist appointment. As I got into the dentist chair, I noticed something was different about my leg. There was such a difference that I had mentioned it to the dental hygienist.

After the dentist, I went home and decided to try walking up the stairs like a regular person. Holy sheep shit! I just walked up the stairs as I did before the accident! Ok, here was an even bigger test. Could I walk down the stairs properly? I could not believe it! I just tried to walk the stairs ten days ago and I could not do it.

Was it really happening? I could not believe it so I continued going up and down the stairs, to make sure it was really happening. Each time I did the flight my eyes got brighter and my smile got bigger. What else could I do?

I decided to try to do a light jog in the hallway of the apartment. You have to be kidding me! I started doing laps up and down the hallway. I screamed with joy, ran to Lorne and Natasha's apartment, and started to frantically knock on the door! Natasha was not there but Lorne was.

I showed him what I could do. I did not want to stop doing laps in the hallway. I had not moved like that since my accident! I screamed and laughed while I jogged back and forth in the hallway like an idiot! Every couple of weeks I had tried to go up and down the stairs like a regular walking person and had been unable to do so until today. I tried the stairs ten days ago and was not successful. Somehow, my leg had straightened enough to be able to move like that. My surgeons told me that it would be highly unlikely that I would ever straighten my leg again. I am happy to say they were wrong!

Lorne suggested that we go to Othello tunnels without the walker today. It was a little dangerous and scary in the tunnels because it was dark and there were many dips on the ground. There was no doubt that my leg was getting better but it was not quite strong enough to walk safely on unlevel ground. I went slowly and made it without the walker.

After the tunnels, I dropped off Lorne and met up with David. I jogged laps in his kitchen to show him what I could do and then we took his dog for a long walk. By the end of the day both my legs hurt so much that I could hardly move. When I lay still in bed, they were throbbing and aching. It was worth it though! The more I work it, the farther I would be able to go. What an amazing day this had been!

October 27

Natasha told me something interesting tonight. She said she had felt what she thought was one of her cats in bed with her one night. She had wondered how they got in her bedroom when the door was closed. She turned on her bedroom light to see what cat was in her room, and to her surprise, there was no cat! She now believed that we had a cat ghost in our building as well.

November 2

I phoned XYZ Radio to speak with the intuitive named June. I explained to June, "A couple of weeks ago, I heard a loud sound in the middle of the night and one of my kitchen lights turned itself on. Was this my guide's way of saying that they haven't left me and to hang on, they are shining the light on me?" This was the feedback she gave me.

"Ok. What I started getting immediately as soon as you started talking and explaining a little bit of what you have been going through, they gave me an example that they often give when they are changing the arena. I don't know if you have heard me talk about this or not where a lot of times, they will show us as sitting like students in a large arena and we are like in the middle of the field. And the guides as they are teaching us and we are learning things, we will go up and down off of the bleachers. They will come in and bring us the new messages. That's what it feels like you have been in, one of those transitional periods.

"Your spirit guide has never left you. Your spirit guide will always be by your side but sometimes they step back and allow us to go through some of the bumps we have to go through because if it was all easy, why would we be here. They are showing me that your guide is very prevalent there.

"They are showing me the significance of the light coming on is a reminder to you to know that in order to chase this dark period away from yourself, that all you have to do is turn on your own personal internal spiritual intuitive light and it is going to chase that darkness away. It is something that is symbolism is what they are telling me. That light coming on and making the noise to get your attention was to give you the awareness that all you have to do is turn that light on.

"Don't feel like you have been left alone. What they are showing me is symbolically almost like you are standing in the middle of this football field and you're standing there about to stretch and all of a sudden, you realize that they are changing places and it is like nobody is there. So you are kind of looking around going, hello, hello. That is what they are showing me is going on and soon it will come back into play. Everyone is going to move into position on your playing field.

"They are actually getting you ready to start you on a whole new learning curve, a whole new development."

Tanya – "I was starting to think that it is some kind of a test to see where my strength is at. To see how far I have come."

"I don't see it as a test but there is that level of patience we have to get a hold of. There is a level of knowing that in order for something highest good and in order for something divine light to come through, we sometimes have to accept that and wait a minute.

"And that is what it feels like they are showing me and for some reason, do you have any Irish heritage or British heritage? I am seeing that I don't even know what it is called. But it is the symbol where the two united hands and the heart around it."

Tanya – "I'm not too sure if I have that kind of heritage."

"Ok. There is something about that that is showing me like there is a union coming within yourself and some of the learning and some of the things that are going to activate within you. It is kind of like the love of the heart uniting an energy."

Tanya – "I feel like I should be doing something on the 11th of this month. Any hints on that?"

"You could do ceremony because that is the perfect time to align energy and in that ceremony can be a time of entering into meditation, bringing yourself into alignment with that energy. We need to ensure that we are letting go of what does not serve our highest good and we draw in that which is for our divine purpose. They may be leading you into that as it is a good time to let go and a good time to draw in."

Tanya – "Thank you so much June."

November 4

I had just found out that Lorne and Natasha broke up, and Lorne moved to Langley to live with his sister. They had fought and broken up before but he usually ended up coming back. Something tells me that might not be happening this time.

That worried me because Lorne was my rock. He had seen me through so much and even though he was the biggest skeptic I knew, he somehow understood me and knew the right words to say. Maybe it was time for me to walk on my own two feet without him. Life would not be the same without him. I knew this day would come and it saddens me.

November 7

Today was the last intuitive training workshop that I would be taking with Deanna. I will be so glad when I was done taking classes with her. What a gong show! I now know why when the very first second I met her, the energy she gave off was the same as Claire Clark's. Of course, I never listened to my instincts and thought that there was no way someone that had been consciously working with angels all their life could have the same energy as Claire. However, as I observed over the months, indeed it was true.

I did not believe that Deanna was here to serve as much as she claimed. I felt that her first and foremost objective was money. She even stated that she only wanted to work one hour a day. She treated her helpers like crap as well, just as Claire did.

I know no one was perfect and I certainly did not claim to be but I guess I just expected more from someone who claimed to be as gifted as she was. She may be gifted but she was not a true light worker. I was having difficulties finding true light workers. The one thing I could definitely take away from those workshops was how not to conduct workshops and how not to treat others.

It seemed to me that my guides had been showing me how not to behave and treat people; also to trust my first instinct. For example, with Deanna, the second I met her I was overwhelmed with the kind of energy that Claire Clark had. I immediately told my instincts that I was wrong because Deanna worked with angels and angels were good.

I am constantly trying to prove my instincts wrong. When I get them, I usually try to deny them because I could not imagine or fathom they would be true. The way I receive information was it just popped into my head unexpectedly. I disregard the information but not fully. That was when I went into observation mode. I eventually figured out that my instincts or predictions were indeed dead on.

November 9

I phoned XYZ Radio to speak with the intuitive named Lilli. She had a guest on her show named Roger. I asked Roger, "Is there any messages for me at this time?" This was the feedback he gave me.

"I have what will come forth for you. Where's your strength? What does that mean to you? Strength? You have lost a sense of power right now. I hear the word strength for you. What does that mean for you? It's almost like you have put it on the side. It's important for you to get more of a deeper sense of self. You're quite powerful by the way. It has something to do with, how do you feel about being a woman that's really umm; let's see how can I say this. A woman that is totally empowered and does not care how she is viewed. How does that look to you?"

Tanya – "That is something that I am trying to achieve right now."

"Yeah. And once you do, look out world."

Tanya – "Exactly!" (I giggled)

"So I sense that your mom, it's interesting, your, I get a sense that your mom had two aspects going on. Its almost like she came one part was really strong and the other part she kind of hid. You were pretty perceptive as a child. Tell me, is that kind of a sense of your mom."

Tanya – "In a sense I always thought mom was weak, and an alcoholic, and I had a rough childhood. But then when I look back now, she left an abusive man with absolutely nothing and me in tow and off we went sort of thing. So I guess she had some sort of power to be able to that."

"Well she, what she did is she gave herself away. What happens with many women and not so much with men, women primarily come into the world as caretakers. So they give from there heart where men are much more independent so they will just say I am going to go do this and they go and do it.

"Where woman as a whole like to have a belonging. I sense that your mom, she left, its almost like you, she gave her power away by giving of herself to this relationship, but there was another part of her that was hidden but it was also strong just like you what you are doing.

"So one of the ways, when you hear the words forgiveness, what does that mean? What does that mean to you? When someone is forgiving, what are they doing?"

Tanya – "When they are forgiving, they are letting go."

"Exactly. It is time for you to let go of that, which has held you back. So my suggestion is to write down all that you have held on to and do a, what would be something that you could do that would be signifying letting go."

Tanya – "Writing it all down, going up to the mountains and burning it."

"There you go. You know who holds the key for you here. Is that part of you that is the child. So she's the one that comes out and feels, so here is something else, I often suggest this to clients, is to. Tell me first what were you called as a child? Do you have a name that you went by?"

Tanya – "Tanya."

"Little Tanya. Oh, she's feisty! Damn!"

Tanya – "Yeah, she is!" (We both have a good long giggle.)

Mystical Puzzle

"That's you too. So you have that as well. So you have this feistiness, so know this about you, this is important to get into, you might want to take some time to write down how you use this part. Feisty is the one that is strong. She is the one that says you know this is who I am and I am going to do just what ever it is regardless of society or man or whoever how they perceive me. She's the one that cares about herself and is not dependent. So you don't have to be, you don't need to be affirmed, ok.

"So here is what I would suggest is to write to the little Tanya and let her know how much you love her, how much you care about her, that whatever she says that you will listen to her, and that what ever she does you are there for her support. Because, you understand?"

Tanya – "I do."

"Oh, before you go, if you have the medicine cards, look up horse energy; that is you."

At that point, Lilli had a message for me as well.

"Tanya, I just have one small message and we have another caller on the line. Just let me give you your message from Archangel Michael. Michael says that you have a lot of sense of humor so try to see the situation with humor, which is very lovingly. You have a wonderful laugh and so just you know, ask Archangel Michael for help and shield you with a lot of white light in certain situations that you going through. So just remember that your humor helps you so much because you are so strong and powerful."

Tanya – "Ok. Thank you so much both of you."

I always found it interesting with the kinds of information that comes through when I talk to intuitives. It was funny that Roger mentioned, "Look out world" because that was something that I said often. I was already planning a burning ceremony, so that was confirmation for me that that was something that I really needed to do.

In addition, Roger mentioned Little Tanya. When I came back from Sedona and started to change my living environment around, I dedicated a corner in my bedroom called the Little Tanya or the child within corner. On a table, I have a black and white picture of me and my cousin Lori. I was three or four, had no shirt on and my face was covered in dirt. The picture was priceless. I have a candle, a few stuffed animals, and a bed of crystal quartz points on the table as well.

In the morning, I light my candle, I tell Little Tanya how lovable she was, and that she had many challenges ahead but to always remember she was never alone. She had me as well as a team of angels and ET's to help her along the way. We would never abandon her.

230

November 10

Natasha came over in the morning claiming that she was officially freaked out because while she was showering, the bathroom light turned itself off. She now, without a doubt, believed that there were indeed spirits in our apartment building. The activity had been unusually high and they were now making themselves known to her, as well as Lorne about a month ago.

I wondered if it was the spirits in the building that were the ones that wrote *S O S* when I was trying to do automatic writing. I had only attempted to try automatic writing twice. Once when I wanted to try it and the other time was when something was making me pick up the pen. I know I am some sort of a beacon to spirits, but I was not sure how to help them yet. Spirits gravitate to me as bugs do to a bright light.

November 11

I started to think about something. November 11th is Remembrance Day. Did that have anything to do with me seeing 11:11 everywhere and that it was supposed to be some kind of trigger to help *remember* something? Or was that just a coincidence?

November 12

I had decided that today was the day that I would share the channeling with my guides with Natasha. I felt like she was ready to hear it and she would not think I was crazy. I had spoken very openly on topics such as spirits, ET's and UFO's around her, and she had taken an interest in the subjects by reading some of my books.

I trusted that she would be honest with me as she had been up until now. She openly tells me that there were many things that I talk about that she did not necessarily believe or understand, but there were also things that resonated with her and had prompted her to give deeper thought. She assured me that what ever my secret was, she was not going to leave me and think I was crazy.

It felt good to finally share with her that I was a starseed. She was only the fourth person I had told in the last six months. She did not look at me as if I was a crazy freak and she accepted what I shared with her. In fact, she told me that she could care less that I thought that I was an ET, but there was no way that she would walk in town with me, if I wore my lime green belly dance coin pants in public. I did not see what the big deal was. I think we should all be able to wear and express who we were regardless of what others thought. One day I would have Natasha convinced to wear a matching pair of coin pants with me.

Now if only it could go that smoothly with everyone else. The people that I had shared with see me on a daily basis so it was obvious to them that I had not gone crazy but for people that simply read my book and were not there to observe me on a regular basis, well I could see how they would think that I had lost it.

November 13

Something strange happened last night when I was in bed. I was not sleeping as it happened a couple of minutes after I had crawled into bed for the night. I was lying on my stomach with my legs slightly spread. The blankets started to curl around my legs as if there was something crawling on top of the blankets but between my legs.

Holy cow! It was the cat ghost! I was not sure if it was my cat Molly or the cat ghost who was here when Molly was alive. It did not scare me at all. I was more curious than anything else. I lay there as still as could be to see what it would do. It was a weird sensation to have the blankets curl around my legs as they were, but nothing was physically there. That was not the first time that the cat ghost had been on my bed.

November 27

Disability cut me off seven weeks ago and I had not had an income since. I had enough money to get me through until the end of the year if I did not buy Christmas presents and I did not have any unplanned emergencies that cost money. I brought a note to my work from my doctor stating to try me back at work for four hours a day and we would go from there.

I had absolutely no intentions of going back to work there. It would mentally, emotionally, physically and spiritually kill me. I would rather dig food out of the garbage than go back to work there! If they found a position for me, I would end up fired for the first time in my life. I needed closure with that company one way or the other. I knew that they were slow and even if my leg were fully healed, they still would not have a position for me to go back to.

It was not that I was lazy and did not want to work; I just knew that I was not meant to work there. Besides, my leg was not fully healed and I would like to concentrate my efforts on healing. I was getting so close that I could taste it!

During my meeting with the Human Resources Manager and Director of the company that I worked for, they informed me that they did not have a job available for me to go back to even if my leg was fully healed. The Director asked the Manager to prepare a leaving the company package.

I put in a prayer to my angels for an amount of money that would last until I decided how I was going to financially take care of myself.

November 29

I phoned XYZ Radio to speak with the intuitive named Marco. I asked him for a general reading. This was the feedback he gave me.

"I will put out what I am feeling. Right away, I am going to finances but I am not sure what they are saying about it. I really do feel like it is going to get better. Some problems will be resolved. Are you wrestling with an issue with finances right now?"

Tanya – "I was on disability for two and a half years and they just cut me off about seven weeks ago. I am meeting my employer tomorrow to pick up my leaving the company package."

"I feel satisfied in your favor for some reason. I feel it going very well.

"Another thing to, did you just fall in love or meet somebody or is it an anniversary? Are you with somebody now?"

Tanya – "No, I have been single for a long time."

"Wow. It feels like you are about to meet somebody. I don't want to ruin your day. (We both started to giggle.) It feels like it doesn't matter or you're not really out there hunting but man I feel like you are going to meet someone."

Tanya – "I am not out there hunting per se, but it would be nice to find an ideal partner."

"It doesn't seem like you are driven crazy by it. It will happen when it happens. Available but not looking; available but not available.

"They keep showing me this guy coming into your life and he rings your bell or fireworks go off. Within the next three months, it's either March or between now and March. I want to say uniform or military, security or law enforcement. It doesn't necessarily mean that he is, just because I am seeing a uniform. It is some type of a clue. It could be him or it could be something else connected to him.

"Because I am also feeling believe it or not is real estate and building. I'm in the building trades. It could be that he is the owner of a business or a foreman or a supervisor. He has authority. Watch for a good looking guy, brown hair, and he carries himself well, he seems very mature about like you. He is a good match. Available but not available, same type of energy.

"It may come about through; I want to say employment or business. I'm not sure about that. Either something with family and property or employment. I don't know what they are trying to say to me with this. Be alert in both areas. If there is something going on with the family and meeting with them be alert or somebody at work or in the course of business, be alert. But it comes from one of those realms like family brings him to you and introduces you or you meet him through work or business.

"Meditation. I keep hearing meditation for some reason. I don't know if you dabble in the arts or if you're into meditation but they want you to increase it or get in to it. It will be very beneficial for you. Did you have any questions?"

Tanya – "Are there any psychic gifts that I should focus on unfolding in the next year?"

Mystical Puzzle

"This is funny because I was going to tell you that you were very psychic and you're the one messing up this phone line right now. You have high energy. You're very psychic."

Tanya – "I blow a lot of electrical items in the home. I constantly have to go to the main breaker after touching electrical things in my apartment. I fried my modem, the kitchen light and the microwave breaker had to be reset the other day."

"What it feels like to me is static electricity all over my skin and it is coming through my phone so you should be dabbling in healing. Especially reiki and anything to do with therapeutic touch and transmission of thought or prayer healing.

"They beat you to it when they said meditation. If you were to focus on anything on the upcoming year, it would be meditation so that you could become more structured and formatted. You're a little all over the place. I wish you luck with it, have fun."

Tanya – "Thank you so much Marco! Blessings!"

I spent the afternoon until sunset on a forest service road in the mountains that I could access with my van. While I was there, I wrote a letter to my mom telling her that even though our lives were brutally challenged, I know that she did the best that she could for us. In fact, I did not know how she managed to take care of us on what little she had. I could not really find the right words to express myself. I just wanted her to know that I had forgiven her for all my hurts.

I also wrote down everything that I wanted to release. My intent was to let go of all that does not serve me. Just as the sun was coming down, I read everything that I had written, burned it and let go.

I brought an offering of fruits and vegetables for Mother Earth and placed them in all four directions. After I grounded myself with the earth and centered myself with the cosmos, I did a world peace prayer before going back home.

Once I was home, I smudged the healing hut and myself and did a twenty-five minute chakra balancing meditation. By the end of the night, I closed my facebook account. I felt like facebook was like reading the newspaper or watching the news. Once in awhile there was something worth reading but the rest was a bunch of negative crap!

December 2

When I woke up in the morning, I remembered having some sort of a dream. I did not remember who was talking to me but they kept saying that I was powerful. I remembered saying I know, that was what everyone kept telling me, but I did not know what it meant or what I was supposed to do with it. I guess in time I would find out.

Aunt Flow from Red River, aka my period, came for a visit. Normally I would not share that with you but you will see why. I was one of those unlucky women that had a lot of cramping during the first couple of days of my period.

Natasha suggested that I try to use some of my crystals to alleviate the cramps. I determined that placing chrysocolla, citrine, magnesite, and rose quartz in a medicine bag and placing the bag over my sacral chakra (four inches below belly button) would work.

Natasha asked if I wanted to go for a walk to the tunnels. I did not think they would be open this time of the year, but thought it would never hurt to try. Maybe someone cut through the gate and we would be able to get through anyways.

The gate was locked and no one had cut through it yet. It was quite cold out anyways. I was not sure we would have lasted walking to the last tunnel and back. We went back to my place to warm up and watch a movie.

I went to the bathroom and something fell out of my pants. Oh yeah, my medicine bag of crystals! That was when I had realized that I did not have any cramps and completely forgot about the medicine bag and my cramps. This was awesome! Now I just needed to find other women with cramps, and try it on them.

December 7

Natasha came over in the morning. She started to talk about the previous night and I said, "There was something in your room, wasn't there?" She nodded yes. We both felt uneasy in our bedrooms at the same time. Our bedrooms were beside each other but we lived in different suites.

She thought the cat ghost was at her place and I thought it had walked on my pillow. I was not sleeping and had just got into bed when something stepped on the pillow that my head was on. I figured it was the cat ghost.

I also felt a snake like thing crawling up my pajama leg. That did not really frighten me as I knew that nothing physical was in my pajama's and I gave my angels and ET's permission every night to continue healing my leg while I was resting and asleep. Just incase, I called Archangel Michael for protection.

December 9

My throat had been bothering me for a few days and I had a killer headache. Natasha suggested I try using my crystals. I determined that I would use amber, angelite, and blue lace agate for fifteen minutes placed on my forehead. I lied down on my meditation mat and my head was pounding more than ever.

After about six or seven minutes my entire body felt like it was having some sort of major anxiety attack. Every millimeter of my body felt like it wanted to go in every direction possible. I did not know what was happening and I did not like it! I felt like I wanted to bolt or throw up or something.

I quickly removed the stones and ran to the bathroom. I felt hot and dizzy but I did not end up getting sick. I realized I still had another eight minutes of lying down with the stones on my forehead. I proceed to lay down with the stones and that weird anxiety feeling came back. My head hurt so much I almost wanted to go to the hospital.

I felt like throwing up again and was completely disoriented. I started to cry because I did not know what was happening. All I did know was I did not feel good at all. I decided to try to sleep it off and went to bed.

December 10

When I woke up this morning, my head felt fine and my throat was no longer sore. I did not know what happened last night but what a violent way of healing. I suppose if there were toxins in my body and they were removed in fifteen minutes instead of a few weeks, I suppose the body could have a violent reaction to that. However, I did not know because I was not a doctor and did not know how the physical body reacted to elimination of toxins or infections.

My friend Sam stopped by for a visit. I asked her when was she going to Costa Rica and she informed me that she had already been and had come back. What!? I just saw you a few days ago. Apparently, my few days ago were actually a month ago. That did not feel like a whole month.

December 17

Upon awakening, I phoned Michelle. She had phoned me last night to let me know that she received my birthday wishes, but I was not home. She told me about her trip to Alberta for her birthday and that they met up with a mutual friend from BC. She started to describe to me how much Tim had changed in the last four months.

I stopped her short and started to tell her that she already told me all that on the trip they went on a couple of weeks ago with Tim and that she and Clay hung out with him for a couple of days and then went on their own for a couple of days.

Michelle then informed me that they never went anywhere on a trip with Tim a couple of weeks ago and that she just got home yesterday on a trip with him. She also confirmed that yes; they did spend some time with him and then went off on their own.

That was trippy, as I could have sworn she told me all that stuff not too long ago. What was even trippier was that I told her stuff that happened that she did not tell me. Whoa! As soon as I figured out what was happening I ended up shutting this déjà vu or intuition thing down. She asked me if I knew about her flight and I could not go any further with whatever just happened.

I froze after that. I knew I was getting information that I should not have known. As soon as I tried to make sense of it all, it went away. I needed to learn to let it flow and not try to make sense of it.

December 19

I tried to sleep but had difficulties as usual. All the two hour alarm intervals that I had set never woke me up because I was already awake, and I shut them off before they went off. I had a strange experience at around 2:30 in the morning. I will try my best to explain it.

I was laying in bed on my side with my back faced to the edge of the bed. I heard what sounded like some people entering my apartment using keys. Only they were not really people. I did not really know what they were but they were walking into my bedroom.

I could hear them whisper as they were getting closer to me, "Do you think she is awake? Do you think she can hear us?" There were three or four of them and I was not exactly sure what *them* was? They hovered all around me and I did not like the feeling that I was getting. They were dark energies of some sort. In my head, I said to them, "Um, hello, I'm not sleeping right now!"

I tried to push them away from me but I was paralyzed and could not move. Now I was really confused! I could feel those things all around me but I could not move. Shit! I hate it when this happened. I was stuck in between states of awareness. It took so much energy to break free from that paralyzed state, not to mention it felt slightly creepy to be awake but paralyzed in my own body.

I broke free and bopped two of them in the shoulder or head area to get away from me. Those things in my room were not physical and they were some how trying to assault me. I started to call for Archangel Michael and then I remembered something. I needed to turn on my light, my eternal light that was.

I closed my eyes and tried to fill my body and my bedroom with white light. I was not going to let those bastards scare me and start using my night light again. It took a little work to make them go away but eventually they left. I dared not try to go to sleep right away because if I did, they might come back and put me in the paralyzed state again.

I almost wanted to try it and learn to work with it and not be afraid of it but it really was a creepy experience. I was not exactly sure what was going on when I experienced those kinds of events. Most of the things that I experienced while I was supposed to be sleeping were too bizarre for words. Sometimes I get messages of some sort and I was aware that it was happening, but I did not know the language. A part of me knew the language but I had not consciously figured out how to decipher it.

Mystical Puzzle

December 21

In exactly three years, the day so many have prophesied about will be here. I do not know what to think about 2012. I have researched and have read so many theories and frankly, any one of them could happen, as anything was possible.

What I did know was that something was definitely going on. Something big would happen in this life time. Something that had every single person on this planet caught with his or her mouth wide open in disbelief. I cannot say that it will happen on 2012 or 2020, but something was definitely going on.

December 26

When I woke up, I checked on a documentary that I had downloaded to see if it turned out ok. I had fast forward into the movie and watched for a couple of minutes to ensure the video and audio were coordinated. I accidently bumped my mouse and that triggered the time into the movie to display. It was 11:11.

I guess I was due for a breakdown because it had been awhile. I had never broken down when I saw the numbers before. This time it triggered me to freak slightly out. What if I did not remember everything that I was supposed to?

I actually sat and bawled my eyes out because I worried that if I did not remember, I might fail my mission. I did not want people to suffer because I forgot what I came here to do. I signed myself up for some crazy ass mission and now I had to remember before it was too late.

So crazy that I refused to come here unless an alarm clock would go off to wake me up. Those kind of thoughts made me realize how alone I was in this world. I have no one to talk about this stuff when it came up because no one had a clue what it really felt like.

How many people do you know that cry at the thought of failing their mission? Exactly! Yes, I know how screwed up that sounds. It would be nice to meet someone in the flesh that really knew what I was going through. Only that would be like looking for a needle in a haystack.

My little breakdown was short lived and I pulled myself together. I was determined that no matter what challenges come my way; I would always get through them.

December 27

I phoned XYZ Radio to speak with the intuitive named Pricilla. I explained to her, "just over a year ago I experienced a dramatic awakening where my highest self had taken over and in the last few months I feel as though she is not in the driver's seat. What happened and where did she go?" This was the feedback she gave me.

"Well, what my feeling is and what I am hearing is that higher self came through to help you through a very difficult period in your life and now it is your time to assume control and to carry on with that change. You are able to do that.

"The withdrawal was so that you don't suffer the abrupt feeling of loss. It is giving you the opportunity to assume the driver's seat. Your higher self came through to help you through a very difficult period of time. To help you with transition in your life and to help reestablish your direction.

"The slow withdrawal from you is to enable you to be able to stand on your own feet. To go forward yourself because enough change has been made and you have grown enough. You have matured enough to be able to move forward and that higher power is with you.

"You also had power from another source and I would say from what I am understanding, not only was your higher self involved but I would say a mentor or guardian angel or teacher was there with you and you felt that entities power in your life.

"Again out of love to help you move forward and now that you have reached a place where you can continue on, that is being slowly withdrawn so that you didn't become completely addicted to it and not live on your own two feet.

"But the thing is you will always have that power to rely on and back you up ok. You will have that power and it is there and available to you. It is not one hundred percent withdrawn and will never be. When you need it, you will get that tremendous feeling back because that entity that helped you out is part of your troop of helpers for you in this life time. You will not be without them. You are just learning to stand more on your own two feet, which is what is important for you to do now. They are still with you in other words.

"They are gradually allowing you to come into your power. Your own power. It is there for you but wasn't it a blessing to have them? It is a wonderful blessing. I have felt that type of interference or help in my life also."

Tanya – "It saved my life."

"Exactly. The same thing happened for me. It saved my life too. It kept me from going over the edge. It helped me through a horrific part of my life that I would not wish on my worst enemy.

"That power is of overwhelming love and that is something now since you have experienced it, you can now develop on your own to share with other people in your life. Did you know that?

"You can use the memory of that love and that power. You can use it to grow in your own life to the extent that you can now help other people with what you learned. You can develop that loving power to help others who are in need because the memory is now a part of who you are and you can develop that love to become a powerful gift to help other people.

"God bless you dear; you have a good life ahead of you. You have a very good life ahead of you. You are coming into your own and there was a reason for having to go through what you went through. If you didn't go through it all, you couldn't come into your own.

"There are times when you have to go through things where you think in your mind, good lord why would I ever want to go through that. Because if you didn't, you wouldn't have gained the strength and the knowledge and the understanding to move ahead on your path in life and to fulfill your mission.

"And it is not all roses and candle light and sweet smelling flowers and sugar candies. It is a hard road to hold but there is a reason for that. The power that we have to grow is exponential and sometimes we have to go through hell before we can reach a place. Again if we didn't know what hell was how would we know what heaven is?"

I thanked Pricilla for her time and all that she provided. There was a lot of static on my end of the phone so a lot of the information I could not hear as she was giving it to me. I had to go to the archive file to retrieve the reading.

Later during the program, the following was what she said.

"The lady who called and said that someone came in and seemed to take care of her during a very difficult period. Without it she would have not have made it. That's true. And now she has grown immeasurably and now she can move forward. It is time for her to be honored in taking her own soul back and moving forward because she has learned many lessons unconsciously that are going to become in good stead because that is in all part of knowledge to her and her unconscious that is going to come to fruit in the future. Again, that is one of the blessings of the gift of a higher soul coming in to help us through these very very difficult times."

The feelings of losing my best friend made so much sense now. The energy that took over me when I came back from Sedona had been slowly leaving me so that I could start to walk on my own two feet. I actually felt it leaving me. Thank god it left me gradually and not in an instant like it did when it came in.

January 4, 2010

I was running a little late for my doctor's appointment and kicked up the speed a notch. I ran down the stairs to the garage. Hey, I just ran down the stairs without thinking twice as if it was something that I had done all along. Did you hear me? I just *ran* down the stairs!

My appointment was to see what the next steps were to figure out why I was soaking the bed in sweat while I slept. All the tests that the endocrinologist took came back normal other than the borderline diabetes. It had also been confirmed that I did not have tuberculosis or HIV. My second twenty-four hour urine collection came back fine. All the blood work, the CAT scan and ultrasound of my liver came back fine as well. My doctor could not find anything physically wrong with me.

I was confident that it had to do with the change and transformation that I had been going through. I could not exactly tell my doctor that angels and ET's work on me during the deepest hours of the night and that was where all the sweating was coming from.

January 9

You would never guess whom I ran into. Bob. I had not talked to him since June. I found out that his phone fell into a pool and he lost all his phone numbers. I was not listed in the phone book and it was not as if he could just knock on my front door as I lived in an apartment building with no intercom. Not to mention he lived in a completely different town. Oh yeah, he was married.

We could not talk freely and openly when we saw each other so he handed me a note with his phone number on it and asked me to call him. I sent him a text later in the day and it turned out that he missed spending time with me. Of course he did, we use to rock each other's world! He also said he was going to try to visit me in the next couple of days. I did not know what it was with him, but we were like magnet and steel.

January 11

Fortunately, Bob was unable to make it because later in the day, Mother Nature came for a visit and I got my period. And hello, I just had my tubes tied and an ovary removed, I did not think I was supposed to be engaging in sexual activity quite yet. Interesting how I was typing about Bob just now, and I just glanced at the time on my computer, and it was 4:44pm.

Well, I still believed that everything happened for a reason. I had no plans of chasing him down. If he happened to contact me when I was healed from my surgery, I would decide what to do then.

January 16

I learned something very valuable today. As my sister was parking her van, I looked over at her confused and asked why was she parking so far away. I thought that maybe she was trying to lose weight and she parked farther away for the extra exercise. I was truly shocked at her response. Read carefully as we could all learn something from this. Her response was, "I always park far away. Someone who has a baby or is elderly might need those spots."

Wow! I never had thought of that myself. Before my accident, whenever I would go somewhere, I would always look for the closest spot for my own selfish needs and never once thought that maybe someone else in need could really use the spot. I thanked my sister for teaching me something very valuable.

January 22

Natasha and Lorne came over, told me that they were in another accident, and totaled her car. Oh my god, I could not believe that! Last night at 9:21pm, I started to have thoughts that she was in an accident again.

The reason I knew exactly what time it was, was because when I had those kinds of thoughts, I look to see what time it was to see if I was predicting something or somehow reading energy after the event. In this case, the information came to me after the accident, just like her last one.

Lorne thought that I was totally making it up that I knew last night that the car was totaled. I asked Natasha if she believed me. She said that she believed that things come to me but because she had never experienced it, it was hard for her to believe me. I looked at her and said, "Why would I make this up? That would just be plain stupid!" It did not matter to me whether they believed me or not. I knew it was true because it was my head that had the thoughts.

One thing that I had noticed was more comes to me when I meditate. I meditated yesterday for the first time in a long time. I also placed a super seven crystal on my third eye while I meditated. Come to think of it, I was sitting on the toilet when the thoughts of Natasha and Lorne were in an accident. For some reason, stuff comes to me while I was sitting on the toilet. Weird!

February 10

I was over at Natasha's place and I randomly brought up that sometimes I wondered if I was receiving the call to be a shaman. I had always thought that only natives could be shamans. I did not know why I would bring up such a topic.

February 12

I was in the hallway of the apartment when Natasha came out of her apartment. She was on her way to the post office so I joined her because I needed to pick up smokes. She needed to go to the bank but I was not joining her to go there because I did not do bank line ups.

I was going to cross the street and just go home while she went to the bank, but then I had the urge to go to the flower shop next to the bank. That was very odd, as I never went in the shop. The prices were outrageous. It was not just that shop that was expensive, I found all flower shops to be over priced.

I walked in and immediately saw a bear sculpture hanging on the wall. I was so drawn to the bear that I felt like it needed to come home with me.

That was odd as I was not into bears but really felt as though that bear was supposed to be mine.

I was afraid to ask how much it cost but thought it never hurt to ask. The bear cost three hundred and twenty-five dollars but the owner said that she would give it to me for fifty percent off. I did not know why but I just had to have the bear and I bought it.

Natasha came into the flower shop after the bank and asked me what I was doing buying the bear when I was on a strict budget. I would eat the food in my cupboard before buying new food if it meant that I could have the bear.

She also asked me where I planned to put it and I had no idea. Natasha suggested that I put it in my bedroom for protection as the bear looked fierce. That was odd coming from Natasha. When I got home I looked up the bear animal totem on the internet, and this was what I found.

* A bear totem or spirit guide symbolizes great strength, security and determination for the Shaman. To American Indians, the Bear has a strong heart and unwavering will, and to Japanese and Siberian Shamans he is the leader of the animals, the animal that taught humans Shamanism.
* The bear as power animal is intuitive and can often manifest healing. Imagine a bear hug. While one might not wish for such a real life encounter with a grizzly bear, the all encompassing strength of a bear animal familiar is a safe and reassuring environment for restoration of both body and spirit. The bear spirit guide thus helps his shaman companion to heal mental, physical and spiritual wounds with intuition and self-assured courage.
* The bear is a symbol of invincibility, offering a secure refuge for those who enjoy the company of a totem bear spirit guide. The Shaman of bear power animal has a determined ally in spiritual work, loyal and utterly dependable.
* The bear is an introspective creature, independent and apparently aloof. He has with little need for fraternity, rather he is self-contained and strong-willed. A Bear spirit guide is of great support and comfort to those who crave human company simply for personal reassurance rather than for the simple pleasure of being with friends. He makes lonely periods of life far easier, and can help the Shaman to work in isolation to gain deep insights.
* The bear represents female energies, hibernating to reconnect with the earth each year, and emerging with answers to spiritual dilemmas. Those with a bear spirit guide can harness this natural connection with the earth to seek insights within. (*Brannan*, 2009)

The other night I questioned whether I was receiving the call of the Shaman and unexpectedly I buy a bear sculpture that Natasha suggested I hung in my bedroom for protection. Bear totem symbolized strength, security, and determination for the Shaman.

Mystical Puzzle

I had just noticed that Lorne had sent a bunch of texts to my cell phone last night. He mentioned that he had not visited with me much while he was in Hope. I sent him the following email.

Lorne,

I got your texts. I was awake then but I do not keep my phone glued to me like the rest of the world, so I did not know that you sent them.

No, you did not see me much when you came to Hope. I expected it to happen eventually. Remember, your mission has been completed. You kept me alive long enough for the switch to turn on. You do not have to be a part of my life anymore and that is what you showed me while you were here.

Even while Natasha was at work, you chose not to visit me. Not to mention after everything that I have shared with you, you still think that I would lie about something as stupid as knowing that you guys were in an accident again only this time the car was totaled. People come and people go. It is all part of the process. You just happened to play a bigger part.

Always remember, when I speak of my experiences, I would never bullshit about that kind of stuff. I know it is weird and I also know that I am not the only one that experiences such events. Just because you have never been to an African jungle, does not mean that it does not exist because you personally never experienced it.

Like others like me, we are ahead of the times. Each and every one of us has a role to play. Humans are so much more capable than they know. A shift is coming and it is time for the truth to come out. The shift is so close. I can taste it. There is something very significant about the time that we are living in. Surely, you can feel something. Like you cannot quite put your finger on it, but you notice that something is different, something is happening.

As I am putting my book together and remembering the different events in my life, my sensitivity to spirits and energy has always been there. I did not really know what it was. I have also learned that I am far stronger and resilient than I give myself credit.

Yes, I have fallen more than once and I have fallen hard, but I always get back up. I just finished writing about my life during 2001 when I went to Asia and I cannot believe I actually lived it and am here to talk about it.

Although there were very good things that happened that year, it ended with me being beaten to the pulp. Not a physical beating, an emotional and mental one. It is those beatings that build us. We do not know it at the time because at the time all we know is hurt and pain. But later is when you build strength and courage from it.

Stubs (his nickname for me)

I ended the email with the lyrics from the song *Superman* by Five For Fighting.

As much as a dumb ass that he could be, he was the glue that kept me together through one of the most difficult periods of my life. He kept me alive until my awakening and then surprisingly, stuck by me during the confusion of my transformation. However, like all my soul mates, his mission was done and he was now not in my life.

February 27

My mom and my nephew Jake came over in the afternoon for an overnight trip. After lunch, I took Jake for a walk to Flood Falls. It had been quite awhile since he was last there and he had asked if I could take him there. After dinner, we made banana bread and cookies together.

Mom had asked me to do her taxes and told me about a benefit that was fairly new. She said that Corrina received extra money at GST time because of it. It sounded like the same form that I threw in my recycling box when I did my taxes the other day. I remembered looking at it and thinking that I had never seen that form before and just assumed that it never applied to me.

My instincts told me to look it up in the explanations book and I totally ignored them and recycled the forms. It turned out that my mom made too much to qualify but I actually did qualify. I pulled the form out of my recycling box and discovered that I was entitled to fifteen hundred dollars!

I unsealed my taxes and adjusted the amount with the new benefit. It made sense why I never mailed my income tax return, because had I done that, I may have missed that benefit. I never listened to my angels when they were trying to show me the form so they went through my sister and mom to get through to me. They were so clever and I was ever so thankful for the extra money!

March 2

I just finished listening to the session with the intuitive named Kylee from start to finish for the first time since it was recorded. She was my very first session when I went to Sedona. As that was my first session, so much of what she was saying, I had no clue what she was talking about, especially when it came to the spiritual stuff and being awake and all.

I had been wondering if I had been receiving the call of the shaman and I think I got my answer. According to Kylee, when I went to Sedona, I did not go there to learn, I went there to remember. "You have to start doing your shaman work is what I am getting at here because that is who you are." she said. When I listen to the reading now, I understand the language. Back then, I did not.

I have to tell you. I have been feeling rather calm lately. Like the calm before the storm, kind of calm. There was no doubt in my mind that I have an incredible journey ahead of me. I have just begun to scratch the surface. I know there was significant information locked within me. I hope I unlock it

Mystical Puzzle

before it was too late. Because when I do, look out World! This is not the end. This is just the beginning.

Did it ever occur to you that the people that you surround yourself with might be closer to my kind than you could ever understand? If it happened to me, buckle your seat belt and hold on. It could happen to you too.

Puzzle Pieces and Other Tidbits

Most of my life I swear to god that I hardly sleep. I can remember that I use to struggle with sleeping as early as ten years old. I toss and turn all night long and by the time I fall asleep, it was time for me to get up for school or work. Even if I do sleep, I do not feel rested when I wake up in the morning.

In my younger years, I was terrified of going to sleep in the dark. I did not start to get bad night terrors until after I tried to commit suicide when I was twenty-two years old. When Brady and I were together, sometimes it happened three times a week and sometimes only once per month. I was never aware when I was having them. Brady would tell me about it the following morning. He usually started out with, "You did one of those things in your sleep last night. You know where you wake up screaming and crying like you are being terrorized. I chased you around the condo last night trying to get you to go back to bed. Your eyes were open but it was not you. It is the creepiest thing."

Another thing that I have never told anyone, I use to always have to go to sleep with the TV on. Several times I have woken up and the TV was still on and I was very confused. It is as though there were messages of some sort coming through the TV, but I could not decipher them. I also jolted out of sleep in confusion like I had just been somewhere and I was given very important information, yet I could not remember where I was or what the information was.

I am positive that a man I use to work with at the college is an Earth Angel. His last name actually has the word angel in it. He is a conservationist and has volunteered countless hours to environmental issues.

I have always been afraid of lightening because for some reason I thought that it was going to strike me down, as if it knew exactly how to find me. I guess that would make sense since I am a portal for energy.

I was always day dreaming about time travel. As though I already knew that it could be done; that you could access the past. I did not know why I had this strange obsession with time travel. I use to always say, "If only I could travel back in time." I guess once I am able to travel into the past, I will then know why I needed to do it.

You know the movie, *The Matrix*. Well I guess you could say that I took the red pill.

I would give my life without thought to see the Earth from space.

I often wondered if we were like the Simm's and we were somewhat controlled by something else and that Earth was a game.

I am in the midst of creating a music video for my Bachelor's creative project. There is a part in the video that describes my suicide attempt, only I do not know where the ideas came from because I have no recollection of when I was in a coma and do not recall a near death experience. I was dead when I was found and brought back to life and sustained with life support. Anyways it shows me running in slow motion and leaping into a big ball of light. Once I was in the light, a brown cloaked figure with no visible face shook his head, no. I acknowledged by nodding my head yes. While doing this I did not look well and my skin around my eyes was blackened. I was so tired. I started to cry tears of blood and then an angel swooped down and the next scene shows me dancing having a great time. When I made this video, I had never heard of Mother Mary statues that cry tears of blood.

I met Misty when I was ten years old over a caterpillar. I strongly believe that she has contributed greatly in transforming me into a butterfly. We did not have a lot of interaction during our teenage and adult years but she managed to pop into my life at a crucial time and encouraged me to backpack in South East Asia by myself for a year in 2001. That was definitely a big turning point in my life.

My awakening never gradually happened. It was instantaneous. It is so hard to find the words to explain what has happened and what is happening. It is as if I lived in a world and we were all oranges. However, one day I woke up, looked in the mirror, and just about shit my pants because it was not an orange staring back at me, it was a banana. I frantically looked for the orange but could not find her. Then my real family of bananas told me that although the world will see me as an orange, I am really a banana. "We have taken away your orange mind and have now given you your banana mind. Congratulations! You made it to the appointed time." Dumped a puzzle in front of me with missing pieces and said not to worry, in time you will learn who you are and you will find the pieces to put the puzzle together. We will stay in contact. Don't do and just be and you will know how to do that. I have been so busy looking for the pieces that I do not know how to just BE. I guess this is where patience comes in as I have been told that there is nothing I can do to stop this, or to make it go any faster. I just need to let go and allow.

One thing that still has a hold on me is changing the toilet paper roll. It has been fifteen years since I have left Ron and I am reminded of him and his abuse every time I change a toilet paper roll. Do you realize how often that is in one's life? If I catch myself trying to make sure that I am putting the toilet paper on the holder to his liking, I will purposely put it on backwards. One day I would like to be able to change the toilet paper without remembering him.

There is not one person in the world that really knows me. My friends and family know parts of me, but not all of me.

One of my missions is to complete this incarnation without getting myself killed. Every time I come to this planet, I am killed!

Are my initials TE a backward code for ET? I have my own certain code that I use when I don't want people to know what I am writing. Following what I have done for years, I would use ET for Tanya Ebert.

I am scared of getting lost while I drive. It is as though I will really be lost and never, ever find my way home for the rest of my life. I get like that every time I have to drive somewhere new. I probably feel this way because in a sense I do feel lost in this 3D world; it is not like the one that I am from. I miss my home planet.

My friend Dexter from work gave me a set of angel cards. He knew that I collected ceramic angels and asked me if I wanted them. They were a special deck of angel cards because they belonged to his fiancé who had passed away suddenly. I never used the cards and just placed them with my display of angels until after Sedona.

My angel cards always tell me what I was lacking and when I was out of balance. If I did not meditate, meditation came up. If I did not spend some time in nature that day, nature came up. It is not as though I needed angel cards to tell me where I was lacking. I knew that without the cards. I just found it fascinating that the cards that do come up were usually dead on to what was going on in my life for that day.

The music card has been coming up a lot. I feel and see music. I get inspired and creative listening to music. However, what was the purpose for it coming up all the time. I was not musically inclined and I did not play an instrument, so I was not sure why it kept coming up. Perhaps I would write a song, and someone famous would sing it. God knows I do not have the voice. Although, if I could just hold a note, I have a pretty good Stevie Nicks voice going on. Oh yeah, I was kidding about writing a song for someone famous to sing.

Kids and animals were usually attracted to me. Quite often the pets of my friends and family got excitedly nuts when I was around. Some of the owners got a little jealous and told me that their pets do not do that when they come home but when I came over they were jumping for joy.

I do not have my own children, but no doubt love hanging out with them. They are brilliant little beings and we could stand to learn a thing or two from them. I try to treat them in such a way that they are little beings with their own thoughts and feelings, not like someone that I can bully because I am older and a little bit taller. They feel safe with me while at the same time having a sense of freedom and joy. That it is ok for them just to be them. My friend Amber actually called me Hitler one day when we were at the lake with Alex because I gave him crap for sticking his sandy hands in the chips that we were all sharing. I am sorry; I did not feel like eating sand that day! It was an easy fix. I pulled out some chips and put them in a baggie for him. Problem solved! He can eat sand if he so chooses and we did not have to. I tried to explain to her that if I was such a Hitler with the kids, why on earth did they get as excited as they did, when they hung out with me and continued to want to hang out with me. My niece and nephews have a choice to pick a gift or date with me when it is their birthday. They always pick date with me.

I was ten years old when the movie ET came out. I loved that movie and I loved ET! I use to cry because I wanted my own real ET. I told my mom that I could take care of my own ET if I got one. Mom tried the next best thing and bought me a stuffed ET for Christmas. She also bought me an ET necklace.

I have a towel that I consider my special towel. It is a huge bath towel of ET when he was getting into the fridge. I have had the towel since 1982. I use it all the time. You would never guess that it was twenty-eight years old! I almost lost this towel forever. In the mid 90's, my boyfriend at the time, Brady had used my towel to clean up a mess of some sort and decided to throw the towel in the dumpster at the condo we were living in. When I came home that day, something made me go look for the towel. I could not find it anywhere so I had asked Brady if he knew where it was. He knew all right, the dumpster. What! I just about hit the roof! Of all towels, my ET towel! I told him to get digging and find me my towel! He found it and washed it and it came out so clean that you would never know what it had just gone through.

I always have an urge to explore. I tend to veer off onto the unbeaten track. There are back mountain roads in and nearby the little town that I live in, that so many do not know exist. My eyes light up every time I find a new road. It is as though I might find something. I do not know what that something is, but I keep looking for it.

I suddenly have a huge fascination with crystals. I cannot wait to start looking for my own. I have always wondered about rocks and have been attracted to them but never had an urge to buy any or find them myself until recently.

Even at five years old, I knew religion was not for me. I was too young to understand my own feelings about religion and where they were coming from. However, I was old enough to figure out that there was something very wrong with church and religion.

When I was five years old, my mom, Ross the sperm donor and I, moved to a new home in Surrey. I remember knocking on everyone's door in the cul-de-sac asking if they had any kids that I could play with. One of the girls I met asked me if I wanted to go to Sunday school with her. She said that it was a lot of fun because you get to make crafts and color. Being five years old, this sounded quite appealing to me. To this day, I do not remember what exactly happened at Sunday school, but I do remember coming home afterwards and telling my mom to *never, ever* let me go there again! I had the distinct feeling that they were lying and that they were bad people! When I was eleven years old and my sister was three years old, all the kids except for me went to Sunday school. I absolutely refused to go and thank god my mom did not make me. There was something about church and religion that I avoided like the plague. At such a young age, with no one to influence me either way, I wanted nothing to do with it!

Nana is Catholic and took me to church with her when I was six years old. I was quite upset that people use to line up and get candy. Or at least I thought it was candy and everyone was getting some except for me. Nana said that it was bread and that only the people who have made there first communion were allowed to have it. Well I had enough of that and told her that I am never going to Church with her again! If I cannot have what everyone else was having, I do not want to be there! I did not understand why everyone but me could have the bread.

I use to walk around with a fear of always needing to know my surroundings. Doors must be kept locked and I was always prepared within a millisecond to fight for my life. I am sure that I was murdered before in past lives. Why? Probably because they thought I was a witch? I feel like I was a very powerful magical being at one time; that I could do the unimaginable. Back in the day, that was considered the work of the devil and quite often, mystics were killed because people could not understand how they were able to do the things they do. How are they able to know the stuff they know? Even today, there are religious groups that think spiritualists are the works of the devil. Give me a break! I pray to god and my angels and seek to find ways of helping humanity and this beautiful planet, Earth. Where is devil worshipping in that?!

There is a warrior in me but there is also an angelic being. The warrior will stop at nothing for the good of humanity. The angel wants to give love and peace.

I use to always tell people, be careful whom you piss off because you never know who they really are. People listen to me and I am five foot nothing. Those who know me well do not want to piss me off. How do you know that the homeless person is not an angel in disguise?

Hurt me or anyone I care about and I will come after you like a savage that you never seen coming. I protect like a mama bear does her cubs! I am not a violent person, nor do I condone violence, but I am no doubt, a protector. You can hurt me but do not dare hurt anyone I love!

In the past, I allowed people to do wrong to me just because I never had solid proof of where I would get my information. You cannot tell someone that you know what they did and you found out through visions in your own head! It happened often when people were treating me poorly behind my back. I would get visions of what they were doing, but most times it was so bad that I would think, no way would that person do that. I would just think it was my imagination in overdrive. I would sit back to see if it would unfold. The sad thing was, those nasty visions I would have turned out not to be an over reactive imagination, but indeed turned out to be facts. I was always right at picking the evil out of people, especially the greedy and people who lie. I have certainly had my share of them!

Approximately ten years ago, I put the word "unity" on my cell phone so that every time I turned it on, unity would pop up on the screen. I do not know why or what it meant at the time, but I did it anyways.

Every person I have ever met has told me that they have never met any one like me before.

There is something about the following that resonates deep in me:

* Noah's Ark
* Helen Keller
* Joan of Arc
* Abraham Lincoln
* Egypt
* Mayan's
* Lemuria
* Atlantis
* Jesus Christ
* Garden of Eden
* Archangel Michael
* Mother Mary
* Orion

Songs that resonate deeply with me:

* Living on a Memory – Alannah Myles
* Battle of Evermore – Led Zeppelin
* Rumours – Lindsay Lohan
* Spirits in the Material World – Police
* Where is this Love – The Payola's
* Wasted Years – Iron Maiden
* The Rose – Bette Middler
* Let It Be – The Beatles
* The Voice – John Farnham
* Superman – Five For Fighting
* Starseed – Our Lady Peace
* Invincible – Pat Benatar
* Fade to Black – Metallica

Closing Comments

During my experience and research, I concluded that we are way more than we know and we are not alone. Someone or something is trying to withhold the truth from us. We are all very gifted only we have forgotten that because we have been programmed since birth to think differently.

Just because you personally have not experienced something, does not mean that it does not exist. Have you ever been to an African Jungle? You might not have seen or experienced it, but it is there. Can you see gamma rays? Can you see electricity?

Mathematicians and physicists drove themselves crazy and some committed suicide back in the day because no one believed them. Two hundred years later, we discovered they were right all along. Keep an open mind. It might just be that some of those people we deem crazy actually know what they are talking about, and are simply ahead of our time.

Some people in mental institutions should not be there. They are psychic not psychotic. Big difference! If someone was there to explain it to them and guide them, they could learn to accept and embrace their gift not only to help themselves, but also to help others.

It is of utmost importance to remember that we are all equal. We are all one. You and I are no better than the drug addicted homeless person down the street. First, you need to love yourself and then love your neighbor regardless of their gender, race, religion, age, etc.

As long as we live our truth, that is all that matters. If living your truth is raising a family, then you are on your right path. If your truth is working a job that does not pay much but you absolutely love what you do, then you are on your right path. It does not matter what we choose to do with ourselves on this Earth as long as you honor yourself, honor your neighbor, and live your truth. If you want to dye your hair purple but are worried about what others will think, you are not living your truth. Your heart will sing when you are on the right path. If you feel like you are constantly being punched in the gut, you need to make a choice and try a different path.

Even though you may be an adult, that does not mean you cannot have any more silly fun. If you feel like skipping down the street, do it! I am sure you will get many looks, but I bet you could not wipe the smile from your face.

Sal was right about me feeling like all seven billion people on Earth were like my babies. You know how a mother would do anything to save her children. Imagine the magnitude of that times seven billion. It is a good thing that I am full of love and not hate. It is a good thing that I am not afraid of telling the truth. It is a good thing that I am no longer afraid of the dark! Hey darkies?

Mystical Puzzle

There have been many times that I no longer wanted to play the human game. I often catch myself saying, I am never coming back here again! Only when I stop to think about it and realize how much of a miracle we are, do I realize that we should all embrace the human experience because once we go to the other side and return to spirit form, we eagerly want to return to Earth.

Forget about yesterday for it is done

Never mind about tomorrow as it has not come

Live in the now and life will become

Peace, Love and Light to all!

About the Author

At age thirty-five, Tanya Ebert experienced a dirt bike accident that left the doctors puzzled and unable to relieve her of the pain that she experienced daily, due to a stuck bent leg. A year after her accident while trying to cope with being disabled and unable to function without daily help, suicide seemed the only option.

After embarking on a journey in Sedona, Arizona, she came back full of life and in a state so blissful it was almost too much for her to handle. After discovering something phenomenal was happening to her, she embarked on another journey to put the pieces together of why she was so different from everyone else. This book is the result of the unfolding process of finding out who she is. Much of it was written in the two and a half years immediately following her dirt bike accident.

Tanya is currently enrolled at the University of Metaphysical Sciences to earn her Bachelors, Masters, and Doctorate Degree. Her passion is to learn as much as she can about the unknown. Not only to understand her own experiences, but to help others with theirs. Tanya has been inspired by many spiritual teachers and various religious teachings but does not follow one in particular.

Tanya currently resides in South West British Columbia, Canada.

Resources

Home Project Documentary

http://www.youtube.com/watch?v=jqxENMKaeCU (*type exactly using upper and lowercase*)

University of Metaphysical Sciences

http://www.umsonline.org/

Picture of Orion Constellation

http://en.wikipedia.org/wiki/Orion_(constellation)

Who are the Starseed Indigos?

http://www.youtube.com/watch?v=D0W8HFDf_hg

11:11 Journey of a Starseed

http://www.youtube.com/watch?v=YXV6q8tEOcQ

Tree of Life

http://en.wikipedia.org/wiki/Tree_of_life

Miriam Delicado: www.alienbluestar.com
Book: Blue Star Fulfilling Prophecy

Rosanna Ienco: Shamanic Practioner, Soul Coach and Past Life Coach
www.rosannaienco.com
Book: Awakening the Divine Soul Finding Your Life Purpose

Doreen Virtue: www.angeltherapy.com
Books: How to Communicate With Your Angels
Realms of the Earth Angels
Earth Angels
Angel Numbers 101

Dan Millman: www.danmillman.com
Book: Way of the Peaceful Warrior

Dolores Cannon: www.ozarkmt.com
Book: The Custodians "Beyond Abduction"

Jean Shinoda Bolen: www.jeanbolen.com
Book: Goddesses in Every Woman

Book: Indigo Adults by Ritama Davidson and Kabir Jaffe
Book: Aliens Among Us by Ruth Montgomery
Book: E.T. 101 by Zoev Jho
Book: From Elsewhere Being E.T. in America by Brad Steiger
Book: Transformation The Breakthrough by Whitley Strieber
Book: Animal Speak by Ted Andrews

References

Chapter 3

Fenn, Celia. <u>What are Indigo and Crystal Children and Adults?</u> Retrieved June 26, 2010, from Indigos and Crystals, What are the New Children? Some Ideas: http://www.starchildglobal.com/

Chapter 4

Virtue, Doreen. (2002) <u>Earth Angels.</u> USA; Hay House Inc., page 99.

Chapter 5

Bauval, Robert. (1995) <u>Orion Correlation Theory.</u> Retrieved June 26, 2010, from http://en.wikipedia.org/wiki/Orion_Correlation_Theory

Chapter 6

Virtue, Doreen. (2008) <u>Angel Numbers 101.</u> USA; Hay House Inc., page 111.

Chapter 8

Mimi.hu. <u>Blocked Toilet.</u> Retrieved June 26, 2010, from http://en.mimi.hu/dreams/toilet.html

Dream Moods. <u>Haircut.</u> Retrieved June 26, 2010, from http://www.dreammoods.com/dreamdictionary/h.htm

Chapter 10

Heal Past Lives. (2000) <u>Walk-Ins – Soul Braiding.</u> Retrieved June 26, 2010, from http://www.healpastlives.com/pastlf/karmdict/kdsbraid.htm

Hornecker, John. (1996) <u>Soul Consolidations and Transfers – Early Retirement.</u> Retrieved June 26, 2010, from http://www.earthscape.net/cosmic/transf.htm

Chapter 11

Brannan, Joanne E. (2009) <u>Totem Bear Sprit Guide.</u> Retrieved June 26, 2010, from http://paganismwicca.suite101.com/article.cfm/totem_bear_spirit_guide